ELECTING THE PRESIDENT

Chandler Publications in
POLITICAL SCIENCE
Victor Jones, *Editor*

ELECTING
THE PRESIDENT

REVISED EDITION

Daniel M. Ogden, Jr.

UNITED STATES DEPARTMENT OF THE INTERIOR

AND

Arthur L. Peterson

THE AMERICAN INSTITUTE FOR FOREIGN TRADE

CHANDLER PUBLISHING COMPANY
124 Spear Street, San Francisco, California 94105

 Science Research Associates, Inc., 259 East Erie Street, Chicago, Illinois 60611
A Subsidiary of IBM   Distributors

To

Val and Connie

CONTENTS

PREFACE

Electing the President describes the process of choosing the chief executive officer of the United States. It reports the experiences of the two major parties in the elections of 1960 and 1964. It includes discussions of history and of constitutional and legal determinants in the detail needed to support its always practical emphasis.

Each of the authors writes from the combined knowledge of a practicing political worker and a scholar in political science. Both write from expert and intimate familiarity with the 1960 campaign, having been Faculty Fellows assigned by the Citizenship Clearing House to the National Committees of the Republican Party (Peterson) and the Democratic Party (Ogden). Dr. Ogden observed the 1964 campaign from the central vantage point of Washington, and Dr. Peterson maintained his connection with the national Republican Party apparatus.

The writing plan for *Electing the President* has assured an objective book as well as a practical and accurate one. The work of each author was scrutinized by the other and also by the series editor and the editorial staff of the publisher. The result has been to develop maximum clarity and accuracy and to eliminate, to the satisfaction of two men with opposed party commitments, any statements challengeable as partisan.

THE PUBLISHER

ELECTING THE PRESIDENT

Chapter I

The Politics of
Electing a President

The election of a President of the United States is perhaps the most dramatic political event in the world. At once the chief executive and the ceremonial leader of the richest and most powerful nation on earth, the President possesses a combination of constitutional powers unparalleled in the free world. Filling the first of the great republican offices created by the Age of Revolution, he also stands as a world symbol of liberty, of constitutional government, and of the will of colonial peoples to be free and independent nations.

The politics of electing a President derive directly from the structure of the Constitution of the United States and from the nature of the political-party system it creates. Any political party which would make a serious bid for power must operate within the system and obey its unspoken rules. Any candidate who would aspire to the presidency must thoroughly understand the nature of American political parties and direct his efforts within his party to the several points where real power lies.

THE NATURE OF AMERICAN
POLITICAL PARTIES

The Constitution's provisions for a federal system with a separation of powers impose upon the United States an "arena-of-compromise" political-party system. Such a system has two basic characteristics. First, only two major political parties can compete seriously for power. Second, both major parties must be "arenas of compromise," united primarily by the desire to win office and so heterogeneous and decentralized that each accommodates a range of political views wide enough to bid for a majority of the American voters.

The two-party system makes an American election a decisive contest for control of the most powerful government in the world. One party or the other gains office for four years and throughout that time rules the Republic. It need not share the honor or the responsibility with any other political organization, and it does not. American elections, then, like elections in the other English-speaking nations which have two-party systems, are real points of decision in public life.

The contrast with elections in nations with multiparty systems is very sharp and most crucial. Multiparty elections merely test shifts in popular support among the parties. Rarely do they change power holders. The dominant coalition may react to an election by adding or dropping a party to strengthen its majority or increase its solidarity, but the electorate takes no action which has decisive consequences for control of governmental power.

The basic constitutional factor causing the two-party system in the United States is the separate election of a single individual to head the executive branch of government. Control of the executive thus is indivisible. No postelection coalitions need be assembled to control executive power, and no postelection political dealings for power need be made. The victor has four years of individual rule in hand. To elect the President is to win all executive power in the national government.

Coalitions, then, are formed *inside* American political parties, not among them. To contest seriously for the presidency, a political party must unite a range of interests broad enough to gain the support of more than half of the American voters. In such a contest there can be but two contenders: the party with the best chance and the party with the next-best chance to win, for only two parties can hope to gain the support of more than half the electorate. In such a system, third parties have no chance at all. A vote for a third-party candidate simply destroys the voter's opportunity to determine who will be President.

This winner-take-all arrangement for the presidency is duplicated in every state for the governorship and also prevails in the election of members of both houses of Congress. Moreover, most state legislators, even those chosen from multimember districts, are selected on the same winner-take-all basis, for the customary American practice is to permit the citizens to cast as many votes for the state legislature as there are members to be elected from their district, rather than to cast one vote each and have the election officials distribute the seats by some form of proportional representation, as in Europe.

Other causes of the two-party system have been suggested. Among them are the two-party tradition stemming from the earliest days of the Republic; widespread agreement among the American people on such potentially explosive issues as separation of church and state and the outlawry of special privilege such as a titled nobility; the division of attitudes between those who favor action by the federal government to achieve public goals and those who advocate preservation of states' rights; and the representation system used in Congress which obliges a political party which would control both houses to hold strength both in the large industrial states of the Northeast and in the sparsely populated states of the West and South.

"Arena-of-compromise" political parties have three fundamental internal characteristics. First, they are multigroup associations united by the desire to win public office in order to advance as much as possible the varied goals of the many groups within their ranks. Second, they are decentralized, with power resting primarily at the local organizational level. Third, they are semipublic associations, not private clubs.

They are semipublic associations, in that every state regulates party organization, qualifications for party membership, the nominating process, and party finance. Yet in every state both major parties retain many private attributes. They take stands on issues as they please, must raise funds privately, and may select their own officers.

Both major American political parties are decentralized, in that power rests with the state and local party organizations and principally with the county central committees. National party committees and national political leaders are unable to compel conformity on issues or oblige local organizations, leaders, or elected officials to support them in campaigns.

Both major parties also are multigroup associations. They are united essentially by a willingness to support common candidates for office. No central philosophy unites the members of either party. Individuals identify themselves with a major American party for a wide variety of reasons. Family preference, sectional tradition, occupation, policy issues, social status, race, and even religion have been important factors in choice. Identification is voluntary. Neither party votes people into membership, imposes dues, or requires any act of political loyalty, even that of voting for its candidates. Yet the members act together voluntarily; for the penalty for failure is that other groups, dominant in the opposing major party, will win and use their public advantage in their own interest.

Public-policy goals—party platforms—are a product of compromise within each party, not the application to a particular election of the party's principles. Policy goals are brought before each party by special-interest groups which seek party approval for their objectives. In the bid for votes for its candidates, each party tries to find "official" positions which will please each group without needlessly offending others. The parties thus act as a first stage in the political process of recognizing the legitimate needs of special groups in society for policy action from government. Groups do not expect policy *pledges* from the political parties, but rather an expression that the group's objectives are in the public interest and deserve serious consideration by elected officials. Party platforms, then, are guidelines, not pledges of action.

Some American political scientists, gazing uncritically at the British political system, have imagined that, ideally, political parties should be associations of people who share a common political philosophy. Such associations would unite to nominate candidates dedicated to the party philosophy. Once in office, the party members would stand together to enact the party program into law and to carry it out. Such parties are said to be "responsible." The voters are presumed to be able to choose between party programs and thus to give a mandate to one party to carry out its philosophy. Individual office holders are viewed simply as agents of the electorate whose task is to translate the party's promises into law. The public would not participate in shaping the parties' programs, but would only choose between them. Competition between such political elites is presumed to be sufficient to protect the public interest. To be effective, such parties would have to be private associations, centralized, and like-minded. The advocates of this "party-responsibility" theory have therefore proposed "reforms" to make American political parties more like the parties in a unitary, parliamentary system such as the British.

American politics long ago developed a quite different rationale, which can be called the "arena-of-compromise" theory. American politics rests upon the premise that in a representative democracy the people freely elect public officers in whom they have confidence. Issues of public policy are then debated by such public officers in full public view and are decided each on its own merits. The American people do not expect competing, disciplined political elites to offer them comprehensive programs of political action for their blanket acceptance or rejection at an election. Moreover, Americans do not conceive of their political parties as seeking or being given mandates to enact comprehensive policy programs based on a body of political theory.

These American attitudes toward the making of public policy, as well as the "arena-of-compromise" characteristics of the major American political parties, stem from two fundamental characteristics of the American constitutional system: the separation of powers and federalism.

The separation of powers both shapes and reflects the American concept of policy formation. Election of the legislature separately from the executive stems from the conviction that the legislature should act independently from the executive. Public-policy issues are to be determined by free votes cast by the legislators following public debate. But the same separation also removes the partisan political question of which party will hold executive power from policy debates in the legislature.

Consequently, policy making in American legislatures is a bipartisan or even a nonpartisan affair. Only on a few highly controversial issues are party lines significant, and even on these, party lines seldom hold.

Since policy questions have no necessary relation to political-power questions, policy questions can be decided on their own merits. Members of both parties of all shades of opinion play a real part in making final decisions.

Accordingly, candidates for public office take personal stands on issues primarily to prove that they are able to exercise independent judgment. Ordinarily they discuss safe issues in which there is widespread interest but a clear public consensus. Occasionally, when it appears profitable, they take vigorous stands on particular controversial issues. But, as often as not, the part of wisdom is to display competence without making commitments which might offend as many voters as they please.

Presidential candidates play this game of winning personal confidence as vigorously as any candidate for Congress. The discussion of issues in a presidential campaign, therefore, often dismays those party-responsibility advocates who believe that the campaign should be a formal confrontation of political ideologies. The candidates, quite logically, are seeking votes, not debate honors. They may not emphasize or even discuss the same "issues" at all!

With policy decisions really left to Congress, another test of presidential capacity to lead—and thus an important campaign appeal—is the ability to work constructively with Congress—on a bipartisan basis—to secure laws in the public interest. In 1964, President Lyndon B. Johnson's long experience and rather considerable reputation as a legislative leader proved to be valuable assets in his campaign. The substantial legislative accomplishments at least during the early portion of his administration will surely be cited by his supporters as further proof of his skill, should he again be a candidate in 1968.

The separation of powers also reenforces and makes profitable the decentralization and heterogeneity of political parties. With an independent executive who does not need to have either a majority in the legislature to win election or a disciplined majority to stay in office, neither party has an effective political whip to compel its elected legislators to vote for the party's platform or to follow the leadership of the President or of a state governor. The set terms of office for legislators as well as for the President and governors further support such independence. Knowing when they must face the voters and knowing they must face them on local issues, members of Congress and of state legislatures serve the needs of their states and districts unless national or party goals are truly overriding.

Federalism also makes American political parties arenas of compromise because it divides political power between the national government and the governments of 50 states. Elections are conducted by the states and won in the states. Only the presidency and vice presidency are filled by putting together the votes of several states. Thus the parties organize to win elections where they must—at the state and local levels.

Each state and local party organization naturally reflects the particular needs and interests of the people within its area. In a nation as large and varied as the United States, differences may be very great. For example, the Democratic Party in Michigan may be intensely interested in labor relations in the automotive industry; the Democratic Party in the state of Arizona, in water supplies for homes and farms; the Democratic Party in Philadelphia, in urban renewal; the Democratic Party in Alaska, in public development of natural resources. The national Democratic Party must therefore recognize and reconcile all these needs as best it can. Thus federalism is a basic cause of decentralization and heterogeneity in both major parties and is greatly reenforced as a cause by the varied social and economic interests of the nation.

The "arena-of-compromise" system thus makes both major parties effective institutions for assembling an electoral majority capable of capturing federal executive power and wielding it successfully. Moreover, both are flexible enough and decentralized enough to bid seriously for a majority of seats in the federal legislature in most of the 50 states, despite their widely varied social and economic conditions. Arena parties enable the American people to govern themselves under a federal, separation-of-powers constitution.

THE ELECTORAL COLLEGE

The strategy of presidential elections was set in 1787 by the Constitutional Convention at Philadelphia. The drafters of the

Constitution provided that the President would be chosen by electors, especially selected for that purpose in such manner as the legislature of each state should prescribe. Each state was to be entitled to "a number of electors, equal to the whole number of Senators and Representatives to which the State may be entitled in the Congress." In 1962, the Twenty-third Amendment added three electoral votes for the District of Columbia.

To win election, a candidate for President must receive a majority of "the whole number of electors appointed." Should no one receive such a majority, selection falls to the House of Representatives, where each state is given but one vote, to be cast as the majority of its representatives shall determine.

The drafters of the Constitution imagined that the electors would be men of high station and independent judgment who would exercise their choices in what they believed to be the best interests of the nation. The device reflected the influence of Montesquieu's praise for the British system of divided powers—as he understood it—with the democratic, aristocratic, and monarchical elements represented in the Commons, Lords, and King respectively. The electoral college was to be a way of designating the chief executive which would obtain for a republic the separation from the passions of the moment that is insured for monarchies by hereditary selection.

Accordingly, the drafters innocently provided that each elector should cast his votes for *two* candidates for President. The candidate receiving the largest number of votes would be President; the candidate having the next-largest number, Vice President.

All went well while George Washington was the leading candidate for President, because all electors voted for him, then scattered their votes for second choice. But after John Adams became President in 1797, the system quickly displayed its faults. When Adams sought a second term in 1800, Thomas Jefferson challenged him. Rallying the widely scattered rural, laboring, and frontier elements of the nation against the trading and financial interests which Adams championed, Jefferson laid the foundations for the party system of today. To assemble a majority coalition, he accepted as his vice-presidential candidate Aaron Burr of New York, an ambitious politician who later killed Alexander Hamilton in a duel, conspired to set up an independent empire in the Mississippi valley, was tried but acquitted of treason, and died in disgrace.

Jefferson and Burr set about assembling slates of candidates for elector in each state who were pledged to vote for them. Their success was phenomenal: they won overwhelmingly, but the result was a tie. Both Jefferson and Burr received 73 electoral votes. The decision fell, therefore, to the House of Representatives, which was still controlled by a majority of Adams' supporters. After prolonged negotiations, Hamilton threw his influence behind Jefferson, and the intended presidential candidate was elected President. The Constitution was promptly amended to provide that electors would henceforth vote separately for President and Vice President.

The election of 1800 set a pattern for the behavior of electors which has been followed ever since. Each candidate for President arranges to have fellow partisans in each state nominate a slate of electors who are pledged to vote for him for President. The procedure varies according to state laws. Most of the states authorize state conventions of the political parties to nominate electors. Nine of the states allow the state central committees to designate them. Arizona nominates electors in the primary election. In Pennsylvania the presidential candidates themselves nominate their electors.

The presidential candidates then campaign, technically, for the election of their electors, because all states now provide that the electors shall be chosen by the people at the general election. But so routine has the role of presidential electors become that two-thirds of the states now provide by law that the names of electors shall not appear on the general-election ballots. Instead, the ballots contain only the names of the candidates for President and Vice President to whom they are pledged. All other states but three list on the ballot both the electors and the candidates to whom they are pledged.[1]

---

[1] Richard D. Hupman and Eiler C. Ravnholt, *Nomination and Election of the President and Vice President of the United States* (Washington: Government Printing Office, 1964), pp. 170-235. A complete, state-by-state exposition is set forth. See also U.S. Congress, Senate, *Nomination and Election of President and Vice President,* Hearings before the Subcommittee on Constitutional Amendments of the Committee on the Judiciary (Washington: Government Printing Office, 1963), pp. 103-104.

Moreover, several states now further require by law that the electors cast their votes only for the candidates to whom they are pledged. Indeed, when the Oregon legislature tried in 1939 to repeal the state law requiring electors to pledge when nominated to cast their votes only for the candidates of their political party, the voters in a referendum repudiated the legislature's change and retained the compulsory requirement. Presidential electors in the United States generally are not expected to exercise independent judgment.

However, a few states in the South do not oblige the electors to vote for the candidates to whom they are pledged. Alabama even provides for slates of electors with no reference to the presidential candidates. Mississippi permits unpledged as well as pledged electors. As a result, some southern electors in three presidential elections since the close of World War II have cast their electoral votes as they pleased, without reference to the people's choice or to the implied pledges contained in their use of a national party label.

In 1948, one Tennessee elector, pledged to Truman, voted for a third-party candidate. In 1956 an Alabama elector, pledged to Stevenson, did likewise. In 1960 one Nixon elector in Oklahoma cast his vote for another candidate, and six Alabama electors who were supposed to vote for Kennedy voted instead for a man who was not even a candidate for President! This sort of irresponsibility on the part of individual electors has occasioned considerable criticism. It could easily be remedied by state laws deleting the names of electors from the ballot and obliging electors to vote only for the candidates nominated by their national political party or simply by abolishing the office of elector altogether and providing that some public official, probably the secretary of state of each state, should cast the electoral vote which the voters direct.

Some southern states have deliberately encouraged elector independence in the hope that enough votes could be wasted on a third-party candidate to throw the election into the House of Representatives, where southern leaders have hoped to wield especially effective bargaining power. The most serious attempt of that kind occurred in 1948, when Strom Thurmond of South Carolina was advanced as a candidate for President on a states'-rights ticket. Given the official Democratic label instead of President Truman in

Alabama, Louisiana, Mississippi, and South Carolina, Thurmond was able to carry these states but was unable to prevent Truman's election. A similar maneuver in 1960 carried only Mississippi for the third-party effort.

THE STRATEGY OF ELECTORAL MAJORITIES

The device of providing slates of pledged candidates for elector has had a profound effect upon the strategy of winning the presidency. Only one slate can win in each state. No states now permit the selection of electors at the congressional-district level, which could result in a divided electoral vote.

Accordingly, each major-party candidate for President ordinarily starts his campaign with certain "safe" states where his party's voters normally are in a majority. Counting on winning all or most of these electoral votes, he next calculates those states in which his party seems to have a good chance of victory. Ordinarily these will be states which his party's presidential candidate carried in the last election and in which his party holds a number of key offices such as governor, United States Senator, and United States Representative. Last, he will look to the "doubtful" or "swing" states which from past performance, the division of party success, and the indications from current public-opinion polls appear likely to go to either candidate.

In 1968 there will be 538 electoral votes: 435 to equal the number of Representatives, 100 to equal the number of Senators, and 3 for the District of Columbia. A successful candidate must have at least 270.

Traditionally, Democratic candidates have been able to count on the electoral votes of the southern states; Republican candidates, on the votes of New England and middle-western states. As the Civil War has faded into history and modern industrial problems have shifted the patterns of party identification, however, the large urban centers of the North have tended to swing toward the Democrats; the urban centers of the South, toward the Republicans. Two-party competition has developed to the point that now no state can be considered "safe" for its traditional party. In 1964, the Republican candidate for President, Senator Barry Goldwater, carried only his home state of Arizona and five traditionally "safe" Democratic states of the deep South: Louisiana, Mississippi, Alabama, Georgia, and South Carolina. President Johnson carried all of the traditionally "safe" Republican states, including rock-ribbed Maine and Vermont, into the Democratic column—a feat even Franklin D. Roosevelt was unable to accomplish.

Despite the topsy-turvy consequences of the 1964 presidential election, each party retains special advantages in certain states which have traditonally been its territory. In congressional, state, and local elections its normal majority usually prevails. Thus Republicans have a solid bloc of loyal adherents upon which to base their bid for the 63 electoral votes of Colorado, Idaho, Indiana, Iowa, Kansas, Maine, Nebraska, New Hampshire, North Dakota, South Dakota, and Vermont. Democrats similarly enjoy large traditional majorities for the 124 electoral votes of Arkansas, Georgia, Louisiana, Mississippi, Missouri, New Mexico, North Carolina, South Carolina, Texas, and West Virginia. Texas with its 25 electoral votes long has been the keystone of the Democratic bloc. Its influence in that party has been especially apparent since the 1930's in the persons of John N. Garner, who was Speaker of the House of Representatives and twice Vice President from 1931 to 1941; Sam Rayburn, who served nearly 17 years as Speaker between 1940 and 1961 (the all-time record); and Lyndon B. Johnson, who has served successively as Democratic Leader of the Senate, Vice President, and President since 1953.

Competition between the candidates for President, then, centers on the "doubtful" states. The reason is twofold: Competition is both possible and profitable. Among the states most likely to be in doubt are those with the largest number of electoral votes: New York, 43 votes; California, 40 votes; Pennsylvania, 29 votes; Illinois, 26 votes; and Ohio, 26 votes. Any candidate, like Franklin D. Roosevelt or Dwight D. Eisenhower or Lyndon B. Johnson, who carries all five of these states with their 164 electoral votes is virtually certain to win the presidency. Without them it is virtually impossible to win. Indeed, only Woodrow Wilson, in 1916, was able to win the presidency by carrying just two of them—and he won election with but 11 electoral votes to spare. Every other victor in a close election has had at least three of these "pivotal" states in his column. In 1960, Kennedy carried Illinois, New York, and Pennsylvania. In 1948, Truman carried California, Illinois, and Ohio.

So important are the pivotal states that both major parties ordinarily select either their candidate for President or their candidate for Vice President from one of them. Many examples can be cited. In 1964, the Republicans named Congressman William Miller of New York as their vice-presidential candidate. In 1960, Richard Nixon of California was the Republican presidential nominee. In 1952 and 1956, the Democratic presidential nominee was Adlai E. Stevenson of Illinois. In 1956, 1952, and 1948, both Republican nominees were from the pivotal states. Since World War II, however, the Democrats have won presidential elections only when they have turned to the middle-sized states for both candidates. In 1948, 1960, and 1964, the Democratic standard-bearers hailed from Missouri, Kentucky, Massachusetts, Texas, and Minnesota.

Can the electoral-college system designate a President who actually has received fewer popular votes than his opponent? Yes, it can; and it has—twice. In 1876, Samuel J. Tilden, the Democratic candidate, polled 4,284,757 votes, while Rutherford B. Hayes, the Republican candidate, received 4,033,950. Hayes received 185 electoral votes, Tilden 184 after a bipartisan commission had decided on a strict party-line vote that the electoral votes of several disputed southern states should go to Hayes. This so-called stolen election was the most serious strain the electoral-college system has received. Again, in 1888, the incumbent President, Grover Cleveland, a Democrat, received 5,540,050 to his opponent's 5,444,337 votes. However, the Republican candidate, Benjamin Harrison, received 233 electoral votes to Cleveland's 168 and was readily acknowledged the winner.

Despite its quirks, the electoral college has a major advantage which has more often proved its worth. Because of its winner-take-all characteristics in each state, the electoral college was able to produce a clear majority for the most popular candidate in 1860, 1912, and 1960 when no candidate had received more than half of all the popular votes cast. Especially in 1860 and 1912, when major third-party candidates were in the field, this quality insured constitutional stability for the United States.

The electoral-college system is unlikely to be changed in substance, even though the office of elector may someday be abolished. The present system permits the small states to cast a vote far in excess of their proportionate share of the total population. Voters in these states will not soon relinquish such an advantage. The very large states, for their part, are equally unlikely to forgo the advantage of being courted. Because the two major parties are of nearly equal strength in all the pivotal states, direct popular election of the President, or even proportionate division of the electoral vote, would wipe them out as decisive factors in the election. A vote would then be a vote wherever it could be won. Now a single popular vote in New York may not count proportionately as much as a single popular vote in Nevada, but that single New York vote can decide all 43 electoral votes and hence is worth a great deal more in the politics of the electoral college.

PRESIDENTIAL CAMPAIGNING WITH "ARENA" PARTIES

Presidential campaigning also is significantly affected in at least five important ways by the "arena-of-compromise" characteristics of American parties.

First, with only two major parties in the field, each presidential candidate has bargaining power with the more extreme factions in his own party. Because in recent years the Republican Party has assumed a generally more conservative posture and the Democratic Party a generally more liberal one, very liberal Democrats and very conservative Republicans find themselves with no serious alternative if they disapprove of a moderate presidential candidate in their own party. In 1952, for example, conservative Taft Republicans were disappointed, but vigorously supported the moderate Republican nominee, Eisenhower, when the alternative was the liberal Democrat Stevenson. In the 1964 campaign, some very liberal Democrats were critical of the moderate record of President Johnson, but the serious alternative was the much more conservative

Republican candidate, Senator Barry Goldwater, who was utterly unacceptable to them.

Second, decentralization and heterogeneity oblige each presidential candidate to deal with a myriad of independent state and local party organizations. In some states, the state central committee will be so well organized that all dealings can be handled through its leaders. In others, some key county central committees will be traditionally independent and important. There the presidential candidate and his representatives will have to work with many separate units. Situations change from election to election, but, for example, the party organizations in the cities of New York, Philadelphia, and Chicago usually must be treated separately from their state organizations.

Some organizations will be so opposed to the presidential candidate that he will be unable to trust them. In that event, he will have to consider establishing separate citizens committees or volunteers to handle local vote-getting and campaign appearances for him.

Other state and local party organizations will prefer to center their efforts on the election or reelection of candidates for Congress, statewide office, or even county office. Holders of those offices commonly control the local organizations and are able to offer them important rewards in the form of policy decisions, jobs, and contracts. Somehow the presidential candidate must convince them that his election will serve their state or local interests, too. Fortunately, because he can easily attract far more attention, and thus far more votes, than can state and local candidates, he is usually able to keep their interest high, especially if it appears likely that he will win.

Third, campaign appeals must reflect state and local concerns and attitudes. For example, natural-resources development is important in the Far West, agriculture is vital in the Middle West, labor-management policy is of continuing concern in the industrial Northeast, and race relations are a major problem in the South. Even foreign policy and defense, though of interest everywhere, traditionally are of more intense concern on the East and West coasts than in the Mississippi valley.

Fourth, "arena" parties are unreliable sources of money. Without effective means to tax the state and local organizations, both national committees wander forever in beggardom. Debts hang over their heads from one presidential campaign to another, threatening the continuity of operations and depriving them of credit. A candidate for President, therefore, must be prepared to raise his own campaign funds and even help to repay past debts.

Fifth, and most significant of all, the presidential candidate must convince the American people that he can lead the nation. He must establish confidence in his competence, honesty, judgment, and maturity. He must demonstrate warmth, human understanding, and concern about people. He must make clear his desire to solve pressing domestic problems of the day and must prove his ability to meet continuing international crises. But he does not have to promise his way into the White House. So long as he is somewhere in the great moderate center of the American ideological spectrum, he can appeal to reasonable men of all political views. His qualities as a person and as a leader are far more important on the whole than are the stands he takes on particular issues. He needs to become, in the eyes of the majority of voters, "the best man for the job."

Bibliography

Hupman, Richard D., and Eiler C. Ravnholt. *Nomination and Election of the President and Vice President of the United States.* Washington: Government Printing Office, 1964.

Johnson, Claudius O., and associates. *American National Government.* 6th ed. New York: Crowell, 1964. Chapters 9 and 10.

Needler, M. "On the Dangers of Copying From the British," *Political Science Quarterly,* LXXVII (September 1962), 379-396.

Polsby, Nelson W., and Aaron B. Wildavsky. *Presidential Elections.* New York: Scribner's, 1964.

U.S. Congress, Senate. *Nomination and Election of President and Vice President.* Hearings before the Subcommittee on Constitutional Amendments of the Committee on the Judiciary. Washington: Government Printing Office, 1963.

Chapter II

The Strategy of a Presidential Campaign

 A presidential candidate shapes his campaign strategy within the limits of two basic political considerations: the relative strength of his party in the electorate, and his own position of leadership within his party. A favorable combination of both gives him an enormous advantage over any opponent. An unfavorable combination of both can create a nearly insurmountable obstacle to victory.

THE STRATEGY OF PARTY POSITION

Throughout American history, one of the two major parties normally has been dominant. The other major party really has been a second party—second in the number of adherents it claims, second in the number of votes its candidates win, and second in the number of elective offices its members fill.

Long periods of one-party ascendancy have been characteristic. From the adoption of the Constitution to the election of 1800, the Federalists generally reigned supreme. A successful challenge in 1800 by the Democratic-Republicans under Thomas Jefferson began a 60-year period of Democratic dominance. During part of that period, especially during James Monroe's administration from 1817 to 1825, the second party virtually disappeared, and thereafter for a time factions of the dominant party vied for power.

17

When a successful second party was revived after 1830, it succeeded only twice, in 1840 and 1848, in breaking through the Democratic majority to elect a President.

The Civil War bitterly divided the Democratic Party and elevated the Republican Party, established in 1856, to the majority. As the party of the Union, the Republican Party remained dominant until the Great Depression broke its hold in 1932. Only four times during that 72-year period did the Democrats capture the presidency: 1884, 1892, 1912, and 1916.

Since 1932, the Democrats have enjoyed a clear majority. Only Dwight D. Eisenhower has managed to win the presidency for the Republicans, in 1952 and 1956, but he managed to gain Republican control of the Congress only during his first two years in office.

The hold of a dominant party can be broken, temporarily, by an extraordinary personality leading the minority, by disunity within the majority, or by very unpopular majority policies at home or abroad. But the second party must usually combine two or all of these elements to overcome its numerical inferiority at the polls.

Presidential elections can therefore be grouped into three types.[1]

Major Shifts of Power come as a result of a crisis event which destroys the coalition supporting the majority party and creates a new majority coalition around the second party. In both major shifts of power in the past century, in 1860 and 1932, the new coalition really displayed its true composition at the next presidential election. In 1864, Lincoln firmly established the Republican Party as "the Party of the Union" and the Democratic Party as "the Party of the Rebellion." In 1936, Roosevelt firmly united a durable majority coalition of labor, farmers, the South, the devel-

---

[1] Various suggestions have been made to classify the nature of American presidential elections. V. O. Key suggests landslides, votes of confidence, and realignments. See V. O. Key, Jr., *Politics, Parties, and Pressure Groups* (5th ed.; New York: Crowell, 1964), pp. 520-536. Angus Campbell and his associates at the Survey Research Center, avowedly basing their analysis on Key's earlier concepts, offer three similar classifications: maintaining elections, deviating elections, and realigning elections. See Angus Campbell *et al.*, *The American Voter* (New York: Wiley, 1960), pp. 531-538. Campbell's people also have offered a variation on the maintaining election: the reinstating election. See Philip E. Converse *et al.*, "Stability and Change in 1960: A Reinstating Election," *American Political Science Review*, LV (June 1961), 269-280.

opment-minded West, disadvantaged ethnic and racial groups, and businessmen who wanted change.

Reaffirmations of Confidence retain the majority party in power or return it to power and are by far the most common type of American presidential election. Of the 26 presidential elections since 1860, 17 clearly are reaffirmations of confidence in the dominant party. Of these, 9 returned the incumbent President to office.

Deviating Elections elect the presidential candidate of the minority party and usually hand the minority control of the Congress as well, but without achieving a lasting realignment of a large enough bloc of voters to alter the balance of power. In the past century, only three men have won the presidency as the minority candidate: Grover Cleveland in 1884 and 1892, Woodrow Wilson in 1912 and 1916, and Dwight D. Eisenhower in 1952 and 1956. Each lost control of Congress during his term of office, and none was able durably to realign enough voters to alter the minority status of his party.

Two elections deserve special mention: 1876 and 1888. From the standpoint of popular votes, both were deviating elections, but in the first instance political manipulation and in the second the regular working of the electoral college retained control for the dominant party.

The election of 1912, although a deviating election in outcome, also is a special case. The dominant Republican Party divided, fielding two candidates: one the incumbent, the other a former President. The Democratic candidate, who would have run a poor second against either, was the easy victor in a three-way race.

A candidate for President accordingly bases his campaign strategy first of all upon the relative strength of his party. The candidate of the majority party normally needs only to muster his own adherents and those friendly to his party to win victory. He must try to avoid major defections, and may choose compromise rather than disunity on issues of deep concern to dissidents within his own party. He must, of course, judge whether compromise with dissidents will cost him more votes among otherwise loyal adherents than the dissidents can deliver against him. However, he has no real need to attract members of the minority party, especially if such appeals might jeopardize his own party's internal harmony.

The candidate of the minority party, on the other hand, must win independents and even make inroads among nominal adherents of the majority if he would win. Appeals designed only to unite his own party—or worse yet, to please only one faction of his own party—are open invitations to defeat. He thus must ascertain which segments of the opposition seem most vulnerable to his appeals and whether winning their support will suffice to carry the day. Unless the gains he can make clearly will carry his party into power, however, he may risk losses among his established supporters who have not heretofore been willing to make common cause with the opposition faction and may not see the value of doing so.[2]

Recent candidates for President afford many excellent examples of "do's" and "don't's." President Harry S. Truman in his campaign of 1948 provided the classic recent illustration of the majority-party candidate mustering his own adherents, rejecting the demands of dissidents whom he could not please, and appealing to other majority-party dissidents so effectively that he undermined a second organized defection.

Alone among majority-party candidates in modern times, Mr. Truman faced open, organized defection from both the right and left wings of his own party. In the South, Strom Thurmond of South Carolina campaigned for President as the candidate of a states'-rights party. In four states of the deep South, he replaced Mr. Truman in the Democratic column and easily carried them. The President wisely perceived that Mr. Thurmond's candidacy would hurt him, but would not help his Republican opponent, Governor Thomas E. Dewey of New York, for Dewey had no chance to best Thurmond without Truman on the ticket to divide the Democratic vote. Mr. Truman also correctly perceived that he could not meet Mr. Thurmond's extreme segregationist and antifederal position without sacrificing the bulk of his support among northern and western liberals, who formed the majority of the

[2] See Philip E. Converse *et al.,* "Electoral Myth and Reality: the 1964 Election," *American Political Science Review,* LXI (June 1965), 323-324.

Democratic Party. He therefore made no serious attempt either to placate Mr. Thurmond or to defeat him.

The other defection was more serious. Henry Wallace—twice Secretary of Agriculture under Franklin D. Roosevelt, and the man Mr. Truman had succeeded as Vice President when Mr. Roosevelt chose to make a change in running mates in 1944—was campaigning as the Progressive Party candidate for President. Appealing primarily to liberals in the Democratic Party, Wallace also had the misfortune of gathering about him extreme left-wing elements which never had been associated with either major party. Because his appeal would pull votes in the pivotal states, President Truman correctly saw Wallace as a major threat to his candidacy.

Truman accordingly barnstormed the nation with great vigor. He energetically espoused a highly progressive program of reform for labor, the aged, the farmer, and the Negro; urged resources development; and advanced an enlightened foreign policy of economic aid to restore the nations of western Europe to economic health. His peppery attacks on the Republican Eightieth Congress, which had enacted over his veto several major pieces of legislation anathematic to Democrats, delighted liberal intellectuals as well as the party rank and file. "Give 'em Hell, Harry!" his partisans would shout, and Mr. Truman, with obvious appreciation, would interrupt his address to reply, "That's what I'm doin'!" Although the pollsters counted him out well before Election Day, the voters did not—and returned him to office with a majority in both houses of Congress.

By contrast, Senator Barry Goldwater, the minority-party candidate in 1964, so grossly misconceived the strategy of a minority candidate for President that he not only brought upon himself the worst defeat any minority-party candidate had received in a generation but also carried down with him many well-entrenched Republican office holders.

Democrats experienced a similar disaster in 1924 when their presidential candidate, John W. Davis, made a conservative appeal which drove liberals in large numbers to support the third-party candidate, Senator Robert M. La Follette of Wisconsin.

Shifts of party allegiance, sometimes durable ones, occur among special groups within the American population from time to time. Sometimes exchanges of groups offset the gains for each major party. At other times shifts may reduce the advantage of the majority party and enable the minority to mount serious challenges.

A series of such shifts away from the Republican Party took place over a long period of time beginning within a decade after the Civil War. Typically the defectors established third parties, sometimes a series of them, over a period of one or two generations. Finally their sons joined the Democratic Party at the time of the Great Depression.

Early versions of dissent took the form of the Greenback Party and centered on schemes for easy credit and the regulation of railroad rates. Free coinage of silver, which had special appeal to the silver-producing Mountain states, became so promising an issue that the Democratic candidate of 1896, William Jennings Bryan, made it a major campaign issue and temporarily pulled to his party's banner many "silver" Republicans.

By 1912, defection took the form of the Progressive Party with former Republican President Theodore Roosevelt as its champion. Roosevelt carried six northern and western states and helped many Progressive candidates win congressional or state offices. Collapse of the Progressive movement nationally with Roosevelt's return to regular Republicanism in 1916 led to state Progressive parties as in Wisconsin or to new Farmer-Labor parties in the northern and far-western states. In several states, these parties became the second party, and in a few the majority.

Union with the Democrats came in 1932, when Franklin D. Roosevelt attracted most Progressives and Farmer-Laborites to his banner. In some states, fusion parties were established. The Minnesota Democratic Party, for example, still also proudly wears the Farmer-Labor title.

A similar series of defections from the Democratic Party began in the South following World War II. Memories of the Civil War and postwar Reconstruction policies, imposed by the dominant Republican party, continue to make adherence to that party label a political liability in most parts of the South. So southern conservatives who despaired of their policy objectives from the liberal-dominated national Democratic Party began doing what liberal Republicans had done two generations earlier: they formed sectional third parties which had a serious chance to win electoral votes.

The Goldwater candidacy of 1964 had the same sort of effect upon conservative southern Democrats which the Bryan candidacy of 1896 had upon liberal western Republicans. They toyed temporarily with membership in the other major party. But the advantages of gaining high station within the majority party remain so great, and the opportunities to use hard-won congressional seniority remain so significant, that practical political advantage outweighs the virtues of greater political homogeneity within the "out" party. As it did with the dissident liberal Republicans of the West, major-party realignment in the South may well come a generation hence from the sons of the Dixiecrats.

THE STRATEGY OF PARTY LEADERSHIP

A presidential candidate's own position of leadership within his party makes another enormous difference in the likelihood of his success and therefore in the way he can conduct his campaign. Normally he finds himself in one of three basic leadership situations: he may be the incumbent seeking a second term; he may be a member of the President's party who is seeking to succeed him; or he may be the challenger sponsored by the Loyal Opposition.

Of the three positions, the greatest advantage lies with the incumbent President. The most trying task befalls the candidate who would succeed an incumbent of his own party. Between the two, stands the challenger. Against an incumbent President, he has a nearly impossible task. Against a would-be successor, he has real hope of success.

THE ADVANTAGES OF INCUMBENCY

An incumbent President of the United States usually can win reelection. Indeed, so great is his advantage that since 1900 only two incumbent Presidents have been defeated when seeking reelection. In 1912, William Howard Taft lost because his Republican Party split. In 1932, Herbert Hoover lost because the Great Depression turned many of his supporters into Democrats. Without such major political catastrophes, even a President of the minority party can win reelection, as Woodrow Wilson proved in 1916 and as Dwight D. Eisenhower confirmed in 1956.

A President seeking reelection has many advantages. Of greatest importance is his famous name. He is known worldwide. Whatever he says, whatever he does, wherever he goes, he makes news. People recognize his picture, listen to what he says, line the streets to see him pass. No challenger can buy enough advertising to match the attention the President gets just by being President.

The incumbent also has experience in being President. Only a former President can claim equal qualification, for the job is unique and solitary. No standard steps of ascent to the presidency have ever been marked out in American politics, as they have to the prime ministership in Britain. Only once in American history has a former President challenged an incumbent President as a major-party candidate—in 1892. Significantly, perhaps, the former President, Grover Cleveland, won.

The incumbent President shapes the issues of the campaign. His proposals for new laws are before the Congress for approval or rejection. The acts of his administration are the subjects of debate. The programs he chooses to emphasize become major issues, by his choice. The statements he makes on them are public policy while he lives in the White House. Singular indeed is the challenger who can create a major issue of his own, as Adlai E. Stevenson did in 1956 with his proposal to ban atomic testing. Most challengers have been content to exploit accumulated dissatisfactions by promising to take the country "back to normalcy," or to "end the Hoover Depression," or to "bring the boys back from Korea," or to "get the country moving again."

A united political party is normally another advantage for the President. Freed from a contest for his party's nomination, he is able to center his preconvention political activities on creating party unity and securing good candidates to join him on the ticket. His status enables him to mediate or settle intraparty rivalries. His patronage summons the regular local party organizations to his cause. His programs attract his party's idealists.

Campaign funds, too, are available for a President. Only Harry

Truman, in 1948, suffered for want of money. Yet this shortage turned to a flood of gold the morning after victory when many a lagging Democrat discovered that he had forgotten to mail his campaign check, which had been written several days before!

Support for an incumbent President's candidacy is provided by the entire administration. His cabinet members are expected to deliver their home states and to campaign elsewhere on his behalf. Congressional leaders solicit his appearance on their behalf, and return the favor by using their personal organizations to assemble votes for both of them.

Despite an incredibly heavy schedule of public work and political appearances, the President can keep abreast of events and can present fresh ideas in well-turned phrases. A large and experienced personal staff is always at his call—to brief him, to write his speeches, to do his research, to handle the press, to conciliate the Congress, to control the administration, and to protect his time. Rare is the challenger who, with uncertain future, can assemble comparable talent to aid him.

One special advantage the President enjoys because of the office he holds. His every move is professionally planned and managed by the Secret Service, which commands the respect and cooperation of law-enforcement officers throughout the land.

One last advantage is drawn from human nature itself, as Thomas Jefferson noted in the Declaration of Independence. Mankind prefers the known to the unknown. The nation knows how the incumbent will perform. It has no such knowledge of the challenger. "Don't change horses in the middle of the stream" can be the President's convincing advice to the people.

THE PROBLEMS OF SUCCESSION

He who would succeed an incumbent President of his own party faces special handicaps which make the task most difficult. So great are they, indeed, that since 1884, when the Democratic Party finally recovered sufficiently from the Civil War to mount a successful presidential campaign, only two of the seven men who have tried have been successful. In 1908, William Howard Taft succeeded Theodore Roosevelt in the White House. Handpicked by the President, he had served in his cabinet and commanded the undivided loyalty of the dominant Republican Party. In 1928, Herbert Hoover similarly succeeded Calvin Coolidge.

Both attempts at succession since World War II have failed. In 1952, Adlai E. Stevenson sought to succeed Harry S. Truman. In 1960, Vice President Richard M. Nixon tried to follow Dwight D. Eisenhower in the presidency. Earlier, James G. Blaine in 1884, William Jennings Bryan in 1896, and James M. Cox in 1920 also had tried and failed.

The successor's basic disadvantage is that he must defend the preceding administration without having been responsible for it. Even a former Vice President or cabinet officer, willing to embrace the administration and all its works, finds himself saddled with its mistakes, but his predecessor credited with its victories. If he chooses to differ with its policies, he risks appearing to repudiate his party's leader and all those who have loyally worked under him. Thus he must pay for the accumulated dissatisfactions with his predecessor without gaining substantially from his achievements. Even the successor who has not been associated with the national administration and chooses to disassociate himself from it finds that he has only invited internal party disharmony without really being able to sway those voters determined to "throw the rascals out."

Another major handicap for a successor is the unavoidable fight for national attention. No matter how hard he tries, he finds that the President continues to command the national limelight and competes with him for public attention. Thus when a loyal successor speaks on issues of policy, he appears to offer a less experienced view of the President's policies, and the public continues to turn to the experienced leader for the authoritative answer. If the President conscientiously shuns the headlines in an effort to avoid competing with his party's new champion (as Dwight D. Eisenhower tried to do in 1960), he appears not to support him or to have reservations about his policy directions. Thus the successor's party unavoidably speaks with two policy voices and presents an appearance of confusion or internal conflict to the electorate.

The successor also finds that his party's national committee is staffed by the President's men. Yet he cannot replace its leaders with his own (as he should if he is to run an effective campaign) without appearing to repudiate the President. He is forced, therefore, to build a duplicate national campaign committee and to use the President's national committee as best he can. Even with the best of goodwill, misunderstanding is almost certain to arise.

The successor may add some handicaps of his own. Unless he has been Vice President, as Richard Nixon had been, or has been a prominent cabinet member like William Howard Taft or Herbert Hoover, he may have no national reputation. In 1952, Adlai E. Stevenson was governor of Illinois, but was unknown nationally. In 1920, James M. Cox was a three-term governor of Ohio with but a limited national political image. If he lacks a national reputation, the successor must build one and thus may face many of the basic problems of the challenger.

Nevertheless, the successor enjoys some of the advantages of the incumbent. He can usually count on the President's help as well as the assistance of the cabinet. He enjoys an inside knowledge of issues and can draw on the detailed expertise of the executive branch for information. Being in power, his party can raise funds more easily. If he has won nomination with the President's support, and without a fight, he may also lead a united party. Such assets, though, have but limited utility against a challenger who escapes the successor's liabilities.

THE STRATEGY OF CHALLENGE

A challenger has both inherent assets and inherent weaknesses. His basic offer to the electorate is a change. He will bring to the White House and the national administration new faces and new vigor and new hopes. He will dispose of rascals and right wrongs. He will "reestablish confidence" in our word or our money.

He also can offer a change in political philosophy, by distinguishing between his principles and the principles of the party in power. If he uses general terms—as Kennedy did with his characterization of the Republican position as "do nothing" and his own as "getting the country moving again"—he can appeal effectively for broad support. If he uses specific issues—as Goldwater did with the Tennessee Valley Authority, field use of nuclear weapons, and the income tax—or slogans with narrow appeal, he risks isolating himself on the left or right.

The challenger's primary weaknesses are his lack of experience as chief executive and his lack of access to the details of policy problems. When he confronts an incumbent, these handicaps are virtually insurmountable. When he challenges a would-be successor, he can assert his own competing qualifications, but he still must depend on his own staff to help identify and help exploit the issues.

A challenger also must build a nationwide political image. Rare indeed is the challenger who enters the race with an established national reputation. He is more likely to be known primarily in his home state and to be associated with state or sectional issues. Building a national image and demonstrating competence in national issues, both domestic and foreign, thus become added hurdles for the challenger. If he already enjoys a national reputation, even a nonpolitical one, as did General Dwight D. Eisenhower in 1952, and has the good fortune to face a would-be successor who does not, he can be a serious contender for power.

Several other advantages also are the challenger's. Having won nomination with his own forces, he can take over the national committee and shape it to his needs. He can praise the achievements of previous Presidents of his own party without having to apologize for their long-forgotten sins. And he faces no competitor for national attention within his own party. Living former Presidents can come to his aid without usurping the limelight or casting doubt on his ability to grapple with current problems.

Even if he has won the nomination after a bitter internal fight, a skillful challenger can use his leadership to unite his party, as Eisenhower did in 1952.

THE NEED FOR FITTING THE TIMES

A presidential candidate must fit the times. If the times call for action, as they did at the depths of the Depression in 1932, a candidate, like Franklin D. Roosevelt, who stands for action fits the times. If the nation has been through a rapid series of great changes and wishes a pause to consolidate and reflect, as in 1920, a candidate who represents a "return to normalcy" and opposes further change, like Warren G. Harding, may fit the times. If the nation is weary of an unpopular war, as it was of the Korean war in

1952, a candidate who can seriously offer to end the conflict, as Eisenhower did, will fit the times.

Sometimes the mood of the nation is unclear. Then arises the rare opportunity for a candidate to interpret the meaning of the times and to lead the country either to action or to consolidation of position. Such was the election of 1960, when either candidate might well have fit the times and the difference between them was less than one vote per precinct across the land.

Many able men have run for President at the wrong time. Their qualities and views fit another year or a different time. Stephen Douglas might well have won the presidency had he been the Democratic candidate in 1856, when the nation was still willing to try compromise on the slavery issue. Indeed, had he then gained the White House, his sense of the possible might well have postponed the Civil War. By 1860, when he did run, the nation was beyond compromise. Lincoln then represented the position of the northern states.

Charles Evans Hughes, one of the nation's leading attorneys, later to serve with great distinction as Chief Justice of the Supreme Court, challenged Woodrow Wilson in the midst of World War I. Had he been the Republican nominee in 1920, he could easily have won the presidency. Cox, the Democratic candidate in 1920, was generally regarded as the better man. Yet he stood for change at a time when a majority wanted a "return to normalcy" and less action from their government.

Herbert Hoover, one of the nation's greatest humanitarians and the incumbent President, represented in the voters' minds a policy of inaction in 1932 when the nation, in the depths of the Depression, was calling upon the government to act.

THE STRATEGY OF APPEAL

A candidate for President must attract a majority of the American voters. No single appeal, however broad, will suffice. The prudent candidate makes both broad, general appeals and specific proposals aimed to please particular groups.

No candidate is free to advocate anything he pleases. He is limited not only by his strategic position and the times, but also by his own past public record, the posture of his opponent, the real issues of the day upon which he is obliged to take a stand, and his own convictions. Only a rare candidate—like General Eisenhower in 1952, who had never been in political life and who had no past record on public issues—can avoid even one of these limits.

The basic appeals must be positive. Attacks on an opposing presidential candidate or even on his program are hazardous. The American public prefers to believe that anyone nominated by either of the two major parties is worthy of the office. The voters are more interested in hearing what a candidate proposes to do than what is wrong with his opponent. Only a challenger usually can make much headway by appealing to accumulated discontents. Seldom can an incumbent gain from attacking the challenger or his program.

Thus broad appeals must go to the basic yearnings of the time. The candidate must have "kept the country out of war" as Wilson claimed in 1916, propose a "return to normalcy" in the manner of Harding in 1920, offer action to end a depression as Roosevelt did in 1932, or wish to end the war in Korea as Eisenhower suggested in 1952. Sometimes broad appeals can exploit the situation, as Johnson's did in 1964 when he called for unity at home and spoke for moderation.

Specific appeals must recognize the legitimate needs of various segments of the nation and offer to meet them. So long as the appeals are within the bounds of accepted accommodation, or even if they are the next step just beyond, they will please the recipients and not offend others. Appeals which sacrifice one group to reward another, however, are highly dangerous. Only if the group to be favored has clearly been the victim of unfair conditions and the group to be penalized has clearly enjoyed unjust privileges can such an appeal hope to win votes.

One rule remains inviolate: Never attack an established institution or an established interest without good cause. If there is no issue and the institution has general support, leave it alone. The candidate who undertakes gratuitous attacks only loses the votes of the friends and beneficiaries of the existing arrangement. He can gain only the votes of the institution's enemies—who necessarily must be fewer than its friends—and he cannot be sure of them.

In modern times, only Senator Goldwater has violated this rule.

He attacked the Tennessee Valley Authority, questioned some aspects of social security, and suggested changes in the income tax. No one who was not already for him was attracted to his cause by these attacks, and many who might have given him serious attention dismissed him as a serious presidential candidate once they heard them. The result was disaster for his cause and for those who sought power in his wake.

These basic circumstances, over which the candidate really has little control, can determine the outcome of a presidential election almost regardless of the adequacy of organization, financing, and personal effort. If his party is dominant, if he is the incumbent, and if he fits the times, a candidate with a well-organized, hard-hitting campaign which unites his party and appeals broadly for public support should gain victory. Analysts would count the election a "reaffirmation of confidence."

If his party is the minority, if he is opposing the incumbent, and if he represents a basic posture which is not in tune with the times, a candidate is likely to fail no matter how well he handles his campaign.

When the advantages of these basic circumstances are divided between the two major-party candidates, however, a deviating election may be in the making. Since the Civil War, all six deviating elections have been marked by a division of the advantages of the basic circumstances between the two major candidates. In two, 1916 and 1956, the minority-party candidate was the incumbent. In two others, 1884 and 1952, the minority-party candidate faced a nonincumbent attempting to succeed an incumbent of his own party.

The other two deviating elections involved very special circumstances which gave the minority party an extraordinary advantage. In 1892, the Democrats nominated Grover Cleveland, who had won a deviating election in 1884 and had lost in 1888 by a quirk of the electoral college. In 1912, the majority party divided, fielding both the incumbent as the Republican candidate and the preceding two-term incumbent as the Progressive Party candidate. With but 42 per cent of the vote, the minority-party candidate had no trouble prevailing in a three-way race. The majority-party candidate actually ran third.

Thus each presidential candidate shapes his strategy to exploit his circumstances. The election system, his political strength in the pivotal states, the relative national strength of his party, his position as party leader, and how well his political image fits the times may all be conditions to which he must adjust but which he cannot significantly alter. The "best man" does not always have the advantage and does not always win.

JOHNSON STRATEGY IN 1964

President Lyndon B. Johnson entered the 1964 campaign as the candidate of the majority party, the incumbent, and the man of the times. The mood of the Republic, still stricken by the tragic assassination of John F. Kennedy, was to fulfill the young President's hopes and aspirations. Johnson, Kennedy's chosen successor, had not only promised to carry forward the Kennedy program, but had delivered a dazzling display of his legislative leadership in the spring of 1964. Much remained to be done, and Johnson could believably lay claim to being the best-qualified American to make it all come true.

To these enormous advantages, his opponent generously donated another: the center of the political spectrum. Isolating himself on the political right, Goldwater invited nonbelievers to leave his cause and, in effect, to join Johnson in the campaign.

Johnson's strategy of appeal, accordingly, had three tactical goals: to keep all regular Democratic voters with him, to attract moderate and liberal Republicans cut adrift by Goldwater's conservatism, and to keep Goldwater isolated on the right by attacking his most vulnerable statements and votes. Goldwater thus also contributed to Johnson's tactics by occupying some positions so vulnerable that the incumbent could safely and profitably attack.

To most Democrats, Johnson appealed as Kennedy's heir. Liberal domestic-policy goals, continued internationalism, and traditional party allegiance were his pleas. He pointed with pride to the legislative performance in the spring and summer of 1964 as proof of his intentions.

He also added a new foundation of Johnsonian idealism—the Great Society—in which Americans would attain the third purpose of government set forth in the Declaration of Independence: the pursuit of happiness. Lyndon Johnson wanted to establish himself as a national leader in his own right with his own creative program.

To confirm his own independent image as a national moderate who could be trusted to carry out a liberal program, he chose Senator Hubert Humphrey as his running mate. Leader of the Senate's liberal Democrats and Majority Whip, Humphrey had also been a contender against Kennedy for the 1960 nomination. Thus, at one stroke, Johnson set a path for using the Kennedy image for the campaign while laying the foundations for his own separate administration in the years ahead.

To win Republican votes, he welcomed all Americans to his cause. "The butcher, the baker, the candlestick maker," to quote the President's use of an old rhyme, all deserved a moderate government which would preserve the gains of the past and build a better world for tomorrow. Thus unity and responsibility both at home and abroad became his second theme.

To keep Senator Goldwater isolated politically, the President vigorously exploited the Arizonan's self-identification with the right wing. He sharpened the policy contrast between them on both foreign and domestic issues. He attacked Goldwater especially for his advocacy of placing tactical nuclear weapons at the disposal of field commanders, selling the TVA, making social security voluntary, and restricting the graduated net income tax.

Johnson's only inherent handicap was his southern power base. Yet he hailed from Texas, the largest, wealthiest, most western, and most modernized of the old Confederate states. And Texas, teeming with new migrants and thriving with new industry, remembered better the Alamo than the Civil War. To end that problem, he needed only to prove his willingness to try to solve the problems facing other sections of the nation. This he did both in his travels and in his appeals.

The strategy worked. Except for the ardent segregationists of the South, who viewed Johnson as a heretic deserting them for larger rewards, virtually all regular Democrats supported him.

A great many Republicans joined his cause as well. Some were active organization leaders, and several had served in the cabinet of the last Republican administration. Chiefly liberals and moderates, they were disturbed by the ideological position of some of Goldwater's sponsors and supporters as well as by several of the Senator's statements on the issues of the day. They were deeply concerned over the potential posture of a Goldwater administration. Accordingly, they actively campaigned on the President's behalf with words, money, and votes, so that they might legitimately claim a voice in the government in the years ahead.

Johnson thus preempted the entire political spectrum from right of center to the liberal left and captured one of the greatest majorities in American two-party history.

GOLDWATER STRATEGY IN 1964

Any Republican candidate faced a major uphill fight for the presidency in 1964. As the minority-party candidate facing an incumbent President, his chief hope to win sufficient votes lay in fitting the times better and in appealing to a wider constituency than did his opponent.

Nevertheless, the Republican Party selected a candidate who did not fit the times and who appealed to a more narrow constituency than did any Republican candidate in a generation. What miscalculations of strategy led to such a selection and to such appeals when the odds against victory were already so great?

Perhaps the basic weakness of the Goldwater strategy was the underlying premise that the Democratic coalition forged by Franklin D. Roosevelt was disintegrating and that the long-term "liberal" trend of the American voter was reversible—indeed was in the process of dramatic reversal. The new consensus, according to conservative theorists, would include historically conservative small businessmen, professional men and women, farmers, and an increased number of suburban and central-city voters, particularly in the West.

To confirm their theory, conservative strategists pointed out that Republican fortunes were on the upswing. Following the substantial Democratic victories in courthouse, Congress, and statehouse in 1958, the Republican percentage of the congressional vote and of state legislative seats had increased significantly in 1960 and 1962.

Leaders of the Draft Goldwater campaign in 1962 and 1963 believed the Arizona Senator would be the ideal candidate to achieve the new consensus. An important consideration in their selection was Goldwater's commitment to the "conservative cause." For, even in the face of the "win-oriented," "nonideological" history and nature of the American two-party system, these conservative strategists felt it imperative and timely to present the American voter with "a choice not an echo."

Architects of the Goldwater strategy contended there was widespread dissatisfaction with the ideological "flabbiness" of recent Republican campaigns. The Goldwater theory held that the "metooist" flavor of recent Republican presidential candidates had actually kept many "real" Republicans home from the polls on Election Day simply because they were offended by the lack of issue differentiation between the Republican and Democratic presidential nominees. If a "true" Republican were nominated—one with strong conservative leanings—their argument ran, a large army of the stay-at-home, conservative Republican voters would march to the polls to make the difference between victory and defeat.

The "stay-at-home" conservatives were a figment of wishful thinking. Philip E. Converse and his associates at the Survey Research Center repudiated the concept with these words:

. . . we know of no reputable sample surveys at any time in this period that gave any shred of reason to believe that this significant pool of stay-at-home Republicans existed. Indeed, such findings as were relevant pointed massively in the opposite direction. . . . Indeed, each time we isolate that polar minority who not only have an intense commitment to the Republican Party, but whose commitment is of a highly sensitive ideological sort, turnout typically reaches proportions staggering for the American system: 96 percent, 98 percent . . . In 1952 those Republicans who reported during the campaign that they would have preferred the "conservative" Taft over the "liberal" Eisenhower—exactly those Republicans to whom the theory refers—actually turned out at much *higher* rates to vote for Eisenhower in the November election (94 percent) than did the set of Republicans who indicated satisfaction with Eisenhower's nomination (84 percent).[3]

Such a strategy, based on a possible consensus of the "new conservative" strength in America, and including the "new and enlightened South" and a heavy number of stay-at-home voters, misjudged both the nature of the American party system and the mood of the American voter in 1964. Moreover, the strategy, boldly conceived on the model of past European political parties, developed costly intraparty conflict when it advanced a candidate as its spokesman who was clearly the minority candidate of a minority party.

Goldwater and his supporters, true to the "party-responsibility" theory upon which their strategy was based, strove mightily to convert the Republican Party from an arena of compromise into an ideological union which would espouse a consistently conservative philosophy.

In his acceptance speech at the Republican national convention, Senator Goldwater called for uncompromising conservatism and basic ideological uniformity.[4] Once nominated, he immediately moved to make the Republican national committee ideologically pure. His conservative associates were placed in all of the key stations. Old-time "arena-style" leaders of the committee were fired outright, given minor tasks, or bypassed.[5]

As the campaign developed, Goldwater handled the three major issues—foreign and defense policy, social-welfare legislation, and civil rights—in an ideological, noncompromising stance. On each of these issues strong and responsible support existed for the position advanced by the Republican standard-bearers. But on each issue the purist political style of an ideological candidate made coalescence of support difficult and subjected the Republican nominee to effective attack from the opposition.

The issue of foreign and defense policy, for example, grew largely from Senator Goldwater's strongly worded attacks concern-

[3] *Ibid.,* pp. 322-323.
[4] See Chapter III.
[5] See *GOP Campaign Organization 1964* (Republican National Committee); and *Washington Post,* November 26, 1964, p. A41.

ing the conduct of the war in South Vietnam. Even though many of the suggestions made by the Republican presidential candidate have since been implemented by President Johnson, the thought of any kind of war escalation was naturally abhorrent to most Americans. Skillfully exploited by mass-communications experts, the prophetic but unpopular Goldwater foreign-policy positions became the focal point for major public anxiety.

The impact of the Goldwater image on voters concerned with social-welfare issues was seen most dramatically in the 13 per cent shift of voters 50 years of age and older (as compared with the 1960 presidential election) from the Republican to the Democratic presidential candidate. This was the largest shift noted among all age groups in the 1964 presidential campaign. Republican strategy here, based on an assumed conservative trend among older voters, appeared to misjudge the level of support for social-welfare programs in general and the support among senior citizens for the social-security program in particular. Even though Senator Goldwater had, in fact, voted in 1956 and 1958 to strengthen social-security programs, his suggestion of making social security voluntary was used by Democratic leaders to raise serious doubts about him in the minds of the millions of voters with a direct or indirect interest in the social-security program.

On the issue of civil rights, Goldwater's straightforward, though purist, position of condemning racial discrimination but questioning the effectiveness and constitutionality of certain civil-rights legislation was immediately susceptible to vastly varying interpretations by detractors and supporters alike.

On the one hand, a Republican pamphlet affirming Goldwater's personal record on civil rights and assailing that of Johnson was used by Democrats in the South to persuade white Southerners to vote for Johnson. On the other hand, Goldwater's Senate vote against the 1964 civil-rights bill was used heavily by Democrats in the North to reduce sharply Goldwater's support among Negro voters and among those white voters with a strong commitment to the civil-rights program.

From the outset, the Republican presidential strategy in 1964 was doomed to failure. It counted on an outpouring of support from stay-at-home voters who turned out to be an electoral myth. Moreover, it attempted to impose an ideological, nonpolitical pattern on a nation which had grown to maturity under a political system in which compromise, bargaining, inconsistencies, and modifications were unashamedly accepted as necessary to bring unity out of diversity.

When such a basic change as was proposed by the Goldwater strategy is attempted, disastrous results are fairly predictable, not only for the party which elects to deviate so drastically from the established pattern of American presidential politics but potentially for the two-party system itself and for the stability of the nation.

Bibliography

Campbell, Angus, *et al. The American Voter.* New York: Wiley, 1960.

Campbell, Angus, *et al. The Voter Decides.* Evanston, Ill.: Row, Peterson, 1954.

Campbell, Angus, and Warren E. Miller. "The Motivational Basis of Straight and Split Ticket Voting," *American Political Science Review,* LI (June 1957), 293-312.

Converse, Philip E., *et al.* "Electoral Myth and Reality: the 1964 Election," *American Political Science Review,* LIX (June 1965), 323-324.

Converse, Philip E., *et al.* "Stability and Change in 1960: A Reinstating Election," *American Political Science Review,* LV (June 1961), 269-280.

David, Paul T., ed. *The Presidential Election and Transition, 1960-1961.* Washington: Brookings Institution, 1961.

Key, V. O., Jr. *Politics, Parties, and Pressure Groups.* 5th ed. New York: Crowell, 1964.

Ogden, Daniel M., Jr. "A Voting Behavior Approach to Split-Ticket Voting in 1952," *Western Political Quarterly,* XI (September 1958), 481-493.

Schattschneider, E. E. *Party Government.* New York: Farrar and Rinehart, 1942.

Stokes, Donald E. "Party Loyalty and the Likelihood of Deviating Elections," *Journal of Politics,* XXIV (November 1962), 689-702.

Stokes, Donald E. "Some Dynamic Elements of Contests for the Presidency," *American Political Science Review,* LX (March 1966), 19-28.

Chapter III

Nominating the Candidate

 American presidential candidates are nominated at national conventions of the major political parties. Customarily national conventions are held in the summer of election years. In 1968 the Republican National Convention will meet in Miami, Florida, from August 5 to 8; the Democratic National Convention, in Chicago, Illinois, from August 26 to 29.

Theoretically, a national convention constitutes a representative assembly of rank-and-file party members. Acting in their name, it nominates candidates for President and Vice President, drafts the party program, adopts rules of procedure to conduct the party's affairs, and establishes the national committee and elects its members.

THE EVOLUTION OF THE NATIONAL CONVENTION

Political-party conventions developed in the United States during the second quarter of the nineteenth century. The earliest method of candidate designation was by a caucus of party members who had been elected to Congress. Similarly, state legislators proposed nominees for governor and other offices at the state level. This "legislative" caucus soon gave way in the states to a "mixed" caucus in which party organizations in those districts represented by a member of the opposition party in the legislature were allowed to select delegates to speak for them in the nominating decision.

The congressional caucus held sway nationally until challenged by Andrew Jackson in the election of 1824. Poor attendance at the Republican-Democratic caucus and the defeat of the Republican-Democratic caucus nominee of that year, William H. Crawford, shattered confidence in the system. By 1832 the convention prevailed for both major parties.

Following the Civil War, party leaders and lobbyists so openly manipulated many state conventions that the system fell into disrepute. Between 1900 and 1910 most states provided by law that candidates would be nominated at a direct primary election conducted by the state. Only five states still permit conventions to nominate a very few important candidates for high office such as governor and congressman. All require nomination by primary for lesser offices.

The national convention has remained the system for presidential nominations, however, and state conventions are still used to select most delegates to the national conventions, to adopt state party platforms, and to conduct party business.

National nominating conventions have remained in style for sound political reasons. First, the convention really has but one nominating decision to make—the one for President. Public attention on that selection is so great that the unsavory practices which plagued state nominating conventions have never developed. The presidential candidate customarily is accorded the privilege of selecting his running mate. In recent times the only exception has been Adlai E. Stevenson's decision in 1956 to permit the Democratic National Convention to name the vice-presidential candidate. A hot contest ensued between Senator Estes Kefauver of Tennessee and Senator John F. Kennedy of Massachusetts. Kefauver won, but Kennedy was catapulted into contention for the presidency in 1960.

Second, a national presidential preference primary for each party would be prohibitively expensive. In 1964, the general-election campaign alone cost the two political parties and their auxiliary committees an estimated $34.8 million.[1] In 1960, they spent $25 million.

---

[1] Herbert E. Alexander, *Financing the 1964 Election* (Princeton, N.J.: Citizens' Research Foundation, 1966), p. 7.

Third, the national conventions afford the state party leaders their only real opportunity to gather together to organize for the presidential campaign. Since the election itself must be conducted separately in each state, winning control of Congress requires no interstate organization, or compromise. Without a presidential candidate to nominate, state party leaders would avoid meeting primarily to adopt a platform because a debate on issues followed by voting could only divide and embitter them. Thus the very ability to unite behind the candidate and to campaign successfully for him turns to a significant degree upon the freedom of state party leaders to choose the candidate after face-to-face bargaining among themselves.

THE MATTER OF "AVAILABILITY"

At the heart of bargaining over the candidate for President is a quality long known in American politics as "availability." A man is "available" to be a candidate for President if he is acceptable to the major groups in his political party, possesses certain attributes which fit the temper of the times, and has personal characteristics which identify him with the broad majority of the people.

Foremost among the requirements of availability is experience in high public office. In this century, only Wendell Willkie, Republican nominee in 1940, has lacked this quality. The governor of one of the "pivotal" states fills this requirement especially well and adds a second: the probable ability to carry a large state. Cabinet officers and United States Senators and outstanding military leaders have occasionally been viewed as available. Ability to project a warm, attractive personality on television and in personal contacts is a third element of being available.

Philosophically, a moderate liberal for the Democrats and a moderate conservative for the Republicans usually fill a fourth requirement of availability. Thus conservatives such as Senator Richard B. Russell of Georgia, the southern preference in 1956, have no real chance to win a Democratic Party nomination.

Personal characteristics also are significant. The candidate has invariably been a man, white, preferably in his early fifties (although in 1960 both John F. Kennedy and Richard M. Nixon were younger), and preferably a Protestant. Kennedy is the only Catholic elected President, and studies of the election reveal that he may have lost about 6.5 per cent of the Protestant Democratic vote for that reason—a margin which can be decisive in almost any presidential election.[2]

THE ALLOCATION OF DELEGATES

The strategy of winning nomination for the presidency at a national convention is greatly influenced by the varied and complex procedures which have developed for the allocation and selection of delegates. The allocation of delegates to both the Republican and Democratic national conventions is determined by their respective national committees. No federal regulations are imposed, so each party uses a slightly different system.

Traditionally, both parties have assigned each state two delegates for each electoral vote. The Democrats adopted the practice in 1852. Since 1896, token votes also have been accorded the organized territories and the outlying possessions of the United States if a local party affiliated with the national party. Thus the District of Columbia, Puerto Rico, and the Virgin Islands are represented at both national conventions. The Democrats also allocate delegates to the Panama Canal Zone and to Guam.[3]

Apportionment of delegates based on the electoral college does not reflect the distribution of party strength, however. To remedy this disparity, both parties have resorted to additional provisions for the assignment of delegate strength. In 1913, the Republican National Committee adopted a penalty system to reduce the influence of the traditionally Democratic southern states in the convention. The move was prompted by the famous Republican Party split in the 1912 election which was occasioned, in part, when the incumbent President, William Howard Taft, won nomination over former President Theodore Roosevelt by controlling delegates from the southern states. Changed several times, the Republican

[2] Philip E. Converse *et al.*, "Stability and Change in 1960: A Reinstating Election," *American Political Science Review*, LV (June 1961), 269-280.

[3] Clarence Cannon, *Democratic Manual for the Democratic National Convention of 1964* (Washington: Democratic National Committee, 1964), p. 17.

rule now obliges each state to "earn" delegates to represent its congressional districts. A district which casts at least 2,000 votes for the Republican candidate for President gets one delegate; a district which casts 10,000 or more gets the customary two. Although the rule decreased southern representation by 76 votes in the 1916 Republican convention,[4] it is now obsolete. In the 1964 Republican National Convention only one congressional district, in Mississippi, was penalized one vote. Goldwater's 1964 success in the South erased all penalties for the 1968 Republican National Convention.

In 1940 the Republicans and in 1944 the Democrats turned instead to bonus votes to reward the faithful. Republicans award six to each state which casts its electoral votes for the Republican candidate for President or has elected a Republican governor or Republican United States Senator since the last Republican national convention. Democrats awarded four bonus votes for the same reasons until 1960. After dropping bonus votes for their 1960 national convention, the Democrats in 1964 yielded to the demands of the big states to add bonus votes in proportion to the popular votes cast for the presidential candidate at the last election. A resolution adopted at the national-committee meeting of January 11, 1964, provided for a national convention of 2,316 votes with a maximum of 3,052 delegates to cast them, some 800 more votes than had been provided at the 1960 convention. Six rules determined the new schedule:

1. Each state was assigned three convention votes for each electoral vote.

2. Each state was given one bonus vote for every 100,000 popular votes cast for the Democratic candidate for President in 1960. Fractions over 50,000 were counted, but no state was to receive less than one such bonus vote. Only Alaska cast fewer than 50,000 Democratic votes for President in 1960. Alabama, which cast only 5 of its 11 electoral votes for John F. Kennedy, was counted as having cast only five-elevenths of its popular votes for him.

[4] See V. O. Key, Jr., *Politics, Parties, and Pressure Groups* (5th ed.; New York: Crowell, 1964), pp. 405-407.

3. States which voted for the Democratic nominee for President in 1960 were given an extra "victory" bonus of 10 votes. Alabama, however, received 5.

4. Each state received two votes for its members of the Democratic National Committee, but no alternates can be appointed for them.

5. No state was to have its representation reduced by the new apportionment system. Two small states, which had voted Democratic in 1948 but had forsaken the party ever since, gained by this provision. Montana, entitled to only 15 votes under the rules, received 2 more votes; Wyoming, entitled to only 12, picked up 3.

6. For the first time in either national convention, Guam was given representation, 3 votes. Since 1960, a Democratic Party had been established on Guam and had asked for affiliation with the national party. The District of Columbia, able henceforth to earn delegates like a state, was given its electoral quota: 2 votes for its members of the national committee, and half of the "victory" bonus.

The Democrats probably will use their new allocation system again in 1968. The big Johnson victory in 1964 therefore will be translated into a convention with 2,624 votes and a maximum of 3,095 delegates. Only Alabama, which had no Johnson electors on the 1964 ballot, will fail to receive bonus votes.

The new Democratic allocation pattern raises another question: Does every delegate have a full vote to cast? All Republican delegates cast a full vote. Democrats, however, traditionally have permitted delegates to cast fractional votes, thus allowing more persons to participate in the convention. In 1960 the Democratic National Committee provided that no delegate could have less than one-half vote. In 1964, to hold down the number of delegates, the Democrats at last adopted the same rule as the Republicans— only one delegate for each vote—but watered it down by permitting each state to send as many individuals as it had been permitted in 1960, in which case some delegates would have to be given one-half a vote. So generous was this rule that only Connecticut, Delaware, Hawaii, and Maryland were obliged to send exclusively

Democratic National Convention, 1964: Allocation of Delegates

State	Convention Votes	Maximum Number of Delegates	Electoral Votes
Alabama	38	58	10
Alaska	12	18	3
Arizona	19	34	5
Arkansas	32	54	6
California	154	162	40
Colorado	23	42	6
Connecticut	43	43	8
Delaware	22	22	3
Florida	51	58	14
Georgia	53	66	12
Hawaii	25	25	4
Idaho	15	26	4
Illinois	114	138	26
Indiana	51	68	13
Iowa	35	52	9
Kansas	27	42	7
Kentucky	34	62	9
Louisiana	46	52	10
Maine	16	30	4
Maryland	48	48	10
Massachusetts	69	82	14
Michigan	92	102	21
Minnesota	50	62	10
Mississippi	24	46	7
Missouri	58	78	12
Montana	17	32	4
Nebraska	19	32	5
Nevada	22	30	3
New Hampshire	15	22	4
New Jersey	77	82	17
New Mexico	26	34	4
New York	179	228	43
North Carolina	58	74	13
North Dakota	15	22	4
Ohio	99	128	26
Oklahoma	30	58	8
Oregon	24	34	6
Pennsylvania	125	162	29
Rhode Island	27	34	4
South Carolina	38	42	8
South Dakota	15	22	4
Tennessee	40	66	11
Texas	99	122	25
Utah	16	26	4
Vermont	12	18	3

State	Convention Votes	Maximum Number of Delegates	Electoral Votes
Virginia	42	66	12
Washington	35	54	9
West Virginia	37	50	7
Wisconsin	46	62	12
Wyoming	15	28	3
Territory			
District of Columbia	16	18	3
Canal Zone	5	8	0
Guam	3	6	0
Puerto Rico	8	14	0
Virgin Islands	5	8	0
Totals	2,316	3,052	538

full-vote delegates. In 1968, however, under the revised allocation system, no more than 944 of the 3,097 Democratic delegates will be assigned half a vote, and 15 states, including California, will have no half-vote delegates. Inasmuch as the use of half-vote delegates is optional, other states may find it far easier to hold to the full-vote rule than to decide which few delegates will get but one-half a vote. The Democrats, therefore, seem headed in practice as well as in theory toward the more easily understood full-vote-only rule.

Because some delegates always prove unable to attend the national conventions, both parties provide for alternate delegates. Each permits only one alternate for each full vote. Thus the 1964 Republican National Convention had a total of 2,616 delegates and alternates, and the Democratic had 5,260. In 1968, the Republicans can have as many as 2,648, the Democrats 5,719.

The great increase in votes at the Democratic National Convention was made for sound political reasons. The assigning of votes strictly in proportion to the electoral vote, even with a bonus for voting Democratic, did not reflect the number of Democratic voters in each state. Finding it less painful to grant votes than to take them away, the national committee simply adopted the obvious alternative to the Republican penalty system. The larger states now feel they have won recognition of their numerical support for the ticket.

Democratic National Convention, 1968: Allocation of Delegates Using 1964 Formula

State	Convention Votes	Maximum Number of Delegates
Alabama	32	56
Alaska	22	22
Arizona	19	34
Arkansas	33	54
California	174	174
Colorado	35	42
Connecticut	44	44
Delaware	22	22
Florida	63	63
Georgia	43	66
Hawaii	26	26
Idaho	25	26
Illinois	118	138
Indiana	63	68
Iowa	46	52
Kansas	38	42
Kentucky	46	62
Louisiana	36	52
Maine	27	30
Maryland	49	49
Massachusetts	72	82
Michigan	96	102
Minnesota	52	62
Mississippi	28	46
Missouri	60	78
Montana	26	32
Nebraska	30	32
Nevada	22	30
New Hampshire	26	26
New Jersey	82	82
New Mexico	26	34
New York	190	228
North Carolina	59	74
North Dakota	25	25
Ohio	115	128
Oklahoma	41	58
Oregon	35	35
Pennsylvania	130	162
Rhode Island	27	34
South Carolina	28	42
South Dakota	26	26
Tennessee	51	66
Texas	104	122
Utah	26	26
Vermont	22	22

State	Convention Votes	Maximum Number of Delegates
Virginia	54	66
Washington	47	54
West Virginia	38	50
Wisconsin	59	62
Wyoming	22	28
Territory		
District of Columbia	23	23
Canal Zone	5	8
Guam	3	6
Puerto Rico	8	14
Virgin Islands	5	8
Totals	2,624	3,095

The larger convention also permits the Democrats to reward more loyal party workers on state and county committees. Moreover, size does not seriously hamper the conduct of a convention's business. No recent national convention has been small enough to engage in policy debate, and none is expected to do so. A large convention has the virtues of allowing more people to participate in demonstrations and other events and of creating a more impressive national spectacle.

THE SELECTION OF DELEGATES

Delegate selection is a complex procedure which varies with the laws of the several states. Two distinctions are of major importance: the types of delegates and the methods by which they are chosen.

TYPES OF DELEGATES

Two types of delegates are recognized by both parties: "district" delegates and "at-large" delegates. District delegates cast the votes assigned a state because of the number of Representatives it has in Congress. A common practice is to distribute a state's district delegates equally among the congressional districts and, if the convention system of selection is used, to have the delegates to the state convention from each congressional district nominate persons to represent them at the national convention. The state convention then ratifies the choices.

"At-large" delegates are assigned a state because of the two electoral votes for its United States Senators and for any United States Representatives who are elected from the state as a whole. Bonus votes also are assigned at large. At-large delegates commonly are chosen by state conventions as a whole or by the people in a statewide primary election.

The practice of distinguishing between district and at-large delegates has led some state Democratic conventions to send full-vote district delegates and half-vote at-large delegates to the Democratic National Convention. It also can result in divided delegations, but gives a substantial advantage to the candidate who has majority support in a majority of a state's congressional districts. For example, in the Republican State Convention in the state of Washington 1952, a sharp fight took place between delegates supporting the candidacy of Senator Robert A. Taft and delegates backing Dwight D. Eisenhower for the Republican nomination for President. Taft delegates were in a majority in two congressional districts, and easily named four delegates to the national convention to represent those districts. Eisenhower delegates were dominant in four districts and similarly won eight delegates. The remaining 12 delegates (4 for the Senators, 2 for a Congressman at Large, and 6 bonus votes) were chosen at large. The Eisenhower delegates, being a majority of the convention as a whole, insisted upon a roll-call vote for each at-large delegate contest, and easily won them all. Eisenhower thereby won 20 of the state's 24 votes at the Republican National Convention.

METHODS OF CHOOSING DELEGATES

Three methods of choosing delegates are provided. Twenty-nine states permit state political-party conventions to choose delegates to the national conventions. Eighteen prescribe or permit primary elections of some sort. Three allow the state central committees of the political parties to name the delegates.[5]

[5] Richard D. Hupman and Eiler C. Ravnholt, *Nomination and Election of the President and Vice President of the United States* (Washington: Government Printing Office, 1964), pp. 43-168.

State conventions constitute an indirect method of delegate selection. Commonly the process begins with precinct caucuses held by the party leader of each such election unit in his own home. The precinct caucuses select delegates to county conventions which in turn name delegates to state conventions.

Running for selection as a national-convention delegate at a state convention often is purely a personal matter. The average delegate spends several hundred dollars of his own money and gives a week or more of his own time to serve. If there is no contest for the presidential nomination, would-be delegates solicit votes among personal friends in their party. Rarely do they promise any sort of action on platform issues or organizational questions which may arise. If there is a fight over convention delegates, as the Republicans had in 1952 and the Democrats in several states in 1960, slates of delegates may be assembled to campaign for votes by pledging support for their favorite candidate.

Presidential preference primaries take several forms. The most common permits each candidate for nomination to put forward a slate of candidates for delegate. Some states even permit slates of unpledged delegates. The voters in the primary then choose among the slates. The entire delegation can thus be won by whichever candidate wins the largest number of votes for his slate of delegates. Because California, the second-largest state, uses this system, its presidential preference primary in June can be a crucial step to the presidency.

Several states permit a variation on the slate of candidates. Wisconsin, for example, provides for the separate election of district and at-large delegates. A divided delegation can result, as was the case in 1960 when Humphrey won four districts and Kennedy carried six and the at-large delegates. Other states permit individual candidates for delegate to indicate candidate preference after their names.

Some states, like New York, elect the delegates in a primary, but do not provide for the designation of candidate preference. Because delegate positions are temporary and unpaid, and because attendance at the convention is at the delegate's personal expense, those running for delegate do not advertise their candidacy and thus are never known to the general electorate. Experience has

Presidential Preference Primary Calendar, 1968

New Hampshire	March 12
Wisconsin	April 2
Illinois	April 9
New Jersey	April 16
Massachusetts	April 23
Pennsylvania	April 23
District of Columbia	May 7
Indiana	May 7
Ohio	May 7
Nebraska	May 14
West Virginia	May 14
Oregon	May 17
Maryland	May 21
Florida	May 28
California	June 4
South Dakota	June 4

Republican National Conventions, 1964 and 1968: Allocation of Delegates

State	Delegates 1964	Delegates 1968	Electoral Votes
Alabama	20	26	10
Alaska	12	12	3
Arizona	16	16	5
Arkansas	12	18	6
California	86	86	40
Colorado	18	18	6
Connecticut	16	16	8
Delaware	12	12	3
Florida	34	34	14
Georgia	24	30	12
Hawaii	8	8	4
Idaho	14	14	4
Illinois	58	58	26
Indiana	32	26	13
Iowa	24	24	9
Kansas	20	20	7
Kentucky	24	24	9
Louisiana	20	26	10
Maine	14	14	4
Maryland	20	26	10
Massachusetts	34	34	14
Michigan	48	48	21
Minnesota	26	26	10

State	Delegates 1964	Delegates 1968	Electoral Votes
Mississippi	13	20	7
Missouri	24	24	12
Montana	14	14	4
Nebraska	16	16	5
Nevada	6	12	3
New Hampshire	14	8	4
New Jersey	40	40	17
New Mexico	14	14	4
New York	92	92	43
North Carolina	26	26	13
North Dakota	14	8	4
Ohio	58	58	26
Oklahoma	22	22	8
Oregon	18	18	6
Pennsylvania	64	64	29
Rhode Island	14	14	4
South Carolina	16	22	8
South Dakota	14	14	4
Tennessee	28	28	11
Texas	56	56	25
Utah	14	8	4
Vermont	12	12	3
Virginia	30	24	12
Washington	24	24	9
West Virginia	14	14	7
Wisconsin	30	30	12
Wyoming	12	12	3
Territory			
District of Columbia	9	6	3
Puerto Rico	5	5	0
Virgin Islands	3	3	0
Totals	1,308	1,324	538

proved that such nondesignation primaries are easily controlled by the regular party organizations.

CORRALLING DELEGATE VOTES

Nomination for President is gained by a majority vote of the delegates at a national convention. The convention ballots as often as is necessary to determine the winner, and in 1924 the Democratic convention voted 103 times before selecting John W. Davis.

Victory is in the hands of the man who can gain the support of a majority—or even a near majority—before the convention opens. Such is the simple principle upon which John F. Kennedy won the Democratic nomination in 1960 and Barry Goldwater the Republican nomination in 1964. But the road to that victory is difficult and complicated as well as very expensive.

The rules of success are: First, see that your friends are elected delegates wherever you can. Second, where you can't control delegate selection, support a neutral leader who can; then work to win his support. Third, fight for delegates openly only where you have to, but avoid picking a fight when you're sure to lose.

The struggle for delegates starts early in election year. Each state sets a different time for the selection of delegates and may permit each party to choose them at different times.

Once the selection timetable is set, each candidate goes after the votes in an orderly sequence. Victory in an early-chosen delegation can snowball into success in states where the outcome is in doubt.

The status of each candidate determines his tactics in winning delegates. An incumbent President, like Lyndon B. Johnson in 1964, is certain of nomination. Any opposition which may be presented will come from candidates who seek to publicize a policy goal or to win notoriety for themselves. In 1964, Governor George Wallace of Alabama challenged Mr. Johnson in the Democratic primaries in Wisconsin, Indiana, and Maryland, principally to demonstrate his belief that there was widespread opposition to the President's civil-rights program outside the South. He polled a surprising 34 per cent in Wisconsin, 30 per cent in Indiana, and 43 per cent in Maryland against state favorite-son candidates who served as stand-ins for the President, thereby revealing that many working-class white people in the North feared Negro competition for their jobs and Negro invasion of their neighborhoods.

In this century the only serious attempt to wrest the nomination from an incumbent President came at the Republican National Convention of 1912, when Theodore Roosevelt, who had served as President from 1901 to 1909, challenged his own handpicked successor, William Howard Taft. Defeated on the floor of the convention, Roosevelt withdrew to form the Progressive Party. The resulting three-way race for the presidency led to the election of the Democratic candidate, Woodrow Wilson.

THE NATIONAL CONVENTIONS

National conventions of both parties follow a traditional pattern of behavior which long has dismayed commentators and critics who do not understand the essentials of American politics. A convention has but one central purpose: to select a candidate for President who can be elected. All else must be subordinated. Above all, the convention must avoid a grand debate on issues of the day which would surely divide and embitter the various elements of the party.

Thus events at a national convention are designed to unite the delegates and to subordinate their differences by centering on the nomination of the candidate for President and by giving each delegate something to do about it. Each state is invited by roll call to place a candidate in nomination. Delegates then seize the spotlight by a "great demonstration" for their favorite candidate when his name is placed before the convention. National attention comes a second time to each state when the roll is called to announce the votes for presidential nominee. Such rituals are not nonsense, as so many have tried to make the American public believe. They serve a fundamental and important political purpose. They attract the attention of the voting public to the task of choosing a President. They dramatically introduce the party's presidential candidate to the nation. And they emotionally commit the rank-and-file party workers on the scene to fight for victory.

Nominating speeches are an artistic specialty. The presidential candidate often seeks a spokesman who hails from a different part of the nation or who represents another wing of his party. The speechmaker extols the virtues of the candidate—his qualities as a leader, his understanding of human needs, his command of the issues of the day, his blameless private life, his capacity to unite the party and the nation, his vigor as a crusader for goodness and justice, his unswerving dedication to freedom and democracy—but carefully refrains from mentioning his name. That comes last and is the signal for the demonstration.

Skilled nominating speakers "telegraph" the coming signal so that the demonstration will virtually explode upon the convention. A master of the art is Senator Everett Dirksen of Illinois, who closed his nomination of Senator Robert A. Taft at the Republican National Convention of 1952 by saying:

And so, my friends and fellow delegates, I present one whom I esteem as the amiable ambassador of our last best hope. I present one who is valiant for truth. I present a defender of the Republican faith. I present Mr. Republican, Mr. Integrity, Mr. American. I present Bob Taft.[6]

Pandemonium reigns. Delegates leap into the aisles, blowing horns, waving state signs, ringing bells, carrying balloons, wearing huge campaign buttons and colorful hats, throwing paper plates or confetti, lifting banners with slogans reading "Madly for Adlai" or "Go With Goldwater"—anything that will attract attention and show how enthusiastically they back their man. Around the convention floor they parade while the convention band or organ strikes up the candidate's theme song—"The Eyes of Texas Are upon You" for Lyndon B. Johnson, for example. Delegates lock arms, sing the theme song, chant "We want——." This is the delegates' hour, their chance to impress the national television audience and perhaps to be picked out of the excited crowd by the folks back home.

The voting follows. In alphabetical order the states are called. The leader of each delegation rises in response to his state's name, and for a brief moment holds the national spotlight while he records for history the decision of his delegation. Candidates' managers, delegates on the floor, and observers in the galleries keep their own running tallies of the count, watching for last-minute changes from their expectations. Delegations toward the end of the alphabet watch for the opportunity to cast the decisive ballots to nominate the candidate. The convention turns the following day to the selection of a vice-presidential candidate.

WINNING THE DEMOCRATIC NOMINATION IN 1960

The Democrats have had only two contested presidential nominating conventions since Franklin D. Roosevelt won the prize in

---

[6] *Official Report of the Proceedings of the Twenty-fifth Republican National Convention Held in Chicago, Illinois, July 7, 8, 9, 10, and 11, 1952* (Washington: Republican National Committee, 1952), p. 353.

1932. The conventions of 1936, 1940, 1944, 1948, and 1964 nominated the incumbent President. In 1956, Adlai E. Stevenson, who had been drafted from his post as governor of Illinois to be the Democratic candidate in 1952, actively campaigned for the nomination and won handily over Senator Estes Kefauver of Tennessee.

In 1960, three United States Senators jousted for the nomination: John F. Kennedy of Massachusetts, Lyndon B. Johnson of Texas, and Hubert H. Humphrey of Minnesota. Lyndon Johnson, Senate Majority Leader, realized that it would be useless for him to contest presidential primaries in northern states. He concentrated instead on marshaling the state organization-chosen delegates from the South and on picking up delegates from the Mountain states and the Pacific Coast, where he had many friends in Congress.

John F. Kennedy, on the other hand, needed to prove that he was a top-notch vote getter. He had to overcome the belief that a Catholic could not be elected President. And he had to become well known. He started with the New Hampshire primary in March and, without serious opposition, swept it. Emboldened, he risked all by entering the Wisconsin primary against Senator Hubert Humphrey from neighboring Minnesota. A narrow victory there on April 5, apparently with the overwhelming help of Republican Catholics who could cross over in the open primary, earned a majority of Wisconsin delegates but obliged him to enter a third key primary, in West Virginia, where Catholics formed but 5 per cent of the voters. Vigorous, well-financed campaigning and a sweeping victory on May 10 established him as a leading vote getter and knocked Humphrey out of the race.[7]

Opposed by no other serious presidential candidate, Kennedy also carried the Indiana, Nebraska, Maryland, and Oregon primaries, netting 134 votes. These, with his block of 103 convention votes from the other five New England states, put him well into the lead.

Two other opponents awaited Kennedy in the wings: Adlai E. Stevenson, still adored by the liberals of the party; and Senator

[7] An excellent description of the 1960 struggle for delegates appears in Theodore H. White, *The Making of the President* (New York: Atheneum, 1961), Chapters 2-5.

Stuart Symington of Missouri, who commanded the very important support of former President Harry S. Truman. Stevenson did not wish to fight for the nomination. Hoping for a draft, he hung back until the very last day before convention balloting, while his supporters dissipated their efforts for want of a determined leader. Symington's hope lay wholly in a convention deadlock. If the Kennedy drive fell short of gaining a majority of the votes, he could step forward as a most acceptable second choice. With few committed delegates, he was in no position to attempt a major show of strength on the first ballot.

Shaping the drive for delegate votes was still another important American political tradition: the favorite-son candidates. When the political leaders of a state deem it advantageous to hold their strength in reserve so that a good bargain can be made at the convention, the traditional step is to pledge their delegation to one of their own political leaders, usually the governor or one of the United States Senators. California, with 81 votes, led the list of favorite-son states at Los Angeles, followed by New Jersey with 41; Minnesota, which Humphrey still held, with 31; Iowa with 26; and Kansas with 21.

Occasionally some delegations actually come uncommitted to a national convention. In 1960 two did, Pennsylvania with 81 votes and Illinois with 69. Thus three of the five big pivotal state delegations were hanging in the balance as the Democratic National Convention of 1960 opened. The strategy of deadlock, which had been Symington's from the start, now became Stevenson's as well. And Stevenson was at this point by far the more serious contender, for he had nationwide support and ready-made international issues in the U-2 debacle and the subsequent collapse of the summit conference.

But the Kennedy forces had not been idle while the convention states were selecting delegates. Michigan, with 51 votes, was the domain of a thoroughly efficient, citizen-led reform Democratic organization which had to be wooed directly, not undermined. After a conference with Senator Kennedy in early June, Governor Williams announced his personal endorsement. The bulk of New York's 114 votes were won by a quiet county-to-county campaign for district delegates. A major inroad was made in the Mountain states, which Johnson had hoped to carry, when Steward L. Udall lined up all 17 of Arizona's votes for Kennedy.

By the time the convention opened, Kennedy had 600 votes of the 761 he needed for nomination. A struggle, brief but spirited, ensued between the Kennedy and Stevenson managers for the remaining uncommitted states. Kennedy had the advantage. He was organized and running. Stevenson wouldn't initiate the challenge. First Illinois, then Pennsylvania, caucused and announced overwhelming support for Kennedy. Minnesota, released by Humphrey, divided. California, strong for Stevenson, divided also.

The Los Angeles convention followed the traditional procedures with gusto. On Tuesday, July 12, it heard the proposals of its platform committee and, after dissent on the civil-rights plank was aired by southern delegates, shouted the program through.

Late Wednesday afternoon the nominating speeches began. Orville Freeman, governor of Minnesota and one of Senator Humphrey's leading supporters, offered the name of John F. Kennedy in a good but routine speech. Johnson's and Symington's names were placed before the convention. All received rousing demonstrations. Meanwhile the galleries were filling with Stevenson followers who had managed by hard work and excellent organization to obtain some 4,000 tickets of admission.[8]

Then rose Senator Eugene McCarthy of Minnesota, also a loyal Humphrey man, to make one of the greatest nominating speeches in American convention history—for Adlai E. Stevenson. Electrified, the crowd responded to his questions. Eloquently he pleaded for the leader who had brought the citizen-politician into his own, who twice had led a revitalized party.

As Stevenson's name was shouted out above the roar of the crowd, there erupted the greatest, most spontaneous, most wildly enthusiastic demonstration within the memory of anyone present. The galleries came alive with signs. Stamping and chanting "We want Stevenson," a solid wall of people marched around the galleries. A huge ball of petitions demanding his nomination was bounced from hand to hand above the delegates' heads across the convention floor. But on the floor many delegates stood at their

[8] *Ibid.,* p. 198.

seats, moved by the demonstration, but knowing that Stevenson could not be nominated.

The roll call of the states followed promptly. As the tally advanced, it became clear that Kennedy was, if anything, running slightly ahead of the more than 700 votes the afternoon papers had predicted. Tension mounted as the count grew. Thirteen votes short of nomination, the call reached Wyoming, the very last state. Wyoming's state chairman held 15 votes and dramatically cast them all for John F. Kennedy, "the next President of the United States."

WINNING THE REPUBLICAN NOMINATION IN 1964

The fight for delegate support for the 1964 Republican presidential nomination began in earnest almost immediately after Nixon lost the 1960 presidential race to John F. Kennedy. Governor Rockefeller appeared at the national committee only days after the election was over. Some of Senator Goldwater's backers, cognizant of the beckoning opportunity, began to plan their campaign even before the President-elect took office.

The contingencies of political life altered the situation drastically between November 1960 and July 1964. For the first two years, Rockefeller clearly was the front runner for the nomination. Then, after the Governor's divorce and remarriage, Goldwater surged into the lead. With Kennedy's assassination, talk of a compromise candidate arose more and more frequently. Some Republicans advanced Senator Thruston B. Morton as the logical choice to fill the compromise role. Others suggested Henry Cabot Lodge, Governor George Romney of Michigan, and Governor William Scranton of Pennsylvania. Yet, as late as January 1964, Republican voters at the grass roots still preferred Richard Nixon, despite his 1962 gubernatorial defeat in California.[9] After some statements denying his interest, Nixon offered to serve again as his party's nominee if called upon to do so.

[9] The Harris poll showed Richard Nixon leading on January 21, 1964.

But, as the new year dawned, what appeared to many casual observers at the beginning of the nomination campaign was really the beginning of the end. Goldwater had spent the previous decade cultivating the party at the grass roots. Now he was to cash in his IOU's.

From January 1955, when he had been elected chairman of the Senatorial Campaign Committee, through the fall of 1963, Goldwater had given extensive personal assistance to congressional and senatorial candidates. Throughout that nine-year period he was in constant contact with party candidates and office holders across the country, and his enthusiastic and effective help was well remembered.

At the 1960 Republican National Convention, Goldwater had loyally called for unity behind Nixon and had acted on his words by assuming a heavy load of campaign speaking in support of the Nixon-Lodge ticket.

After 1960, Goldwater became the party's top fund raiser and made an average of from 160 to 200 speeches annually at fund-raising dinners and rallies. His vigorous leadership won him many true and lasting friends in the ranks of top state and national party organization leaders.

Now, as he stepped forward as the conservative champion, he was greeted by a corps of effective and tireless workers who had started nearly three years before the convention systematically to capture delegates for their cause. In early October 1961, a group of 22 men assembled in a conference room in Chicago to discuss the feasibility of a "conservative" Republican presidential campaign in 1964. This group shortly selected Barry Goldwater as a likely candidate to head such an effort, and soon the Draft Goldwater Committee was formed.

When the Senator announced his candidacy on January 1, 1964, a formal Goldwater for President Committee immediately organized openly to garner sufficient delegate support to win the nomination at the July convention. Two separate types of drives for delegate votes were set in motion, with two quite different results. With many debts to collect, Goldwater had an enormous advantage at state conventions. His forces systematically moved to control as many convention-chosen delegations as possible, and they managed to gather virtually all but those controlled by powerful moderate governors like Scranton, Romney, and Rockefeller.

Preference primaries proved a different story. In uncontested primaries—as in Illinois, Indiana, Ohio, and Nebraska—Goldwater swept to victory. Three primary contests, however, signaled danger.

In New Hampshire, which on March 10 held the first presidential primary in the nation, a doughty band of moderates sponsored a write-in campaign for Ambassador Henry Cabot Lodge. Although their candidate never agreed to run and stayed on his job in Vietnam, he carried the primary. Goldwater's poor showing was attributed in part to overexposure; it also came in part because on three separate occasions he urged that social security be made "voluntary." Rockefeller promptly exploited this opening, charging that such a change would bankrupt the system and would be a "personal disaster to millions of senior citizens and their families." Although Goldwater tried to recoup by announcing, "I favor a sound social-security program and I want to strengthen it," the damage was done. Neither Rockefeller, nor later President Johnson, let him forget his "voluntary" suggestion.

The New Hampshire defeat did not discourage Goldwater's organization leaders. They continued to seek support at state conventions and in states where primary elections could be entered to their advantage. As a result, delegates friendly to Goldwater were selected in South Carolina, Wisconsin, North Dakota, Kentucky, Illinois, Arizona, Louisiana, and Kansas. During one brief fifteen-day period between the last days of April and the early part of May, Barry Goldwater won 200 delegates in seven primaries and six state conventions. Clif White, codirector of the Goldwater for President field operations, claimed 250 delegates. His personal view was that at least 400 delegates could already be counted on—about four-fifths of all the delegates named to that date.

By May 5, even though many moderate and liberal Republicans still assumed that there was a chance to stop Goldwater, some national political commentators were well aware of the massive delegate support he had developed. In its issue of May 8, *Time* reported:

Suddenly like a forest fire racing out of control, the word crackled among informed Republicans: Goldwater's almost got it! It seemed hardly possible. Here was Arizona's Barry Goldwater, who only a few weeks ago appeared to be flat on his back in his quest for the GOP Presidential nomination . . . yet, as of last week, Goldwater is clearly the man to beat in San Francisco . . .[10]

Then came two primaries of major importance, Oregon and California. Under Oregon law Goldwater could not withdraw his name from the ballot; but sensing defeat and preferring to concentrate on the California primary three weeks later, he visited Oregon briefly. Rockefeller seized the opportunity to stump the state vigorously, and on May 15 won all of Oregon's delegates. Polls showed, moreover, that had Lodge been the candidate, he would have fared even better.

Calfornia was to ballot on June 2. With 86 delegates, it was the greatest prize at issue. A victory there for Goldwater would all but seal the nomination. A victory for any moderate might stop the Goldwater bandwagon.

Rockefeller joined the fray as the moderates' only candidate. Both he and Senator Goldwater campaigned vigorously with the support of tens of thousands of volunteer workers and millions of dollars. Public-opinion polls showed the contest to be very close.

Then, on the day before the California primary, Mrs. Margaretta Fitler Murphy Rockefeller presented her new husband with a son. This reminder of the difficulty in Rockefeller's personal life was enough, according to many commentators, to give Goldwater the extra advantage he needed. On June 2, Goldwater won by a few more than 60,000 votes.

The true proportions of Goldwater's strength for nomination were now clear. Yet the warnings for elections had been sounded. In the only real contests he had faced, he had lost twice and had barely won once, entirely within the minority party.

Moderate and liberal Republicans, although foreseeing impending disaster at the polls if Goldwater were their candidate, proved unable to act. At the governors' conference in Cleveland in early

[10] F. Clifton White, *Suite 3505* (New Rochelle, N.Y.: Arlington House, 1967), pp. 319-320.

June, Scranton, Rockefeller, Romney, and Nixon all made some effort to stop Goldwater, but none was really willing to declare himself leader in the battle.

Finally, on June 12, Scranton accepted the mantle of leadership. Speaking to the Maryland State Republican Convention, he announced his active candidacy. His entry into the race apparently had little effect. Steven Shadegg, one of Goldwater's strategists observed:

Between the day Scranton announced and the day the Convention opened in San Francisco, not a single delegate we had counted for Goldwater switched to the Pennsylvania Governor. Our private polls indicated that for all his efforts this Johnny-come-lately in the race failed to gain as many as ten votes.[11]

Thus the so-called moderate and liberal Republicans had failed to organize their support when it counted, and the few, feeble last-minute efforts to coalesce behind Governor Scranton merely highlighted the virtually complete control of the convention delegates and machinery by pro-Goldwater forces.

Before officially convening at the convention, Republican delegates entered into spirited discussions in the convention's rules and credentials committees. Rejection of some motions (concerning the imposition of the unit rule by state or congressional-district organizations and automatic delegate status for national committeemen and committeewomen) offered by pro-Goldwater leaders demonstrated that even normally cohesive convention delegates can have their differences on procedural and organizational matters.

In the process of writing and adopting a platform, the Goldwater delegates left no doubt that they intended to conduct an ideologically oriented campaign.

Additional proof of the overwhelming power of the Goldwater forces came on the first day of the convention proper (July 13), when attempts to bar the seating of "lily-white" southern delegations were defeated by a resounding voice vote.

On July 14, moderate Republicans failed in their efforts to

[11] Steven Shadegg, *What Happened to Goldwater?* (New York: Rinehart, 1965), p. 128.

incorporate into the platform amendments strengthening the civil-rights provisions, adding a plank condemning extremist groups of the left and right by name, and adding a plank asserting traditional presidential control over the use and deployment of nuclear weapons.

The Goldwater nomination came on the first ballot on July 15. He received 883 votes; Governor William Scranton of Pennsylvania, 214; Governor Nelson Rockefeller of New York, 114; Governor George Romney of Michigan, 41; Senator Margaret Chase Smith of Maine, 27; former Congressman Walter Judd of Minnesota, 21; Senator Hiram Fong of Hawaii, 5; and former Senator Henry Cabot Lodge of Massachusetts, 3.

With the voting ended, nearly all the states, including Pennsylvania, switched their entire delegations to the Senator. Governor Scranton made his way to the rostrum to enter an eloquent plea for Republican harmony. Using almost the same words Goldwater had employed in Chicago four years before when he had pledged himself to work for the election of the party's presidential nominee, Scranton opened the door through which he hoped Goldwater might walk on the following night when he gave his acceptance speech.

The moderates were destined to disappointment. The following day, Goldwater solidified the ideological image of his ticket by selecting conservative Republican National Chairman William Miller of New York as his running mate. Undaunted, Richard Nixon, who introduced the candidate for his acceptance speech, also sought to keep his party an arena of compromise. In one of his most eloquent moments, the former Vice President pointed to the high road the Republicans must travel, urged them to unite behind their new leader, and begged them to remember that the party was big enough for men and women of vastly differing ideological positions.

Goldwater responded by defining Republican philosophy as the philosophy of conservatism. Republicans, he declared, believe in constitutional government, private property, a stable monetary and fiscal climate, and government at the lowest level possible.

Then, to make certain there would be no mistake about his insistence upon basic ideological uniformity, he invited those who did not agree with him to leave the party and threw party liberals and moderates a stinging rebuke:

> Any who join us in all sincerity, we welcome. Those who do not care for our cause we do not expect to enter our ranks in any case.
> And let our Republicanism, so focused and so dedicated, not be made fuzzy and futile by unthinking labels.
> Extremism in the defense of liberty is no vice. Moderation in the pursuit of justice is no virtue.[12]

Party moderates and liberals on the convention floor were flabbergasted. Senator Jacob Javits, a leading party liberal, pointedly walked from the floor and thereafter offered the ticket no further support. Democrats, viewing the scene on television, were unbelieving. No candidate in their memory had so torpedoed his own ship on its launching night.

The fatal lines had come from the pen of Dr. Harry Jaffa, a political scientist and Aristotelian. They had never been intended as part of an acceptance speech, certainly not within the context of the battle over extremism which had been taking place at the convention during the week which had preceded. But the Goldwater speech was a product of the thinking of many men, and several felt strongly that this point should be interjected into the speech itself as a strong reminder that this campaign would be run on ideological grounds. Thus it was that an abstract philosophic pronouncement, voiced in true ideological style, came to typify the general mood of the initiation of the Senator's campaign. It was as if it were a sign of things to come in the ideological campaign planned by the Goldwater architects.

THE REPUBLICAN CONVENTION IN 1968

Following the devastating defeat of 1964, Republican office holders and organization leaders began the painful process of reexamination and rebuilding. The 1964 election was scarcely over before the Republican Governors' Association, dominated by moderate-to-liberal big-state governors, announced their intention to enter the national-issue field by developing a constructive program looking toward the 1966 and 1968 elections. Similar sugges-

[12] *San Francisco Chronicle,* July 17, 1964, p. 18.

tions had come from the Republican Senate-House Joint Leadership Committee and from Ohio Chairmen Ray C. Bliss. As a result a Party Coordinating Committee representing an ideological cross section of party leaders was formed. In April of 1965, Ohio's highly respected, sixteen-year chairman, Ray Bliss, became the chairman of the Republican National Committee. All of these developments indicated that the rebuilding process would aim at those objectives which had historically been the basis of partisan victory in America: broad-based support, flexibility, and party unity.

Victories in such major big-city elections as New York, Philadelphia, Louisville, and Akron in the fall of 1965 saw the return to the Republican Party of a larger share of the Negro vote, increased support from labor wards, and an expected return to the Republican column of a majority of voters from the professions.

The startling Republican gains in the 1966 gubernatorial, congressional, state-legislative, and county-courthouse elections across the country gave final and convincing proof that, as Chairman Ray Bliss put it on election night, "The elephant is very much alive."

How would the Republican resurgence affect the 1968 Republican presidential nomination?

First, it was more than obvious that the so-called southern strategy of the Goldwater campaign had been abandoned. So determined were Republican leaders to publicly divorce themselves from this ill-fated plan that in May of 1967 Congressman Gerald Ford, Minority Leader in the House of Representatives, stated that House Republicans would no longer team up with southern Democrats to support or defeat particular pieces of legislation.

Second, sensing the very real possibility of defeating Lyndon B. Johnson in the 1968 presidential contest, Republicans of all ideological backgrounds appeared to be searching for a candidate with broad popular support rather than for an ideological candidate.

Third, because party leaders had returned to the "arena of compromise" and because they were optimistic about their chances if a popular candidate with broad appeal was nominated, the selection of that candidate in 1968 would hinge largely upon the presidential preference primaries.

Front-runner Richard Nixon was so bold as to say in April 1967 that the 1968 nomination would be won in the presidential preference primaries. But would it? And, if so, who would do well in the primaries? Nixon already had built a storehouse of goodwill and an impressive fund of campaign debts among party leaders, office holders, and candidates by his tireless efforts to assist in crucial contests from 1963 to 1967. To what extent would these political IOU's be convertible to effective primary support in the critical presidential preference contests? And to what extent would party leaders in convention states put their leadership on the line for Nixon prior to the establishment of a primary trend, if one should develop?

Governor George Romney, whose presidential star shone brightly ·immediately after the 1964 debacle, had by 1967 lost a significant measure of support in opinion polls. He was nonetheless a certain and a strong contender and, like Nixon, had a full-blown campaign headquarters established in Washington more than a year before the national convention would take place.

Despite New York Governor Nelson Rockefeller's emphatic denials of any interest in the 1968 Republican presidential nomination, few political savants were counting him out of the 1968 Republican sweepstakes.

The fact that newcomers to the political scene, such as Illinois Senator Charles Percy and California Governor Ronald Reagan, were seriously mentioned as "dark-horse" or "impasse" candidates indicated how rapidly mass communications can acquaint the American voter with new faces.

Every development since 1964 pointed toward a Republican candidate and campaign exhibiting the flexibility and responsiveness which have always been the keys to victory in American presidential elections.

Bibliography

Bain, Richard C. *Convention Decisions and Voting Records*. Washington: Brookings Institution, 1960.

David, Paul T., *et al. The Politics of National Party Conventions.*

Washington: Brookings Institution, 1960.

David, Paul T., *et al. Presidential Nominating Politics in 1952.* 5 vols. Baltimore: Johns Hopkins Press, 1954.

Hupman, Richard D., and Eiler C. Ravnholt. *Nomination and Election of the President and Vice President of the United States.* Washington: Government Printing Office, 1964.

Martin, Ralph G. *Ballots and Bandwagons.* New York: Rand McNally, 1964.

Marvick, Dwaine, and Samuel J. Eldersveld. "National Convention Leadership: 1952 and 1956," *Western Political Quarterly,* XIV (March 1961), 176-194.

Munger, Frank, and J. Blackburst. "Factionalism in the National Conventions, 1940-1964," *Journal of Politics,* XXVII (May 1965), 375-394.

Pomper, Gerald. *Nominating the President.* Evanston, Ill.: Northwestern University Press, 1963.

Samson, W. A. "Coalition Formation at Presidential Nominating Conventions," *American Journal of Sociology,* LXVIII (September 1962), 157-171.

Stone, Irving. *They Also Ran.* New York: Pyramid Books, 1964.

Tillett, Paul, ed. *Inside Politics: The National Conventions of 1960.* Dobbs Ferry, N.Y.: Oceana Publications, 1962.

Wildavsky, Aaron. "On the Superiority of National Conventions," *Review of Politics,* XXIV (July 1962), 307-319.

Chapter IV

Drafting the Platform

 National party platforms are illustrations, par excellence, of the basic characteristic of compromise which underlies the American two-party system. Every four years the two major parties attempt to find and to state a series of official positions which will unite as many as possible of the disparate interests which have been uneasily allied to the party during the preceding four years.

The notable exception to this rule was the 1964 Republican platform, which bore an indisputable ideological imprint and unquestionably created some major rifts among the party faithful. The results of this deviation from historical precedent stress the wisdom of the traditional practice of drafting a platform which helps enlarge rather than restrict the size of the partisan tent.

WHAT PLATFORMS ARE

The writing of the national platforms becomes, in one sense, the first stage in the legitimization of certain positions advanced by various groups in society. These groups do not expect specific policy pledges from the political parties in the platform document; they do hope, however, that the party leaders will, through the platform, indicate that their special objectives are also in the public interest. Through such recognition political leaders serve notice on the nation as a whole that certain policy proposals deserve serious consideration by elected officials.

Party platforms, then, are guidelines, not pledges of action. They are, moreover, guidelines which are set down by only a small segment of the membership of a political party—a segment which, incidentally, is not necessarily representative of the inarticulate attitudes of the millions of nominal Democrats or Republicans back in Everytown, U.S.A., or even representative of the delegates to the conventions.

Party platforms, of course, are only one aspect in the development of national party policy. More important, perhaps, are the policy pronouncements by the candidates for the presidency, vice presidency, and Congress during the campaign and the party action taken at the national levels of officialdom following the election.

Even though national party platforms do not establish definitive party positions on all major campaign issues, they cannot be dismissed as having no importance. Significant contrasts between them indicate important differences between the parties in direction, emphasis, and approach.

Most platforms have contained certain basic items: eulogies of the party's record, some general declarations denouncing the opposition and favoring democracy and Americanism, reference to some current crucial nonparty issues, and a limited number of definite pledges.

For the party in power, the President determines the contents of the platform. The Democratic platforms in 1936, 1940, 1944, 1948, and 1964 and the Republican platform of 1956 were essentially products of the White House staff. In 1968, if President Johnson is the Democratic nominee, he and his staff probably will shape the basic content of the Democratic platform long before the resolutions committee assembles at the Democratic National Convention.

The opposition party, by contrast, usually expands its platform-writing effort to obtain the thinking of its various segments and of the community at large. This expansion can be accomplished in several ways. The Democrats in 1960 staged a series of regional public hearings so that all interested persons could make their views known. Republican Party leaders that same year asked the public at large to communicate opinions regarding the platform by letter or telegram. Preconvention hearings by the platform committee are also ordinarily held just prior to the formal convening of the national convention. Sometimes these are pro-forma meetings with only a few hours devoted to the process. On other occasions, the preconvention platform hearings have lasted as long as a week, as was the case with the Republicans in 1960.

Even when extensive preconvention public platform hearings are held, however, the platform itself ordinarily has been hammered out in rough outline long before the resolutions committee first convenes. The Democrats in 1960, for example, assigned the task of drafting the platform to four skilled writers in Washington weeks before the Los Angeles convention.

It should be noted that the platform written by the resolutions committee is not always accepted. Notable floor debates on the content of the platform marked the Democratic conventions of 1920, 1924, 1928, and 1948. At times, dissenters have proved that the positions espoused by the resolutions committee did not reflect the thinking of the majority of the convention. In 1948, for example, a liberal faction in the Democratic Party succeeded in gaining a majority of the delegate support to adopt a civil-rights plank over the vigorous objections of the so-called Dixiecrat group.

THE REPUBLICAN PLATFORM IN 1960

Unlike a number of his predecessors, Republican Chairman Thruston B. Morton took a very great interest in the preparations for the platform phase of the 1960 Republican National Convention. Early in 1960, in line with the desires of President Eisenhower and other White House leaders, Morton selected Charles A. Percy to be temporary chairman of the resolutions committee.

Percy, a young Chicago industrialist, was best known to Republicans as the chairman of a special long-range study committee on Republican program and progress which had met throughout 1959. His study group, which included Republican leaders from widely varied vocational backgrounds and ideological positions, ultimately published a report entitled *Decisions for a Better America*. Ostensibly, Percy had the friendship and support of a large number of the nation's top Republicans. Yet, when his selection was made known, there was marked dissatisfaction with Percy's appointment on the part of several high-ranking House and Senate

members. To satisfy these Republicans on Capitol Hill, Chairman Morton appointed Congressman Melvin Laird of Wisconsin to assist Percy with the work of the resolutions (platform) committee.

Each state selects its two-member delegation to the platform committee. Chairman Morton, however, in consultation with Percy and Laird, carefully picked the chairmen of eight platform subcommittees. More than past party national chairmen, Senator Morton took a deep personal interest in the background and the quality of the men and women who were to determine the basic nature of the 1960 Republican campaign document.

THE PUBLIC'S SUGGESTIONS

As chairman of the resolutions committee, Percy approached the problem of public involvement in a different way from his Democratic counterpart, Chester Bowles. Bowles had held a number of regional public hearings on platform content. Percy, in contrast, issued a release on January 19, 1960, inviting the American people to take part in the development of the Republican platform through two devices. He stated, in part:

We urge and will welcome suggestions from individuals and national and regional groups. We want to consider a wide range of opinion from every segment of American life.

He asked individuals to write to him indicating their personal views, and he promised that the eight subcommittees of the resolutions committee would give every opportunity for individual and group hearings in Chicago.

The number of letters, telegrams, and telephone calls which came to Chairman Percy was indeed impressive. They came from individuals in every walk of life and represented all shades of political opinion. Some were written in Chinese. Some were extremely lengthy and costly telegrams. Still others were written by cranks and came in most imaginative shapes and on an endless variety of writing materials.

Meanwhile, in order to assess the kind of platform which the members of the resolutions committee desired, Percy had mailed to each of them a mimeographed letter requesting information from them on this matter. It was an interesting letter for it suggested, among other things, that the members of the resolutions committee choose between (1) a long, a brief, or some-thing-in-between platform; (2) a platform with a central theme or one with a catalog of items; and (3) a platform which promised many things to interest groups or one which would serve the general interest of the nation.

Forty-two of the eighty-four who responded to Percy's questionnaire wanted a brief platform, whereas forty-two wanted something in between. Seventy-three wanted a central theme; four wanted a catalog. Seventy-eight wanted a platform basically addressing itself to the general interest of the nation, whereas two wanted a platform with promises to interest groups and two wanted to involve both. The theory that a multitude of special interests may constitute the general interest seems to have been overlooked by most of Percy's respondents.

THE DRAFTING PROCESS

The official program for the 1960 Republican resolutions committee began at 10 a.m. on July 19 with a coffee hour at the Sheraton-Blackstone Hotel in downtown Chicago. At 10:30 the temporary officers selected by Chairman Morton were officially installed as the permanent officers of the resolutions committee. (The resolutions committee is more popularly known as the platform committee.)

Addresses were given by Chairman Morton, Mr. Percy, Dr. Lee A. DuBridge, Dr. Lawrence Gould, and Secretary of the Treasury Anderson. After a brief lunch period, the full committee heard from Governor Rockefeller, Admiral Radford, Representative John Byrnes of Wisconsin, Senator Barry Goldwater, and Clarence B. Randall.

After these opening speeches, the committee reconvened at 5 p.m. to organize their subcommittee hearings for the following day. It is interesting to examine one or two of the subcommittee hearing schedules to see who, in fact, does appear before a typical platform committee at one of its preconvention hearings.

On Wednesday, July 20, the following individuals and groups appeared before the Foreign Policy Subcommittee: United Presbyterian Church, Friends Committee on National Legislation, American Association for the United Nations, Inc., League of Women Voters, National Committee on Captive Nations Week, American Israel Public Affairs Committee, American Council for Judaism, Major General Julius Klein, American Legion, AMVETS, 1960 Campaign for Disarmament, Polish-American Congress, American Farm Bureau Federation, Republican State Committee in and for the District of Columbia, International Economic Policy Association, Inc., American-Latvian Association, the National Council for Jewish Women, Americans for Democratic Action, the American Friends of the Captive Nations, and Norman Raise, President of the Cedar Society.

On the same day, the following groups appeared before the Agricultural and Natural Resources Subcommittee: Keep America Beautiful, League of Women Voters, Investors League, Inc., Save the Dunes Council, National Rural Electric Cooperative Association, Water Pollution Control Advisory Board, National Association of Soil Conservation Districts, and the Utah Mining Association.

The hearings of these and the six other subcommittees went on from Wednesday morning through Friday afternoon. By Friday evening, July 22, the eight subcommittees had drafted what they felt were sound statements on which to base the national Republican campaign of 1960.

THE REVISION PROCESS

Back in Washington, however, Richard Nixon had just decided to take an action which would soon complicate the work of the platform committee. On this same Friday evening after the platform-subcommittee chairmen had retired, confident that the bulk of their tedious task was over, Richard Nixon met with Governor Nelson Rockefeller in New York to discuss changes in certain of the subcommittee drafts.

When the Saturday-morning newspapers revealed the nature of the momentous midnight meeting in Governor Rockefeller's apartment, even the Vice President's convention-advisory staff appeared stunned (Meade Alcorn, Len Hall, Ray Bliss, Mort Frayn, Lee Potter, Bob Finch, and others).

The true story of the events leading up to this amazing meeting of the Vice President and the governor of New York and the personalities involved has remained a mystery to the newsmen and commentators who otherwise have written fairly accurate and complete accounts of the election of the President in 1960.

In any case, the platform committee was thrown into utter confusion by the events which had transpired the night before in New York City. The members of the committee were angry and they were tired. They were resentful and some of them were on the verge of mutiny. From Senator Barry Goldwater's headquarters in Chicago came the following statement:

Unprecedented last minute attempts to impose upon the Republican Platform Committee platform provisions from a point 1,000 miles away from the Convention has caused deep concern on the part of conscientious Republicans attending the Convention at Chicago.

If a spokesman for the ultra-liberals is to be permitted to dictate the Republican Platform, it seems logical that this same spokesman should become an announced candidate for the presidency and thus be prepared to assume the responsibility for carrying out the ultra-liberal positions of his Platform.

What are we doing to the men and women of good conscience who have labored on the Platform Committee in Chicago for more than a full week, if we now give in to this pressure and accept cut and dried Platform provisions. . . .

I have great confidence in the integrity of the men and women on the Platform Committee. I am encouraged by statements made to me by members of the Platform Committee during the noon recess today. Several members of the Committee for whom I have the highest regard have assured me that the Platform Committee can well write the provisions of the Republican Platform and will refuse to accept this last minute pressure technique.

Had it not been for Chairman Morton's straight-from-the shoulder talk to the platform committee on Saturday morning, it is likely that at least two men might have walked out of the committee and taken their entire state delegations back home with them. Following Morton's effective plea for party unity, and for a facing-up to the situation at hand, the subcommittees (particularly those on defense, civil rights, and immigration) went back into executive session in an attempt to rewrite the provisions of their plans in accordance with the wishes of the Vice President and Governor Rockefeller.

All during Saturday and Sunday the platform committee was in turmoil. Introduced into the grim atmosphere were comic situations created by a shortage of meeting space. The housing arrangements for the hearings had been made only through Saturday, at which time it was assumed that the platform would have been written and the work of the platform committee completed. Consequently, many of the needed meeting rooms and other facilities had been scheduled for weddings, parties, and dances. On one occasion, a wedding party was almost shocked into sobriety when harassed subcommittee members marched into their former meeting room and demanded the quarters now occupied by gay and slightly inebriated celebrants.

What some reporters called the "total chaos of Saturday and Sunday" was, in a sense, made official when the platform committee formally voted by a two-to-one majority to stand by the platform which had been drafted and approved on Friday evening. This was on Sunday, July 24.

While the committee members argued and threatened on the second floor, quite different activities were taking place on the seventh floor of the Sheraton-Blackstone. Here, in the luxurious set of suites which had been assigned for the final drafting of the platform, representatives of the various ideological wings of the party gathered to attempt to work out a solution to their dilemma.

Here, for example, were such leaders as Gabriel Hauge, former economic advisor to the President; Bob Merriam, representing the President; George Grassmuck, in attendance as a spokesman for the Vice President; and Emmett Hughes, an emissary of Governor Rockefeller. The conflicts were real and at times appeared irreconcilable during that trying Sunday.

When it appeared that the defense subcommittee, partially through the urging of Eisenhower's man, Bob Merriam, would stand fast on defense, and the civil-rights subcommittee was unlikely to alter its statement on civil rights, the local Nixon team announced a decision of its own to go to the full platform committee on Monday regarding both civil rights and defense. If need be, the Vice President promised a floor fight at the side of Rockefeller before the entire convention on Tuesday.

When the platform committee reassembled for a Sunday-night session, irate and weary members threatened to revolt. Tempers flared. It was fortunate that the steady hand of Congressman Laird was on the gavel. Percy, undoubtedly a skilled leader with boards of trustees and business concerns, was not prepared nor politically experienced enough to handle the excited members of the platform committee.

The pressures which were brought to bear on certain members of the platform committee during the Sunday and Monday sessions came from the highest possible sources in American government and party life.

During those last few agonizing hours of the platform committee's work, the tension in the air was palpable. Deeply held convictions—both liberal and conservative—were straining to be free of the bonds of party unity. But as a result of the stubborn insistence on the part of the Vice President, the platform committee was left no choice. With bitterness in the hearts of many members, the committee, after the Sunday marathon session, now voted by another two-to-one majority to reverse its previous decision and to accept the rewritten planks on civil rights and defense. Governor Rockefeller and Vice President Nixon had won their battle.

The Vice President, hurrying out to Chicago days earlier than planned, had followed Senator Morton's appeal for unity and patience by a personal visit with small groups of recalcitrant members of the platform committee and by presenting, with deep conviction, his personal justification for the altered platform planks. He insisted that the rewriting of certain segments of the platform was not only a moral requirement from his standpoint, but a political necessity if he were to win the 1960 campaign. Thus the Vice President's own role in the writing of the strong civil-rights and defense planks which ultimately became part of the 1960 platform cannot be overemphasized.

But there were other key personalities who operated effectively behind the scenes to help resolve the platform-committee fight and to restore unity out of irate diversity and order out of chaos. Among them, Ohio State Chairman Ray Bliss must be ranked extremely high; so too must Dr. Gabriel Hauge. The constructive roles played by these men, known to only a few people, were indeed crucial.

It is interesting to note the extent to which academic leaders were used in the platform-drafting process in 1960. Of the 28 men and women who worked closely with the Republican platform committee, more than half were academicians by training or profession. Such names as Dave Abshire, Bob Forsythe, Bob Goldwin, Steve Hess, Karl Lamb, Bill MacComber, Floyd McCaffree, Bill Prendergast, and Guy Waterman suggest the extent of utilization of academic people who, though perhaps holding other positions during the summer of 1960, were actually trained for and had instructional experience in American academic institutions.

THE REPUBLICAN PLATFORM IN 1964

Contrary to predictions, it was not the presidential nomination but rather the resolutions (platform) committee which became the center of controversy at the 1964 Republican National Convention.

Because it was obvious to most delegates weeks before the convention convened that Senator Barry Goldwater would be the Republican standard-bearer in 1964, attention in early July turned to the platform. Would it be in general agreement with the compromise campaign document of 1960, or would it reflect the conservative, ideological position of the majority of 1964 delegates and platform-committee members?

As the platform committee commenced its hearings on July 7, every outward indication was that the 1964 platform would bear a strong resemblance to the 1960 document.

Congressman Mel Laird, assistant to platform-committee chairman Charles A. Percy in 1960, had been appointed chairman. Moderate Congressman Charles E. Goodell of New York had been named by Laird as assistant to the chairman for domestic policy, while conservative Congressman Glenard P. Lipscomb of California had been appointed assistant to the chairman for national security.

The 1964 staff, though smaller than in 1960, contained many of the same specialists who has assisted in 1960. Dr. William Prendergast, research director at the Republican National Committee, had been named to serve a second time as executive director. Dr. Arthur Peterson, Dr. Malcolm Moos, and Mr. Bryce Harlow were again on hand to assist with administrative and drafting chores.

Platform-committee procedures, under Laird, were also strongly reminiscent of 1960. Months prior to the convention, former Eisenhower aide Robert E. Merriam had been named national coordinator of a Party-to-People Program. Merriam's assignment was to determine the attitudes of Americans of all backgrounds and political leanings through regional public hearings and through correspondence.

Along with Clare Boothe Luce, who represented an Eisenhower-sponsored issue-study group called the Critical Issues Council, Merriam opened the first full session of the platform committee with a report to the committee on what he had found to be the major concerns of the American people in 1964.

Subsequent speakers before the open-session, full committee meetings were New York Governor Nelson Rockefeller; Mayor William B. Cowger of Louisville; former Governor of Minnesota Harold Stassen; Governor George Romney of Michigan; George Meany, president of the AFL-CIO; W. P. Gullander, president of the National Association of Manufacturers; former U.S. Senator Henry Cabot Lodge of Massachusetts; Pennsylvania Governor William Scranton; Senator Bourke Hickenlooper of Iowa; Illinois Congressman Leslie Arends; Dr. Alan Waterman, former director of the National Science Foundation; Senator Barry Goldwater of Arizona; former Chief of Naval Operations, Admiral Arleigh Burke; former Congressman Walter Judd of Minnesota; and Walter F. Carey, president of the U.S. Chamber of Commerce.

Of the political speakers eight were moderate or liberal Republicans while eight were generally considered conservatives.

There were some slight variations in the hearing procedures in 1964 for those other individuals and groups making a presentation. Instead of the eight subcommittees of 1960, four "panels" were named by Laird. These met every afternoon from Tuesday through Friday, recording their findings for later use in the final full-committee discussions.

Shortly after the last of the Friday afternoon (July 18) panel hearings had concluded, the full committee began considering amendments to a draft document. From this point forward the similarity between 1960 and 1964 ceased. Although a number of amendments from the moderate Republicans were accepted and incorporated into the final platform, the suggested liberalization of the civil-rights plank, the inclusion of a statement condemning extremist groups, and the assurance of presidential control over nuclear weapons were flatly rejected.

These issues were of grave concern to the moderates. They were well aware of the implications of the Goldwater platform positions for all Republican candidates in the forthcoming elections.

Having failed to amend the platform to their satisfaction in committee, the moderates now took their exceptions to the convention floor. Ultimately five amendments were offered and all of them were defeated by a two-to-one standing vote.

The first amendment, condemning extremist groups by name, was offered by Nelson Rockefeller. During his presentation the New York governor was booed and taunted before a nationwide television audience of millions.

A similar amendment, without specifically naming the extremist groups in question (the Communist Party, the Ku Klux Klan, and the John Birch Society), was offered by a Romney assistant.

The third amendment would have added to the platform a statement of pride in Republican support of the 1964 civil-rights legislation and specific pledges on strengthening various national civil-rights programs.

Senator Hugh Scott's amendment supported presidential control over nuclear weapons.

The final amendment was a Romney civil-rights plank pledging action at the state, local, and private levels to eliminate discrimination in all fields.

The 1964 Republican platform was unquestionably a more conservative document than its predecessor of 1960, but a careful reading does not reveal the virtual repudiation of modern Republicanism which was alleged during the heat of the presidential campaign by some estranged Republicans and many interested Democrats.

It is true, however, that the tactics and manners of some of the

Goldwater forces during the convention debate of the platform and its suggested amendment did prove to be a continuing and costly embarrassment to the Goldwater-Miller ticket in the campaign which followed.

So determined were some Goldwater leaders and supporters to make the platform reflect the ideological posture of the entire campaign effort that they were apparently unaware of the damage being done to their cause through the highly visible intransigence and rudeness to moderate and liberal party spokesmen.

Even though the contents of the platform were accepted by former President Eisenhower, he expressed grave disappointment over the tactics used by some of the Goldwater delegates in their response to the two Romney amendments. To Eisenhower the mood and methods of the Goldwater delegates represented "a rigid position . . . that is really not the democratic method, as I see it."

Questioned after the platform was adopted, Chairman Laird insisted that the platform was "not a Goldwater platform, not a Rockefeller platform, not a Scranton platform, but a Republican platform." He later agreed, however, that it was a Republican platform reflecting the mainstream of thought at the 1964 convention.

In most particulars, the Republican platform conformed to a typical "outparty" statement. It gave considerable attention to alleged Democratic failure in foreign and domestic policy, voicing sharp disagreement with recent developments concerning United States relations with the Soviet Union and citing the failure of the Democratic administration to maintain national preparedness at a level consistent with continued military superiority for the United States.

In domestic policy the 1964 platform charged the Johnson administration with failure to meet its goal of reducing unemployment to 4 per cent, refusal to take adequate and practical measures to help the poor, betrayal of the farmer (by dropping the parity level to its lowest level since 1939), fiscal irresponsibility, and governmental inefficiency.

These attacks in both foreign and domestic fields were actually less strident than were similar allegations of 1952, but a number of explicit and implicit progressive positions of the 1960 platform were challenged.

The ascendancy of the Republican conservatives in the resolutions committee and in the convention as a whole was nowhere more clearly illustrated than in the platform's civil-rights planks. As adopted, even though the platform pledged full implementation and faithful execution of the civil-rights act of 1964, it conformed in spirit to the election plan developed earlier by Goldwater strategists calling for the capture of sufficient votes in the South, West, and Midwest to offset losses in the more rights-conscious North.

THE REPUBLICAN PLATFORM IN 1968

The creation of the Republican Coordinating Committee in January 1965 and the highly successful operation of this group since then have introduced a totally new element into the Republican platform plans for 1968. Composed of the five living Republican presidential nominees, five prominent governors (selected by the Republican Governors' Association), the twelve members of the Senate-House Joint Leadership, a representative of the Republican State Legislators' Association, and five members of the Republican National Committee, the quarterly meetings of this unusual political assemblage produced eighteen unanimously approved advisory statements on policy in the first twenty months of its existence.

Although the Coordinating Committee is not the first party advisory group on policy to draw support from all ideological wings, it is the first successful coordinated involvement of governors, state legislators, congressmen, national-committee members, and presidential nominees.

These sometimes divisive elements have gathered faithfully every three months to advance positions on all of the major issues of the day, ranging from civil rights and the war in Vietnam to job opportunities and the problems of the aging.

Despite the fact that the positions advanced on these issues were merely advisory, they, in fact, became the "official" party positions for many candidates in the midterm elections.

It would be difficult indeed for any platform committee to

completely cast aside the position papers prepared by such an impressive and representative group as the Coordinating Committee, particularly since these positions appeared to serve candidates so well in the highly successful Republican campaign of 1966.

It is of more than passing interest that the positions of the Coordinating Committee, on most issues, and on civil rights and extremism particularly, were far closer to the tone of the minority report of the 1964 platform committee than they were to the "mainstream of Convention thought" reflected in the 1964 platform itself.

Illustrative was the position paper on human rights, approved by the Coordinating Committee August 30, 1965. It began with a recital of the historical Republican position on civil rights and included references to the 80 per cent support given the civil-rights legislation of 1964 by Republicans in Congress. The report, entitled "Equality in America, A Promise Unfulfilled," then proceeded to examine areas of inequality in voting, education, employment, and public accommodations. At several points the report called the Johnson administration to task for its failure to enforce fully and faithfully existing civil-rights laws.

Reflecting the tone of the entire report is the opening paragraph on education and employment:

> Every American deserves and should have a full and fair chance to fulfill his God-given capacity to learn, to work, to earn . . . all without regard to race, or creed or color. He deserves and should have a full and fair chance to own a decent home, at a price he can afford, in a decent neighborhood. He deserves and should have a full and fair chance, with all his fellows, to go to the places and do the things for himself and his family as his earnings will permit.

On December 13, 1965, the Coordinating Committee stamped unanimous approval on the position taken by Republican National Chairman Ray Bliss regarding political extremism. Bliss's position was announced originally in Albuquerque, New Mexico, on November 5, 1965. The Coordinating Committee's resolution of December 13 asserted:

The Republican Coordinating Committee endorses the position of Republican National Committee Chairman Ray C. Bliss that all Republicans should reject membership in any radical or extremist organization including any which attempts to use the Republican Party for its own ends or any which seeks to undermine the basic principles of American freedom and constitutional government.

Thus it was that the moderate position on civil rights and extremism, defeated in 1964, came to be the official "advisory" position for Republicans in 1965.

THE DEMOCRATIC PLATFORM IN 1964

The differing contents and the contrasting methods of writing the Democratic platforms of 1964 and 1960 illustrate well the principle that American party platforms are campaign documents, not systematic applications of party philosophy to the issues of the day. This section will discuss the Johnson platform of 1964, and the next reviews the Democratic platform of 1960.

In 1964, President Johnson based his campaign on three simple themes:

1. Complete the unfinished tasks of President Kennedy's New Frontier.
2. Use President Johnson's great experience in political leadership to get the job done.
3. Achieve consensus by meeting the many varied needs of the American people.

The platform spoke of all three purposes. Its title, "One Nation, One People," laid consensus as the cornerstone. Its opening phrases sounded the consensus theme:

America is *One Nation, One People.*
The welfare, progress, security and survival of each of us reside in the common good—the sharing of responsibilities as well as benefits by all our people.

. . .

Accordingly, we offer this platform as a *covenant* of unity.
We invite all to join us who believe that narrow partisanship takes too small account of the size of our task, the penalties for failure and the boundless rewards to all our people for success.

Repeatedly the 1964 platform spoke of President Kennedy's innovations and of President Johnson's follow-through in peace, in defense, in economic growth, and in other fields. It closed with the Kennedy theme:

On November 22, 1963, John Fitzgerald Kennedy was shot down in our land.

We honor his memory best—and as he would wish—by devoting ourselves anew to the larger purposes for which he lived.

It pledged President Johnson's skills to achieve the goals set forth:

The leadership we offer has already been tested in the crucible of crisis and challenge. To this Nation and to all the world we reaffirm President Johnson's resolve to "use every resource at the command of the Government . . . and the people . . . to find the road to peace."

We offer this platform as a guide for that journey.

The White House staff, in close collaboration with trusted lieutenants at the Democratic National Committee, wrote the 1964 platform. Bill Moyers, then Special Counsel to the President, coordinated the drafting and the preparation of position papers to support the various planks. He worked closely with Frederick G. Dutton, a key organizer of Citizens for Kennedy in 1960, who was sent to the Democratic National Committee from the State Department to be staff director for the resolutions committee.

In early summer, Moyers called upon each cabinet officer to prepare position papers proposing platform planks in the fields for which he was responsible. Thus, for example, Interior Secretary Stewart L. Udall was asked to prepare papers in the field of natural resources. In most instances this logical distribution of subject-matter assignments touched off elaborate interagency efforts, for responsibility is widely distributed among federal agencies in many fields of public endeavor.

Moyers called for five specific types of information in preparing position papers for the platform: (1) the specific points the cabinet officer would propose be included in the platform; (2) supporting documentation, including statements by the President, pertinent facts, and other source materials; (3) an appraisal of the major arguments against the proposals; (4) a comparison of the proposals to the 1960 platform commitments; and (5) an analysis of the extent to which the 1960 platform had been carried out on related points.

Position papers were assembled in Moyers' office by July 17, and the central drafting effort was set in motion. A complete rewrite proved unavoidable. Differences in style and emphasis, the need for balance in the platform presentation, and agency tendencies to advocate "strengthening" all going programs dictated considerable weeding and trimming before the platform was ready for presidential review. The result was a single compact document in which each cabinet officer won his major objectives, but recognized only occasional bits of his language.

The resolutions committee of the national convention, with a well-researched and readable platform draft in hand, assembled in Washington, D.C., a week before the convention's opening to hear cabinet officers and a wide range of key individuals and private groups suggest platform goals. For three days the committee sat in bloc, listening to scheduled speakers by subject-matter groupings. At the civil-rights hearings, for example, Attorney General Robert F. Kennedy urged a strong law-and-order plank denouncing racial violence. Roy Wilkins, executive secretary of the National Association for the Advancement of Colored People and the Reverend Dr. Martin Luther King, Jr., president of the Southern Christian Leadership Conference, urged vigorous enforcement of the 1964 civil-rights law. James Farmer, national director of the Congress of Racial Equality, urged a massive federal public-works program to provide housing, schools, and hospitals, and at the same time to create jobs for the nation's unemployed.[1]

On Thursday, August 20, the committee flew to Atlantic City for another day and a half of hearings. In all, nearly 180 representatives of various groups appeared before the committee out of some 200 who sought the opportunity. Candidates for office, however, were uniformly turned down.[2] With the coming of the weekend, the committee turned to final consideration of the 1964 platform.

---

[1] *Washington Post,* August 20, 1964, pp. A1-A2.
[2] *Ibid.,* p. A2.

Do the formal hearings change platforms? Rarely. Well before the hearings take place, the key ideas usually are given to the men charged with drafting the platform. Yet many ideas presented at the hearings are reflected in the platform, and the groups presenting the ideas receive welcome national publicity for their goals.

Organized labor, for example, got needed publicity from its appearances at both 1964 platform hearings, to present a well-written 24-page statement of platform proposals. Although the statement covered the whole range of public concerns, the key issue appeared on page 18 under "Labor-Employer Relations" and centered on the provisions of section 14 (b) of the Taft-Hartley Act which permits states to outlaw the union shop. The labor statement urged:

Congress should enact legislation based in fact on the principles of the Wagner Act. It should begin by repealing Section 14 (b).

The Democratic platform of 1964 responded:

The industrial democracy of free, private collective bargaining and the security of American trade unions must be strengthened by repealing Section 14 (b) of the Taft-Hartley Act.

THE DEMOCRATIC PLATFORM IN 1960

The Democratic national platform of 1960, entitled "The Rights of Man," was designed to portray the Democratic Party as a union of liberals. Paul M. Butler, then chairman of the Democratic National Committee, believed firmly in the theory that political parties are united by political philosophy. Accordingly, he deliberately set about to convey that image to the nation through his party's platform. Charges by former President Harry S. Truman that the 1960 convention was "rigged" were widely circulated but generally misunderstood. As Paul Butler testified to the convention, there was no rigging in favor of any candidate, nor could there have been. The rigging, if such it can be called, was purely ideological. It was an attempt to make sure that the platform would state the issues of the day as liberals saw them and would propose solutions to the issues which liberals would approve.

Liberals were given charge of the Committee on Resolutions and Platform by the appointment of Representative Chester Bowles of

Connecticut and Philip Perlman of Maryland as cochairmen. Before the convention opened, drafts of possible planks for the platform were prepared by subject-matter specialists who were drawn almost entirely from the liberal wing of the party. A draft of the platform itself was prepared at national party headquarters by a handpicked team of liberals who paid slight heed to previous national platforms and who made no use at all of state and county platforms adopted in 1960. The drafting team depended for content material primarily upon pamphlets which had been prepared by the Democratic Advisory Council, a liberal-wing group; upon the draft planks submitted by the liberal subject-matter specialists; upon the summaries of ten preconvention platform hearings which were held in the late spring of 1960; and upon their own knowledge of the goals of liberal members of Congress.

The Democratic Advisory Council was a major source of ideas for the platform. When it was formed in 1956, Speaker of the House of Representatives Sam Rayburn and Senate Majority Leader Lyndon B. Johnson had declined membership. Significantly, however, the 1956 presidential and vice-presidential candidates, Governor Adlai E. Stevenson and Senator Estes Kefauver, had accepted membership. They later were joined by Senators John F. Kennedy and Hubert Humphrey. Beginning in 1957, the council had published 13 pamphlets on foreign affairs, on domestic problems, and on defense.

Ideas and materials for the advisory-council pamphlets came from many sources. For example, in preparing a pamphlet on natural resources for 1960 publication, the advisory council's subcommittee on natural resources made an especially elaborate effort to gather widespread contributions. In the fall of 1959 a series of "position papers," each covering in detail one major phase of resource conservation and development, such as energy, water, lands, forests, and recreation, was prepared by experts in those fields. The position papers were used as source material in the preparation of a platform on resources adopted by the Western States Democratic Conference in Albuquerque, New Mexico, February 6, 1960. The conference platform and the position papers were then used as the starting point for a new pamphlet by the advisory council which sought to make a coherent, parallel statement of needs, problems, and objectives within a single framework. This effort formed the foundation from which the "long-form" platform plank on natural resources was drawn. The final product was published in mid-October 1960 as a campaign pamphlet, "Resources for the People," and appeared to be an elaboration of the platform plank on conservation. In fact, the platform plank was a summary of the pamphlet.

A second major source of platform material was the preconvention platform hearings, which began April 28, 1960, at Philadelphia. Nine more were sponsored by the Democratic National Committee in rapid succession: May 6 at Minneapolis, May 12 at Detroit, May 27 at Denver, May 31 at St. Louis, June 3 at Salt Lake City, June 17 in Los Angeles, June 21 in New York City, June 24 in Seattle, and June 27 in Miami.

At each, attention was focused on one major field of interest, but local people were welcomed to speak on any subject they wished during one of the three hearing sessions. Thus foreign policy was highlighted at Philadelphia, farm problems at Minneapolis, natural resources at Denver, education at Salt Lake City, and urban and suburban problems at St. Louis. Hearings ran morning, afternoon, and evening, and were deluged with requests to testify. Many persons had to be content with submitting written statements for the record.

Each preconvention hearing was conducted by a panel of four or five distinguished Democrats which usually included a governor and a United States Senator. But, because there was no way to be sure that panelists would also be members of the Resolutions and Platform Committee at the national convention, a special staff man was employed to summarize the findings of each hearing and prepare the materials for presentation to the platform committee.

The large volume and variety of ideas, suggestions, statements, and proposals which emerged from these two processes posed a dilemma for the party's leaders: How could they satisfy most of the legitimate desires expressed and yet keep the platform of reasonable length as a campaign document? Indeed, the need to present the platform to the convention and, through television, to the nation made length an urgent consideration. Experience in 1952 and 1956 showed that the reading of a long platform bored the convention and rapidly reduced the viewing audience. Chairman Butler, with the concurrence of Congressman Bowles and Mr. Perlman, decided to illustrate the platform with three short movies covering foreign affairs, domestic affairs, and civil rights. With the making of this concession to audience attention, Mr. Bowles appears to have been the man who decided that the platform to be read to the convention should not exceed 3,000 words.

A 3,000-word platform, however, could not begin to express the objectives which the varied component groups within the Democratic Party would surely expect, particularly on domestic matters. It soon became clear that a second, and much longer, version would somehow have to be provided. Accordingly, efforts were undertaken to draft two platforms—a "short form" and a "long form"—with the long form presumably to be presented to the convention in written form and debated and adopted without being read verbatim from the rostrum.

Drafting of the two versions was undertaken in mid-June. Staff specialists with Congress, with the national committee, and with the interest groups which identify themselves principally with the Democratic Party undertook to prepare preliminary drafts of both a short-form and a long-form platform. Many of these people had helped with pamphlets from the advisory council, written background position papers on these subjects, or had prepared statements for the preconvention hearings. Most of them were conversant with the pressing controversies in their areas of specialization and could be depended upon to put into the proposed platform language calculated to cover the field yet avoid unnecessary antagonisms.

To prepare a final, integrated, smooth-flowing product, a special four-man drafting crew was brought into national-committee headquarters. One was Mr. Bowles' administrative assistant; two were administrative assistants to prominent liberal Senators; one was a member of the Harvard University faculty of law. All had long experience in political affairs.

Chairman Bowles himself proceeded to prepare an integrated draft of the 3,000-word short-form platform. Reflecting his concerns and his New England residence, Bowles' draft concentrated almost entirely upon foreign policy, civil rights, and pressing social and economic problems of urban areas. Final preparation of the long form was left to the drafting team.

Two of the administrative assistants on the drafting team quickly perceived the gross imbalance which would result if other areas of domestic policy were not covered, such as agricultural policy, education, labor, natural resources, public power, and veterans' affairs. Without time to consult adequately with the subject-matter specialists who had prepared the draft versions, they rewrote most of what had been given them to provide a single, coherent style. Occasionally consultation was taken with the specialists, but more often they grumbled that they were not permitted to be of assistance.

The result was a serious imbalance in the platform which is apparent in its final version, despite rather extensive revisions following the hearings by the full resolutions committee at Los Angeles. Domestic policy, always the area requiring the most delicate phrasing and most specific statements, was treated hastily and in some aspects inadequately. For example, natural resources and labor policy—two of the most complicated and explosive areas of controversy—were handled so inadequately in the short form and were covered so weakly in the long form that it became necessary to have specialists make rather extensive revisions of the drafts at the last minute in Los Angeles.

The Committee on Resolutions and Platform assembled in the Grand Ballroom of the Biltmore Hotel in Los Angeles on Tuesday, July 5. There, in plenary session, until Friday afternoon, it heard testimony from individuals and groups wishing to have their views included in the platform. No subcommittees on special subject-matter areas were set up, and no separate subject-matter hearings were held.

At the end of the week, a 19-man drafting subcommittee was appointed from among the committee members to work over the weekend. Once behind closed doors, the drafting committee was handed both the short-form and the long-form drafts. Chairman Bowles indicated that the long-form material would be in the nature of an appendix to the short form which was really to be the platform. A quick review of content, however, promptly disclosed the urgent need to have both as parts of the platform. Discussion resulted in which Chairman Bowles agreed to treat both forms equally as parts of the platform.

Debate in the drafting subcommittee centered on the strong civil-rights plank. Occasionally other gaps were uncovered—for instance, the need for a plank on women's rights. By and large, however, the work of the four-man liberal drafting crew stood unchallenged. The resolutions committee's hearings in Los Angeles had contributed nothing of significance to the preparation of the platform.

Through long hours of the weekend, the drafting crew then undertook to combine the two forms so that the short form would appear in the final version as boldface introductions to the more detailed long-form provisions, which were to be printed in regular type.

Security was tight. Only five or six professional staff people from the drafting crew, the preplatform-hearings staff, and the advisory-council staff appear to have joined the drafting subcommittee. Nationally known lobbyists hovered about the committee rooms but could get only assurances like, "You'll have nothing to worry about." Even an attempt by a nationally prominent Democrat to smuggle a copy of the platform to the *New York Times* was thwarted by an alert staff member.

Tuesday night, July 12, the resolutions committee brought out an "integrated" document. Lack of time had precluded extensive revision of the short-form draft, but the commitments to present the three short movies had compelled its use. Printed copies of the entire document were passed out to the delegates. Mr. Bowles then simply read the boldface portions of the committee's report to the convention, stopping three times for the short film interludes. The entire platform was adopted by approval of the motion to accept the committee's report.

Only on the vigorous civil-rights plank was there formal, organized dissent. Delegates from nine southern states presented a minority report which pleaded their cause in impassioned language. Yet it was in no sense an alternative platform proposal and was predictably shouted down.

Thus the complete 1960 Democratic platform was a fairly typical major-party platform. It indicated the direction in which the

Democratic Party hoped to go without making specific promises to reach the destination. It reflected the objectives of the groups having significant power within the party. And, by "glittering generalities," it also reflected the issues upon which the party was so divided that no firm position could be taken. Yet, over-all, it was a platform with a strong liberal tone.

On the other hand, the version of the platform which was presented to the nation over television was not a typical major-party platform. The short-form passages and the movies were designed to portray a "responsible" party united by liberal principles; particularly concerned about foreign affairs, civil rights, and urban problems; proud of its past; and prepared to act cohesively in the future.

Bibliography

Tillett, Paul, ed. *Inside Politics: The National Conventions, 1960.* Dobbs Ferry, N.Y.: Oceana Publications, 1962. Part III, "Kennedy and Nixon Leadership on Party Platform," Articles 6, 7, 8, and 9.

Chapter V

Organizing the Campaign

There can be only one boss in a political campaign. Democratic and Republican leaders alike have learned this rule the hard way.

When an incumbent President seeks reelection, the White House runs the campaign. The President puts the task into the hands of a trusted lieutenant who has all the powers of the office to back him up. The national committee of the President's party is either turned over to the campaign manager, who becomes its chairman, or it obeys his orders. Thus did the Republicans win reelection in 1956 and the Democrats in 1936, 1940, 1944, 1948, and, with special modifications, 1964.

A challenger faces tougher going. He must be prepared to take over his own national committee lock, stock, and barrel or else face never-ending problems of coordination, duplication, and rivalry, to say nothing of unnecessary expense.

The organizational problem for a challenger is caused by a simple fact of political life: national committees are neither geared nor staffed to handle a presidential campaign. They are set up to provide year-round services to state and county central committees. They grind out political propaganda; they stimulate auxiliary groups for youth, women, and special minorities; they do political research; they provide tips to improve local political organization; they assist in fund raising; and they do other related tasks.

During presidential campaigns, other talents are needed.

95

Speeches must be written, campaign appearances must be advanced, separate "citizens" organizations must be established for the candidate, and money must be raised in large quantities. Moreover, the candidate needs the undivided loyalty of his staff; and the national-committee staffs, like federal civil servants, have remained neutral in the struggle for the nomination.

THE PATTERNS OF CAMPAIGN STRUCTURE

A nominee for President dares not depend upon the old national-committee staff to handle his campaign. He must either leave the old staff intact to serve him as best it can while he depends upon his own separate and personal organization (the "divided" system); or else he must construct a new, "unified" national-committee staff from his own team and fit the old people in wherever they can be used. Ordinarily it is impractical to fire the old staff outright when all good men must be called to the aid of their party.

The divided system enables the candidate to throw his campaign into high gear quickly and economically. He can depend upon his own preconvention organization and he knows how to use it. Division of responsibility leaves him free to call upon the national committee as opportunity arises without having to disrupt his own team. If the national committee is headed by a chairman over whom he has little control or influence, especially if the chairman is a member of Congress (as Republican chairmen were during the late 1950's and early 1960's), the candidate is very likely indeed to find the divided system better than a unified operation which he might have difficulty commanding.

The divided system is fraught with perils, however. Inevitably the national committee and its staff become aware of their secondary role in the campaign. As plans are made and actions are taken by the candidate's team without their advice, they conclude that they are being "ignored" or that the candidate is "refusing to work with the regular organization." In what they regard as self-defense, they may shift their efforts to their regular clientele or even divert their help to congressional contests. If they try to aid the presidential campaign anyway, they may dissipate much of their energy by enlarging their own regular activities; they may duplicate work of the candidate's team, or they may inadvertently upset some hard-won gain. Worst of all, they are likely to fritter away badly needed campaign funds on projects which never receive a priority rating from the candidate.

The unified system has superior virtues and fewer problems. The party speaks only with the candidate's voice. National effort is concentrated on winning the presidency. The strengths of the regular organization are added to those of the campaign team, and thus the campaign efforts are legitimized in the eyes of the regular organizations at state and county levels. Finance can be centralized and spending limited to high-priority tasks in the campaign.

If the candidate and his manager act decisively to establish and maintain their leadership, the problems of the unified system can be confined to individual reactions of the old-time staff of the national committee. Although there appears to be a new professionalism developing in the staffing of national party headquarters, many staff members in the past have held their positions because of special support from key party figures. When these men and women were unceremoniously relegated to subordinate roles during the campaign period, considerable pressure was brought to bear to force reconsideration of their new assignments. Thus internal jockeying for position, bickering and even foot dragging have frequently accompanied the establishment of a new campaign regime at national headquarters. Although this problem will probably never be completely solved, the detrimental effects of these quadrennial personnel adjustments can be reduced through judicious, equitable, and firm assignments for career personnel at the national committee.

Few challengers have had the organization or the will to set up a unified campaign. Franklin D. Roosevelt was equal to the occasion in 1932. With James A. Farley as his manager, Roosevelt cleaned out the old Democratic national-committee personnel and installed his own high command. Farley ran a unified, centralized campaign which swept the Democrats into power for a twenty-year stay.

The ratification of the Twenty-second Amendment, however, appears to have narrowed the choices in campaign organization for a candidate who seeks to succeed a two-term President of his own party. Somehow, he must take over the party organization and run it without offending the President, who unavoidably retains the power to control the party and who may also retain the desire as well. Both candidates who have attempted succession—Stevenson and Nixon—have lost. Neither was able to solve the basic problems of integrating his own organization with that of the incumbent President.

THE DEMOCRATIC ORGANIZATION IN 1964

The organization of President Johnson's campaign in 1964 presented a unique political problem. His unexpected accession to the presidency less than a year before the next presidential election and only nine months before the nominating convention precluded his moving to take over the executive branch and the national committee with his own people, as most new Presidents would. Needing the Kennedy men in 1964 to help carry the North and East as they needed Johnson and his men in 1960 to help carry the South, President Johnson promptly asked the entire Kennedy team to stay, in the cabinet, on the White House staff, and at the national committee.

His request accomplished two other vital political objectives: it signified the sincerity of his embrace of the Kennedy domestic program, and it put on his team the only organization equipped to lead a revolt against him within the Democratic Party.

Between January 1961 and November 1963, the Democratic National Committee had been converted into a thoroughgoing Kennedy organization. Its chairman was John Bailey of Connecticut, who gathered in the New England delegates for Kennedy before the 1960 convention. Treasurer Richard Maguire had headed the Washington scheduling office for the Kennedy campaign. Other Kennedy men held virtually all the important committee posts.

Even so, the Democratic National Committee had always expected that the 1964 presidential campaign would be run from the White House, even if President Kennedy had lived. President Johnson therefore had no need to reorganize the committee to run a unified campaign. He needed only to place a few key men on the committee's staff to direct its support for his efforts.

The President adroitly used both his own men and Kennedy men from the White House staff to tie the national committee to the White House for the campaign. Some were transferred to the committee payroll; others stayed with the White House staff to pilot part of the campaign.

Four key men—two Johnson men and two from the old Kennedy team—led the campaign organization effort:

Clifton F. Carter, a long-time Johnson lieutenant, early took up the role of liaison officer between the White House and the committee. As the national convention neared, he left the White House and went to the committee full time.

Lawrence O'Brien, White House congressional-relations expert, who had headed political organization for the 1960 Kennedy campaign, again became director of campaign organization. As he had in 1960, O'Brien toured the states, beginning in late September, to scout the political currents and to encourage state and local campaign efforts. From Washington he was supported by John H. Crooker, Jr., of Houston, and David Clarke, a 1960 Kennedy advance man.

Kenneth O'Donnell, Kennedy's campaign scheduler, left the White House staff to become executive director of the national committee.

Until his resignation October 14, Walter Jenkins, Johnson's administrative assistant since 1939, served as a direct tie between the President and the campaign organization. Bill Moyers, also a Johnson man, replaced him.

Speech writing and media work also had leadership from both staffs. In addition to his other duties, Moyers worked with the networks and newspapers and led the speech writers, who included such Johnson and Kennedy staffers as Douglass Cater, Richard Goodwin, and Horace Busby. Myer Feldman, who had led Kennedy's research efforts from Senate days, handled research at the White House and maintained liaison with the federal departments to supply information and material on issues. Feldman also worked closely with Frederick Dutton, research director of the national committee, an experienced political writer from the Brown campaigns in California, who had helped head Citizens for Kennedy in 1960.

President Johnson, however, was his own campaign manager. More than any other recent President, he refused to delegate responsibility on important campaign matters and even on many minor ones. No one else really was campaign manager as was Robert Kennedy in 1960.[1] Moreover, the President frequently kept his decisions to himself until he was ready to announce them. So pronounced did this practice become that by the time of the convention some Democratic leaders were urging the President to move more rapidly to organize his campaign.[2]

Although the President's decision to be his own campaign manager brought him criticism, it fit both the tactical situation which he faced and his personal style of leadership. The selection of a single campaign manager would have given the campaign leadership to either a Kennedy man or a Johnson man. No one was available who could truly be said to have been identified with both or with neither during or after the 1960 campaign. To choose a campaign manager, then, was to invite the opening of a breach between the Kennedy and Johnson staffs which the President neither wanted nor could afford. Under the circumstances, his decision was probably the wisest possible course.

The President may, however, have decided to be his own campaign manager because he wanted to control the details of his campaign. He thoroughly enjoyed the contest and repeatedly was reported to be delving into details of its organization and conduct. He especially took a keen interest in the public-opinion polls and in the interpretations of their meaning.

Having both the form and the substance of a unified campaign, even though it was directed by the President himself, the experienced staff men leading the campaign introduced several organizational improvements.

First, they held regular staff meetings at 9:30 each morning.

---

[1] See *Congressional Quarterly Reports,* October 16, 1964, pp. 2447 and 2448.

[2] See Carroll Kilpatrick, "Some Democrats Feel Johnson Should Step Up Campaign Pace," *Washington Post,* August 17, 1964, p. A2.

Usually meeting with Chairman John Bailey were Carter, O'Brien, O'Donnell, and Feldman from the White House liaison group; Robert Short from the Humphrey staff; and six national-committee leaders: Mrs. Margaret Price, vice chairman; Fred Dutton; Wayne Phillips, director of news and information; Samuel C. Brightman, long-time deputy chairman for public affairs; Charles D. Roche, deputy chairman, who handled congressional-campaign liaison; and Louis Martin, deputy chairman for minorities. Others joined them as the occasion required.

Second, a system of state and regional coordinators was instituted to cover the nation. In many instances, state coordinators were the Democratic state chairmen, in contrast to the 1960 arrangement, a change which was welcomed by the state organizations. The seven regional coordinators were experienced political organizers, including William Dunfey, a former full-time regional coordinator for the national committee in Butler days; Irvin Hoff, former administrative assistant to Senator Warren G. Magnuson of Washington, who had aided Johnson's preconvention campaign in 1960; and Ivan Nestingen, former Mayor of Madison, Wisconsin, who had been a leading Kennedy organizer in 1960.[3]

Third, a strong registration and get-out-the-vote drive was inaugurated. Led by Matthew Reese, who was Kennedy's campaign manager for the crucial West Virginia primary in 1960, the drive centered especially on reaching the Negro vote.

Fourth, the national committee's news service was substantially expanded and improved under the guidance of Wayne Phillips, a former reporter for the *New York Times* and information director of the Housing and Home Finance Agency.[4]

Fifth, national-committee treasurer Richard Maquire maintained fiscal control. Although President Johnson could, and did, order additional spending, the 1960 experience of having several centers of budgetary decision making was eliminated.

Thus did Johnson organize to win one of the greatest electoral victories of the century. His organizational improvements probably merit retention. His failure to use a campaign manager does not. In

[3] See *Congressional Quarterly Reports,* October 16, 1964, p. 2450 for the names of the other regional coordinators.

[4] See Chapter VIII for details.

1964, Lyndon Johnson would have won no matter how he organized his campaign. His organization, however, was a unique structure to fit a unique situation. It produced what may well be a unique result in this century.

THE "UNIFIED" DEMOCRATIC ORGANIZATION IN 1960

In 1960, Senator John F. Kennedy had an easier organizational task than his Republican opponent. He had no incumbent President as a rival to his leadership and the outgoing chairman of the Democratic National Committee, Paul M. Butler, no longer commanded a substantial following of his own.

With such a tailor-made opportunity to take over the national committee, John F. Kennedy should have had clear sailing to use the 1932 unified system of Franklin Roosevelt. But, for reasons of high policy, he made a preliminary decision that contained the seeds of organizational trouble.

Kennedy's preconvention campaign manager was his brother Robert. They agreed that to name him national chairman would be a political blunder of the first magnitude. To "balance" the leadership, a Protestant Westerner seemed ideal. Senator Henry M. Jackson of Washington, who had supported Kennedy's drive for the nomination and campaigned openly to be his running mate, was a logical choice. Thus the East, the South, and the West were served.

While still in Los Angeles, the Kennedy team reviewed with Jackson the experience of previous Democratic candidates. Organization of the two most recent campaigns had been unsatisfactory. In 1952, although Stephen Mitchell was made national chairman, Governor Stevenson ran his campaign from Springfield. Liaison with the national committee in Washington and with the White House was inadequate. In 1956, in an attempt to correct this weakness, Mr. Stevenson ran his campaign from Washington, D.C., under the leadership of James A. Finnegan, but Mr. Butler remained as national chairman. Physical proximity helped coordination, but divided responsibility continued the weaknesses of 1952.

Without hesitation, the Kennedys turned to the 1932 unified-campaign system of James A. Farley as the key to success. The national committee would be reorganized to serve the campaign. There would be one central staff, divided on functional lines. But Jackson was chairman and Robert Kennedy was campaign manager. If the campaign really were to be unified and organizational discord avoided, one or the other had to be boss.

The organization did operate as a unified system and the boss was Robert Kennedy. Henry Jackson went on the road to give campaign speeches and left his lieutenants in Washington to handle the routine national-committee functions of acquiring space, purchasing supplies and materials, employing temporary personnel, and organizing such auxiliary services as telephones, mail, duplicating, and materials distribution. Robert Kennedy took over national-committee headquarters and adapted the existing staff to his campaign needs.

Such an arrangement was necessary, wise, and probably inevitable. The Kennedys brought a going campaign organization with them. Jackson had no team beyond his own office staff. Unfortunately, clear-cut organizational procedures to formalize the arrangement were never specifically adopted and promulgated.

For a time, two views were held of the structure of the campaign organization. The Jackson forces thought of the national committee as operating in five parts: The regular committee staff under Jackson was to continue essential services to the state and local committees and to congressional candidates while bending every effort to aid the presidential campaign. Robert Kennedy, using the preconvention Kennedy team, was to direct the presidential campaign proper. Senator Lyndon Johnson and his lieutenants, using their preconvention organization, were to run the vice-presidential campaign in coordination with the others. Matthew H. McCloskey, the committee treasurer, was to raise and disburse the money. Mrs. Margaret Price, newly elected vice chairman of the committee, was to direct women's activities.

The Kennedy team, on the other hand, appears to have viewed the organization functionally, as a family affair. Fundamentally, it also had five parts:

First, Senator John F. Kennedy made the speeches and did the barnstorming. Four important campaign units reported directly to him without accounting to other officers of the national committee or to the family team: (a) the Kennedy research team represented by Theodore Sorensen on the campaign plane and managed by Myer Feldman at committee headquarters; (b) the Kennedy speech-writing team under Archibald Cox; (c) the Kennedy press team headed by Pierre Salinger; and (d) the media department under Leonard Reinsch, which was responsible primarily for negotiating with Nixon headquarters concerning the television debates.

Second, Robert F. Kennedy served as campaign manager for the presidential campaign and had general supervision over all other phases of the work of the national committee and its auxiliaries. Control was accomplished through "campaign coordinators" from the preconvention Kennedy staff, who were made responsible for the over-all direction of major parts of the national committee. Three units appear to have been assigned as the immediate responsibility of the campaign manager: (a) the Organization Division, headed by Lawrence O'Brien, which stimulated efforts by regular state and local Democratic organizations and maintained a general check on the work of all divisions of the national committee except those reporting directly to Senator Kennedy; (b) the Scheduling Office, which also reported directly to Senator Kennedy through Kenneth O'Donnell on the candidate's plane; and (c) the Publicity Division, which was entrusted to Roger Tubby as campaign coordinator.

Third, R. Sargent Shriver, Senator Kennedy's brother-in-law, formed various special-interest groups for Kennedy-Johnson. Shriver's job essentially was to create such units for the campaign. The specialized committees of the Democratic Advisory Council offered a nucleus from which to begin, so Mr. Shriver originally located himself in the chambers of the council and drew heavily upon its staff for names and advice. Once the several divisions were under way, separate quarters were provided for them.

Fourth, Stephen Smith, also a brother-in-law of Senator Kennedy, was asked to raise money. He did so principally as treasurer for the Citizens for Kennedy-Johnson. Because of the $3-million spending limit imposed on national committees by the Hatch Act, his role became vital about the middle of October, when the Democratic National Committee reached its spending limit and all income and expenditures had to be processed by Citizens for Kennedy-Johnson.

Fifth, Byron White, an old friend, headed the separate Citizens for Kennedy-Johnson to corral persons who wished to work exclusively for the national ticket. The citizens organization coordinated its efforts closely with the Democratic National Committee and especially cooperated with Sargent Shriver's special-interest units. Some such units were housed with "Citizens" and often put out material for "Citizens."

The candidate's sisters appeared at women's meetings and, after Mrs. Kennedy (expecting a second child) could no longer accompany the Senator on tour, went with their brother as hostesses.

Neither the Kennedy nor the Jackson system was ever formalized. Indeed, informality in organization was deliberately retained and was defended on the theory that to structure the campaign organization would be to introduce red tape which would restrict flexibility, hamstring prompt decision making, and prevent quick action. In practice, after much trial and effort, both theories of organization were meshed together after a fashion.

Each division of the national committee, whether long established or created for the campaign, was virtually turned loose to do all it could to win the election. Coordination among units was called for only when a joint enterprise was required. Big expenses were to be cleared with the Organization Division—Lawrence O'Brien, or his lieutenants Ralph Dungan or Dick Donohue—and each unit was supposed to have a budget within which it was expected to live. Policy statements were to be cleared with Senator Kennedy's personal research staff headed by Myer Feldman. Coordination with the Johnson team was handled by William Welsh, a former research director of the national committee.

Such an arrangement suited the well-established and close-knit Kennedy family campaign organization. For the newly created special-interest adjuncts, such as Farmers for Kennedy-Johnson, Viva Kennedy, or Business and Professional Men and Women for Kennedy and Johnson, such provisions were not inadequate. They had no ongoing function to perform and could concentrate on a few well-selected mailings.

For the old national-committee staff, accustomed to minute

control by the chairman over every step of the work, the new arrangement was bewildering. Where were they to report? What sort of guidance could they expect? By trial and error they discovered that they were free to follow whichever program they deemed best. For approval of funds and policy statements, they cleared with O'Brien and Feldman respectively. For personnel, equipment, supplies, and services, they notified John Salter or Dan Martin in Jackson's office. They ended up reporting both to Robert Kennedy and to Henry Jackson. But many old staff people felt they were bypassing the chairman and that this bypassing was unwise.

Major shifts in staff assignments and location were made early in August. Left intact were the treasurer's functions, both fund raising and accounting. Similarly treated were the Women's Division, the Young Democrats, the Speakers' Bureau, the Voters' Service Bureau, and the "headquarters" services such as duplicating, telephones, and mail room. All were useful and created no conflict with the main thrust of the campaign.

On the other hand, the old Department of Political Organization and the advisory council were abolished and their personnel temporarily put to other and much less important campaign work.

As the campaign unfolded and the national-committee payroll swelled from 100 to nearly 500 paid employees, who were aided by untold numbers of volunteers, it became plain that the ordinary tools of administrative management were to be used primarily as emergency devices. Staff meetings were held when needed by those division chiefs who faced a problem. Some division chiefs, especially those concerned with policy statements and publicity for such statements, got together regularly for breakfast meetings on their own initiative.

Although a central clearing station for volunteer help was in operation, each unit was left to hire and fire paid personnel independently. As a result, one incompetent girl was hired and fired by six different divisions of the committee.

As might be expected, performances of the divisions varied widely. The Community Relations Division, which concentrated on the religious issue, achieved remarkable success by distributing widely Senator Kennedy's well-received address to Protestant ministers at Houston. The Nationalities Division made deep inroads into the Polish vote by effective use of Prince Stanislaw Radziwill, a brother-in-law of Mrs. Kennedy. By contrast, the Veterans' Division program, run for all practical purposes by one weak secretary, was a near debacle. Having accumulated a list of veterans, which turned out to be well laced with Republicans, Veterans for Kennedy-Johnson mailed each veteran an invitation to volunteer as a worker in the Kennedy cause. Each respondent was sent a pamphlet and was referred to his *state* Citizens for Kennedy-Johnson chairman, who usually was located in a distant city. The state chairman, however, was never notified of the existence of the volunteer! Worse, the burden of this "activity" proved so great that no other mail was handled. In January 1961, a large box full of unanswered letters to Senator Kennedy from veterans around the nation turned up in the division's files!

The imposition of budget controls was attempted on behalf of Chairman Jackson by William Perkins, but with only limited effect. Individual division heads were able to secure approval for spending projects variously from Treasurer McCloskey, Stephen Smith, Robert Kennedy, or his lieutenants; and some units, such as Labor's Committee for Kennedy and Johnson, Business and Professional Men and Women for Kennedy-Johnson, and Citizens for Kennedy-Johnson, had their own treasuries. One resulting minor crisis created some amusement: An end-of-campaign car caravan by the Young Democrats was scheduled, canceled the night before its departure, then reauthorized the following morning—all by different people able to make fiscal decisions.

Thus did the Kennedys take over the Democratic National Committee and confine the problems of the adjustment to the two most vulnerable of the old units. Fortunately, long hours, devotion, and real talent marked the efforts of most campaign operations. The success gained may have come, in part, through unified campaign organization, concentration on essentials, tight organization of key units, and flexible administration of auxiliary activities.

THE REPUBLICAN ORGANIZATION IN 1964

The Republican presidential-campaign organization in 1964 reflected the same ideological tone as did the candidates' general strategy and the new party platform.

On the very day of his nomination, July 15, Senator Goldwater announced that he would run his campaign from the Republican National Committee in Washington. He had decided to fuse his personal campaign staff with that of the national committee for two reasons: to avoid the overlap, duplication, and waste so often characteristic of a divided-campaign effort; and to harness effectively the considerable talents available among his preconvention supporters.

In very short order he appointed trusted colleagues to fill key positions both in the national-committee staff and in the newly organized Citizens for Goldwater-Miller Committee.

As over-all campaign chairman he chose Denison Kitchel, Arizona attorney and long-time friend. As chairman of the national committee he selected his former administrative assistant, Dean Burch. Alabaman John Grenier, former director of the Draft Goldwater group's southern region, became the national committee's executive director, while Wayne Hood, another regional director for the Draft Goldwater movement, was named director of the campaign organization at the national committee.

With the appointment of Goldwater men to every key policy post at the national committee came the necessary demotions and replacements among the committee's permanent personnel. Research Director William Pendergast, for example, had earlier turned down a post with the Draft Goldwater group. Now he was replaced with a Washington attorney and offered, a subordinate position which he refused.

Albert B. "Ab" Hermann, former executive director and director of campaign organization at the committee, was relegated to answering mail. National Committeeman I. Lee Potter, former director of "Operation Dixie," found himself scheduling trips for Nixon and Eisenhower rather than assisting with the development of support in the South. Some second-echelon personnel in research and public relations were given subordinate roles to play; others were dismissed outright.

Since the grand strategy of the campaign included heavy emphasis on sectional appeals, leaders at the national committee and citizens group alike made provision for a decentralized field operation centering in seven regional offices. National-committee regional directors, who worked closely with official Republican leaders of the states under their jurisdiction, reported to John Grenier, while regional directors of the Citizens for Goldwater-Miller reported to F. Clifton White, executive director of the citizens organization.

The close contact between the staffs of the citizens committee and the national committee eliminated much of the overlap and duplication usually found in such parallel field operations.

The Goldwater-Miller citizens organization created a remarkable number and variety of special-interest groups at national and state levels to broaden the base of support for the candidate by appealing to nonparty members through personal, vocational, or avocational interests. Some of these efforts were highly successful, but in too many cases the necessarily "political" approach of these programs was blunted by the zealous idealism of top citizens leadership.

An interview with a prominent Citizens for Goldwater-Miller leader revealed that in his opinion "special-interest appeals" were inappropriate for the Goldwater campaign since:

We are endeavoring to appeal to America's voters as a whole and not in relation to the various individual factions which tend to draw them into separate groups. The material which we are disseminating is related only to various issues which we feel are of importance to all Americans.[5]

Thus with both the national party organization and the associated citizens group in the hands of sincere and dedicated conservative ideologists, there was little room for the pragmatic innovations which have historically marked successful American presidential campaigns.

The impact of this ideologically oriented campaign was seen clearly in the reorganization of the national committee's Campaign Division, traditionally composed of farm, labor, arts and sciences, minorities, senior citizens, veterans, nationalities, and similar special-interest sections.

In 1964 the arts and sciences section was placed in the Research Division, and most of the others (farm, senior citizens, labor,

[5] Interview with citizens leader in charge of special-interest groups in a major midwestern state.

veterans) were simply deactivated or eliminated as autonomous campaign organizations.

Only the Nationalities Division remained as a separate entity in the national committee's Campaign Division. The function of attracting voters through special-interest appeals was transferred largely to the citizens committee's state organizations.

With much of its former responsibility transferred to the citizens committee, Wayne Hood's Campaign Division now became the coordinator of two ostensibly autonomous organizations, the Women's Federation and the Young Republicans. In addition, Hood assumed responsibility for the Political Education and Training Program (concerned with ballot security, door-to-door canvassing, and election-day activity), the Tour Committee (which handled Goldwater-Miller, Eisenhower, and Nixon appearances), the Speakers' Bureau, the Nationalities Division, and the Truth Squad.

The immediate responsibilities of Executive Director John Grenier were administrative: communications, campaign mail, visitors, office management, and the comptroller function.

Significantly omitted from Grenier's control were the Research Division and the Public Relations Division, both of whose directors reported directly to Chairman Dean Burch. Lou Guylay, who had directed the national committee's Public Relations Division in the 1956 and 1960 presidential campaigns, was asked to assume again the directorship of this division in 1964. Edward A. McCabe, a Washington attorney and a White House aide during the Eisenhower administration, became the director of research.

In both these divisions the major innovations in 1964 were technological in nature. National politics entered the electronic data-processing age with the use by the Research Division of the Recordak information-retrieval machines. Thousands of man-hours were consumed in the clipping, indexing, and processing of every possible speech, statement, or activity by leading Democratic candidates. Once processed and properly indexed, these items could be retrieved in a matter of seconds for use by the Research Division.

Although similar data-processing equipment had been used by

various state party leaders prior to 1964 for voter data and contributions records, the Goldwater campaign was the first to use these machines for research purposes in a national campaign.

In the Public Relations Division, electronic devices also played an important role. In order to expedite communications between national and state campaign headquarters, TWX teletypewriters were installed in virtually every state. These machines transmitted literally thousands of pages of press statements, speeches, and accounts of major campaign developments—so much material, in fact, that few state headquarters could keep an up-to-date file on this vast ocean of data. Effective use of related parts of this continuous flow of words was virtually impossible. Because of the volume of material flowing outward from Washington, the second purpose of the TWX teletypewriter system—an inexpensive two-way communications link between national and state headquarters—was largely defeated.

Despite whatever other organizational weaknesses may be laid at the door of the Goldwater campaign directors, they proved both at the convention and during the campaign that they had mastered at least the technical side of campaign communications. Their extensive use of two-way radios, Recordak equipment, and the TWX teletypewriter system will undoubtedly have its impact on leaders from both political parties.

Senator Goldwater and other close personal advisors were aware that the Republican National Committee and the citizens committee were in the hands of leaders with a basically ideological orientation. They were aware, too, that it was imperative to bring other top Republican leaders actively into the campaign. To accomplish this purpose a steering committee was appointed, consisting of Kitchel, Burch, Grenier, Hood Guylay, and McCabe, F. Clifton White, national director of the Citizens for Goldwater-Miller; William S. Warner, vice-presidential nominee William Miller's campaign director; Ray C. Bliss, Ohio state chairman and chairman of the Republican State Chairmen's Association; Ralph Cordiner, chairman of the Republican National Finance Committee; and William F. Knowland, former U.S. Senate Majority Leader from California. Goldwater campaign aides William Baroody and Tony

Smith also attended the meetings when their schedules permitted. The stated purpose of this high-level group was to meet weekly to formulate political strategy and prepare the campaign calendar.

The Sunday meetings of the steering committee did indeed focus on central campaign problems, but the inability of either of the candidates to attend even one of these sessions minimized the impact of the suggestions and solutions developed therein.

Actually, neither the unified and rationalized national-committee campaign organization, nor the associated Citizens for Goldwater-Miller, nor the high-level steering committee had as much influence on the critical decisions of the campaign as a small group of individuals who occupied offices on the third floor of the Cafritz Building in downtown Washington.

Known as the "think tank," these offices provided the working space for three groups of Goldwater campaign intimates: First, there were those individuals who traveled frequently with the presidential candidate—Denison Kitchel, campaign director; Tony Smith, Goldwater's former press secretary; and Karl Hess, a professional speech writer and journalist. Second, a small coterie of idea men or brain trusters, headed by William A. Baroody, of the American Enterprise Association. Finally, a group of academic luminaries, most of whom contributed occasional position papers or suggested possible responses to developing issues, but who seldom frequented the offices themselves. Among this group of distinguished intellectuals were Karl Brandt and W. Glenn Campbell of Stanford, G. Warren Nutter of the University of Virginia, Richard A. Ware of the RELM Foundation in Michigan, Raymond Saulnier and Arthur Burns of Columbia, Gerhard Neimeyer of Notre Dame University, Edward Teller of the University of California at Los Angeles, Milton Friedman of the University of Chicago, Robert Strausz-Hupé of the University of Pennsylvania, Dave Nelson Rowe of Yale University, Paul McCracken of the University of Michigan, and Harry Jaffa of Pomona College.

The fact that the really important decisions of the campaign were hammered out in this so-called think tank was most disturbing to those Goldwater lieutenants who had labored long and hard for their leader and who were now excluded from the inner circle. The bitterness expressed by F. Clifton White on this point is representative. Referring to the nearly inaccessible third-floor offices where "Denison Kitchel, Bill Baroody, and their stable of writers and research experts held court," White opined:

It was a court that was notably unreceptive to ideas from outside its own circle. Senator Goldwater's office adjoining the "tank" was open only to a select few.[6]

In organization and technical innovation the Goldwater campaign had much to commend it. In the utilization of available, experienced, and skilled leadership both within and without the integrated campaign structure, it was woefully weak. As with the 1964 Republican platform, pragmatic politics gave way to ideological considerations, and experienced political leaders were replaced by well-meaning but inadequate novices.

THE "DUAL" REPUBLICAN ORGANIZATION IN 1960

The problems faced by the Republican Party in 1960 were quite different from those faced by the Democrats. By January of the election year, it was assumed by most Republican state and national leaders that Vice President Richard M. Nixon would surely be the presidential nominee. Although some of Nixon's lieutenants were strangely uncertain of the Republican nomination so freely predicted for their candidate, a number of them were optimistic enough to move into Washington to "set up shop" with the coming of the new year. Nixon's lieutenants had done their work well. In the fall of 1959 they had anticipated an extended conflict in several presidential-primary states and at the convention as well. But through their skillful planning, and through careful engineering by sympathetic Republican organization leaders in key presidential-primary states, they had been highly successful in discouraging the anticipated Rockefeller candidacy.

Early in January, many of these same men came to Washington to establish the framework of the Vice President's campaign organization. The several offices which were established were dedicated essentially to the capture of the Republican presidential nomina-

[6] F. Clifton White, *Suite 3505* (New Rochelle, N.Y.: Arlington House, 1967), p. 416.

tion for the Vice President; but they also foreshadowed the Vice President's personal campaign organization which was basically to direct the national Republican campaign after the national convention. In the Washington Building, scarcely four blocks from the national Republican headquarters, a team of writers, researchers, and subject-matter experts was already turning out work as 1960 began. As this staff expanded, another office, housing a Dick Nixon Club, was opened close by at the Shoreham Building for the purpose of raising money and developing "personal-follower-group" strength in all of the 50 states.

At the swank Sheraton Park Hotel, two miles out Connecticut Avenue, Leonard Hall, former Republican National Chairman, had also established his headquarters. It was assumed that because of his prominent role in the successful containment of the Rockefeller movement, his wide party contacts, and his management of the 1956 presidential campaign, he would help fashion the strategy of the Nixon campaign.

On Capitol Hill close friends and associates of the Vice President arrived from California. Bob Finch, young, aggressive, former Los Angeles County Republican Chairman; Stan McCaffrey, a former vice president of the University of California; and Herb Klein, California newspaperman, came to supplement the forces working close to the Vice President in the Senate Office Building.

Over at the Republican National Committee during this period early in 1960, the development of this Nixon campaign organization was duly noted. It was obvious to many of the long-time staff members at the committee that the Vice President was not likely to replace these trusted lieutenants with professional committee staff men once the nomination was secured. Nevertheless, while Nixon's campaign staff was building, plans were also being made at the national committee for the waging of the campaign which would mark the centenary of Abraham Lincoln's candidacy.

The chairman of the Republican National Committee, Senator Thruston B. Morton of Kentucky, had proved to be one of the ablest the Republican Party had ever called to its top position. Possessed with an unusual ability to mediate between the liberal and the conservative wings of the party, Senator Morton also had a sparkling sense of humor and exceptional speaking skill which soon catapulted him into great favor as one of the party's most popular and most articulate spokesmen.

Senator Morton, speaking in February 1959 in Wheeling, West Virginia, had publicly announced that he was committed to the candidacy of Richard Nixon. When he assumed the party chairmanship, however, he indicated in unmistakable terms that he considered it his responsibility to see that the facilities of the national-committee staff were made available on equal terms to all potential candidates for the presidential nomination.

During the early months of 1960, the national-committee staff was, indeed, reminded on several occasions that their services were to be made available to all leading presidential aspirants. It is true, however, that the personal relationships that existed between national-committee staff members and the omnipresent Nixon aides made it quite natural for the Vice President's assistants to request and to receive more help than was tendered to the staff of any other potential candidate.

As the winter turned into spring, the liaison between many of the Nixon people and their counterparts in all divisions at the national committee increased. Speculations arose anew that perhaps once the convention had nominated the Vice President a unified campaign organization might ensue.

In looking forward to the 1960 campaign, Chairman Morton continually asserted in a 49-state speaking tour that the Republican Party was the minority party and that if it were to be successful in 1960 and thereafter, it must broaden its base. Consequently, several new programs were established and several old programs were strengthened.

If the organization chart used in the successful 1956 campaign were compared with that projected for the 1960 campaign, it would appear that there were to be relatively few personnel changes. In 1960, many of the top-echelon personalities of 1956 were back at their posts or were in roughly parallel positions in the rapidly developing Nixon campaign headquarters.

Leonard Hall, for example, the national chairman in 1956, was now actively assisting in the direction of Nixon's campaign strategy. Robert Carter served as executive assistant to Mr. Hall, a post he had occupied in 1956. Cliff Folger, the Republican National

Finance Committee Chairman in 1956, was now functioning as the chief money raiser for the Vice President.

In the line divisions, a 1956 public-relations director, Lou Guylay, had been brought back by Chairman Morton to direct the national committee's public-relations program for the 1960 campaign. Albert B. Hermann, considered to be one of the better "professional" staff men in party politics, assumed control of the campaign division. A Southern Division, not existing in 1956, had been added under the direction of I. Lee Potter, the Republican state chairman for Virginia. New programs had been instituted by the creation of Business Men in Politics, Senior Republicans, and the Arts and Sciences Division.

During the period from January through July, old and new programs alike were far ahead of similar developments in 1956, according to some long-time staff members. In the businessmen's division, for example, a list of graduates of businessmen's public-affairs courses had been developed in the hope that many of these people might be successfully drawn into the coming campaign. Likewise, in the Senior Republicans Division, a program to inform senior citizens of the accomplishments of the Eisenhower administration was linked with an active solicitation of the support of these people for the election of the Republican presidential candidate in 1960. The Arts and Sciences Division was identifying Republican-oriented academicians on campuses across the land and was attempting to recruit them for precampaign and campaign tasks.

Similar efforts were being made in the Labor, Agriculture, Veterans, Minorities, and Nationalities Divisions. The Young Republicans were busy preparing a number of their young men for campaign field-work assignments, and the Women's Division staged a "campaign countdown" April 2 through April 5, which was designed to inform the leaders of women's Republican groups across the nation of the issues in the coming campaign and of successful campaign techniques.

So it was that as spring ended and summer came to Washington, the national-committee staff was functioning essentially in the same manner that it had under the leadership of Chairman Len Hall in 1956. The organization chart which had been developed for the 1960 campaign by national-committee personnel suggested that the over-all campaign strategy would be determined by a group including the Vice President, the national chairman, the director of a citizens committee, a representative of the White House, the chairman of the Senatorial Campaign Committee, the chairman of the Congressional Campaign Committee, and the vice-presidential candidate for 1960.

There were many sound reasons for believing that the 1960 presidential campaign would be virtually a rerun of 1956. In the first place, many of the top Nixon staff members were formerly of the national-committee staff, including a former national chairman, his chief assistant, and a number of former division heads. Likewise, the close relationship which had developed between January and June among the various Nixon offices and clubs and the national-committee staff personnel suggested at the very least a close cooperation between the top Nixon campaign lieutenants and the regular national-committee staff.

But some seasoned hands at the national committee had noted certain signs as early as May and June which indicated that the 1960 campaign might well differ markedly from the 1956 effort in terms of direction and management.

The Vice President had demonstrated an unwillingness to brook criticism of his own campaign strategy; he had refused to delegate responsibility, and some members of the ever-increasing Nixon staff were extremely young and politically inexperienced. As the convention approached, there was growing concern at the committee over the shape of things to come.

After the national convention had come and gone, and the national-committee staff had returned to Washington, some of the more experienced, whose forebodings had preceded the convention, were now even more deeply disturbed. A number of events, largely unnoticed by the casual observer during the convention, had convinced these national-committee staff people that the campaign indeed might be a disappointing one.

Nevertheless, when the various Washington offices resumed operation in early August, there was still considerable hope, in most quarters, that a unified campaign organization might be developed and that victory in 1960 was within easy reach.

And then things began to happen. First the Vice President injured himself and lost valuable campaign time. Next came the decision to debate Kennedy and the demoralizing effect of the first joint television appearance. Division after division at the national committee found itself rebuffed by Nixon organization people when they offered their services and suggested programs. What was happening? What was going wrong?

It had now become obvious to all that the Republican national campaign of 1960, from an organizational standpoint, was to be based upon a dual effort. The Vice President and his staff were obviously trying to create a new Nixon image and a new image for the Republican Party. Mr. Nixon had insisted on a stronger civil-rights plank and a more vigorous approach to national defense because he believed firmly in these positions, and he believed that the Republican Party had to move ahead on these fronts. Now as the campaign proper got under way, it was his announced intention to woo votes which were not ordinarily cast for Republican candidates. He understood quite well that the Republican Party was a minority party. He felt his only chance for victory was to be found in the regular Republican vote plus the votes of millions of Americans who are quadrennially undecided as between the Republican and Democratic candidate.

And so Nixon turned away from the leadership and the programs of the Republican National Committee because he felt that this leadership and these programs would be too partisan in orientation. Because he had great faith in those lieutenants who had done such a skillful job in obtaining the nomination for him, Nixon determined to lean heavily on his own personal campaign organization and to use the national-committee staff almost as an auxiliary to his own campaign.

Just as it was quite natural for candidate Nixon to make a "candidate-type" decision as to the nature of his campaign organization, so it was quite natural for the members of the national-committee staff to react adversely to such a decision. They were, by virtue of background and experience, opposed to a dual campaign organizational structure. It was a firmly held conviction among these men that the Vice President could have found campaign-management skills in abundance and much of the kind of program he needed at the national committee itself.

With the development of a dual campaign organization, the question always arises as to which programs are to be directed from which organization. In the Republican campaign of 1960, all divisions and programs considered basic to the success of the campaign were directed by the Vice President's own immediate staff.

In some campaign areas there was almost complete control of a given campaign effort from the Nixon headquarters, with the staff personnel from the national committee physically relocating and becoming an integral part of the Nixon-Lodge campaign staff. One thus shifted, for example, was the top agriculture specialist at the national committee—Mr. Rollis Nelson, a talented and trusted speech writer and expert in the politics of agriculture.

In other areas such as nationalities, the national committee retained its own division personnel but the leadership for the campaign effort was transferred to the Nixon-Lodge headquarters where a newly appointed leader managed the division effort.

A third pattern in the dual organization structure developed where the national-committee staff was given direction of the campaign effort for both organizations. This pattern developed in the campaign for support of the academic community. For example, the executive director of the national committee's Arts and Sciences Division was given the additional responsibility for directing the Nixon-Lodge Scholars Program.

In certain other areas where dual efforts existed, such as in minorities, labor, and the Senior Republicans, the programs and proposals of the national-committee staff were very often entirely overlooked. Postmortems of the election often pointed to the costly bypass of the talents and experience available in some of these crucial fields. Labor and minorities, for example, had no budget. Without any real demonstration of interest on the part of the Nixon-Lodge headquarters, both divisions suffered from gross underutilization during the entire postconvention campaign.

Another of the great weaknesses which is likely to develop when a dual organization is employed concerns delegation of authority and assignment. Inefficiency and duplication often result. Professor Neil Cotter notes this dilemma in his example of the Republican organization's research efforts in the 1960 campaign:

. . . I find that a friend of mine who attempted to analyze in shorthand terms the allocation of responsibility for research in the Republican campaign effort for 1960 made the following note: "Grassmuck vs.

Hamlin vs. Shepley vs. GOP." The reference is to the fact that George Grassmuck, a political scientist from the University of Michigan, was taken on by the Nixon campaign staff in a research capacity. Prior to George's joining the Nixon campaign group, John Hamlin, formerly an assistant to the President with an office in the Executive Office Building, had moved into a suite in the Sheraton-Park Hotel, where he proceeded to put together a file on Kennedy for the use of the Vice President. For a time, many people regarded Hamlin as the Nixon research man. When Professor Grassmuck came along, many people regarded Professor Grassmuck as having replaced Hamlin. Then along came Mr. James Shepley from the *Time-Life* organization. At this point many persons wondered who had replaced whom. Cordial as this trio's relations were with personnel on the Republican National Committee staff, there was always a question in the Committee as to whether the Research Division of the Republican National Committee was working with, for, or being worked against by the research staff of the Nixon campaign organization.[7]

The illustration of the difficulty of coordination in the research field could be multiplied many times over as between the Nixon-Lodge campaign staff and the national-committee operation. There appeared to be very little coordination among state Nixon-Lodge headquarters and the national Nixon-Lodge office as well. As director of a campaign division at the national committee, Arthur Peterson attempted to coordinate his activities with those of the Nixon-Lodge national headquarters but seldom was able to meet with success. As director of one of the divisions in the Nixon-Lodge operation, he attempted to develop coordination and communication between the state Nixon-Lodge headquarters and the national Nixon-Lodge office, but again his efforts met with extreme frustration.

The budget problems created by the dual campaign organization constitute one of the most unfortunate aspects of the entire campaign. Thus at the end of October in 1960, with Election Day imminent, the Republican Party found itself with a debt of $1.183 million. In January 1961, the national committee found itself with a

[7] Cornelius P. Cotter, *Technical Specialists in the 1960 Republican Campaign,* unpublished paper delivered at the 1960 convention of the American Political Science Association, St. Louis, Missouri, September 8, 1961, pp. 4f.

postelection debt of staggering proportions. The figure exceeded $700,000.

Issues, candidates, financial support, and the party image are all well-known essentials to a successful political campaign. An analysis of the 1960 campaign reveals, however, that the element of campaign organization and management can also be crucial.

One can easily understand the difficulties of a candidate in quest of a new party image. Vice President Nixon's decision to set up a dual campaign organization was probably made to facilitate the building of this new party image. Some political leaders would insist, however, that the Republican candidate for the presidency in 1960, as in 1964, would have been well advised to utilize more extensively and effectively the available party organizational support and time-tested leadership.

Bibliography

Cotter, Cornelius P. *Technical Specialists in the 1960 Republican Campaign.* Unpublished paper delivered at the 1960 convention of the American Political Science Association, St. Louis, Missouri, September 8, 1961.

Ogden, Daniel M., Jr. "The Democratic National Committee in the Campaign of 1960," *Western Political Quarterly,* XIV (September 1961), 27-28. Summary of a paper presented at the annual meeting of the Western Political Science Association.

Sorensen, Theodore C. *Kennedy.* New York: Harper, 1965. See especially pp. 170-177.

White, F. Clifton. *Suite 3505.* New Rochelle, N.Y.: Arlington House, 1967.

Chapter VI

Enlisting State and Local Support

Support for a presidential candidate from his own state and local party organizations is related directly to his chances for victory. If he looks like a sure winner, his party's organizations and their candidates for lesser offices will "jump on his bandwagon" in the expectation that his victory will carry them, too, into office and power. If he looks like a loser, they will avoid identification with him and with the national committee in the hope of salvaging a state or local victory from the impending national disaster. If the race is close, the candidate must make strenuous efforts to reassure the loyal and to keep the fainthearted with him, for their efforts can make the difference between victory and defeat.

The role of the national committee remains much the same in each of these three circumstances, but the ease of its work and the probability of its success vary among them. When the candidate seems sure to win, the committee is deluged with requests for pictures with the presidential candidate, for national materials with which the local organizations and candidates can identify, and for direct assistance from national workers. The committee must respond positively to such overtures and need urge only a few state and local organizations to cooperate in the national campaign.

If the candidate looks like a loser, the national committee must seek support as it can. Within some states, it must turn to loyalists who hold no official party posts. Personal efforts by key committee leaders may be necessary to get even the most rudimentary efforts under way on behalf of the national ticket.

When the contest is close, the national committee must both respond and urge. From those areas where the candidate is strongest, the initiative for cooperation will come from the state and local organizations and candidates. In areas where he is weakest, the national committee, the candidate's personal representatives, or even the candidate himself must initiate the effort. If, as with the Democrats in 1960, the presidential candidate has special appeal to one section of the nation and the vice-presidential candidate to another, they may divide the work.

Both the Republican Party and the Democratic Party have been in all three situations in the last three presidential campaigns. In 1956, President Dwight D. Eisenhower was a sure winner. Republican organizations and candidates countrywide flocked to his support and sought to identify with his name. "Back Ike, elect Jones," was a typical slogan. Adlai E. Stevenson, repeat Democratic nominee, was cold-shouldered by hardheaded state and local organizations and candidates who sought their own salvation in state and local personalities and issues. Only among the liberal intellectuals did Stevenson find a solid band of enthusiastic believers, and they frequently had to forsake the state or local efforts to campaign in his behalf.

In 1964, the party positions were reversed. President Lyndon B. Johnson was an obvious winner from the day the Republican Party nominated Senator Barry Goldwater, the spokesman for its right wing. A full-page ad in the *New York Times* of October 23, 1964, tells the story. Across the bottom in large black letters it implored, "On Nov. 3, Vote for Robert Kennedy—for the Johnson, Humphrey, Kennedy Team." Only in his own Southland was Johnson's name unwanted. There Barry Goldwater proved a major asset to the emerging conservative Republican organizations.

The 1960 campaign, then, with its tight race between Senator John F. Kennedy and Vice President Richard M. Nixon, was the contest which really tried the organizational mettle of both national committees. It therefore deserves special description and analysis.

THE PAROCHIALISM OF STATE AND LOCAL ORGANIZATIONS

The independent behavior of state and local party organizations in a presidential campaign, and thus the need for both national committees to adapt their organizational efforts to the circumstances in each election, stems from the decentralized and heterogeneous nature of both major parties.

The American political-party system is differentiated from the so-called ideological parties of Europe in three key ways: (1) The two major parties are loosely knit associations composed of individuals and groups with widely divergent interests, backgrounds, and ideologies. (2) In the main these associations gain direction and thrust only during elections. (3) The power to make decisions concerning candidates, financial support, and such party policy as does exist is largely in the hands of state and local party leaders and elected public officials.

Presidential elections in American politics accordingly constitute a periodic and sometimes painful wrenching of the sinews and muscles of party organization. The conflict has grown as the party system has grown; for although a major goal of parties in America is to win elections, more particularly presidential elections, the state and local organizations are not basically oriented in the direction of national concerns. Their day-to-day problems quite naturally center in state and local politics; yet once every four years, they are expected to completely readjust their focus for a period of from three to six months.

This decentralized party system is quadrennially forced to become, at least in part, a centralized party system with campaign plans, party propaganda, and issue accentuation dictated from the national level. To many career politicians, the change means an invasion of their province. Organizations geared to local, congressional, and state contests are asked to redirect their thinking, to tie into their staffs the amateurs from the so-called presidential party, and to attempt to implement the most recent innovations in campaign organization and extension suggested by the campaign masterminds in Washington. In some states, where circumstances appear to warrant it, the local organizations may even be expected to "stand by" while the "citizen" or "volunteer" organizations move in to direct the presidential campaign efforts with such assists as they request from the regular party organization.

From the perspective of the national party organization the conflict is seen in a different light. Programs which the national committee has spent considerable time and money to initiate and develop are never tried; party propaganda which could have tremendous impact on the outcome of the campaign is never completely distributed; the presidential and vice-presidential candidates' time is partially wasted on the wrong kinds of meetings. In short, the tools which might bring victory in November are not properly utilized.

After almost any national campaign, a third interpretation of the problems of developing presidential support at the state and local levels is advanced by the leaders of the volunteer or citizens groups. These men and women are ordinarily relative amateurs in politics. They are, on the other hand, usually prominent people, selected to reflect the support the presidential aspirant has from certain important groups in the community. Accustomed to community deference, these leading businessmen, educators, agriculturists, labor leaders, doctors, and the like are frequently quite unhappy when they are forced to subordinate their judgment about running the campaign to that of some junior staff man attached to either the national committee or the state organization. When the candidate loses, the local chairman of the Volunteers for X remembers his effort to present the "future President" at his alma mater, Public School No. 5, and feels that the professional party leaders were unknowing as well as ungrateful. He feels humiliated even if the candidate wins.

Out of this triangle of interests and approaches a presidential campaign must be fashioned at the state and local levels. During the four years between presidential elections the scant contact between the state or local party leaders and the national-committee staff reinforces the sense of remoteness caused by the keenly felt differences between state and national interests in practical and ideological concerns.

Open conflict between what has been called the "presidential party" and the state and local organizations appears early in the presidential year. As soon as the discussion of possible candidates begins, state leaders clearly perceive that their interests are at stake. They are naturally wary of nominees who might hurt their state ticket, or perhaps jeopardize the reelection of their delegation to Congress. For that reason, candidates who occupy the more extreme positions along the liberal-conservative continuum are bound to have ardent supporters and equally determined detractors. Many southern Republican leaders had made known their desire for Goldwater as the 1964 candidate because they believed he would substantially strengthen their state Republican organizations. Most New York Republicans, on the other hand, were convinced that a Goldwater nomination would hurt their state ticket considerably and would diminish significantly Senator Keating's chances for reelection.

Southern Democrats used the same kind of argument against the selection of Senator Hubert Humphrey or Attorney General Robert Kennedy as President Johnson's running mate in 1964, while northern Democrats insisted that a well-known liberal was needed on the ticket to offset what some feared was a "conservative" Johnson image.

A second conflict arises between the presidential campaign managers and the state and local leaders in the area of campaign strategy and propaganda. Leaders in each state and in each locality have their own intelligence systems. The day when the morning "coffee break" constituted the public exposure of the organization politician has long since passed. In many state committees and in more than a few city headquarters, long before the campaign year begins, party chairmen and their staffs are busy reading and rereading reports of professional pollsters, scrutinizing key precinct election returns, and conferring with various community leaders in order to understand and prepare for the political climate of primaries, conventions, and campaigns.

Regardless of how sophisticated or how unsophisticated the means employed to detect current political opinion may be, the local and state leaders feel that they have a better understanding of their area than do the staff people from the national committee or from the nominee's own inner circle. Thus controversy develops over such matters as what kind of speech the candidate should give; whether a whistle-stop train tour of the state would be better than a car caravan; whether the appearances in a central city should be under the auspices of the volunteers or of the regular organization; whether the local candidates should appear with the presidential nominee.

All of these questions involve the presidential campaign triangle mentioned above: the national committee's interests and plans, the desires of state and local party headquarters, and the involvement of the ubiquitous volunteers. In anticipation of these very problems, the national committee—as the official headquarters for the "presidential party"—continually attempts to develop programs which will facilitate a unity of approach and an understanding of the difficulties involved in a presidential campaign. To a lesser extent, and during a much shorter period, the national volunteer organizations also make a concerted effort to enlist and develop effective support at the grass roots.

REPUBLICAN NATIONAL-COMMITTEE EFFORTS IN 1960

In January 1959, after the decisive Republican defeat of 1958, Meade Alcorn, then chairman of the Republican National Committee, looked forward to the 1960 election and strongly recommended that the national committee channel an increased portion of its resources and a larger number of its staff in the direction of improving state and local organizations. Speaking to the members of the Republican National Committee in Des Moines on January 22, Alcorn stated:

A political party without precinct manpower is like a ship without a crew. It may stay afloat, but isn't going anywhere. . . . We need a drastic overhaul of our manpower situation.

Chairman Alcorn went on to suggest nine specific programs which, in his opinion, should be put into effect immediately in preparation for the 1960 campaign. Among these proposals were a *nationwide recruiting program* to enlist two million additional precinct workers by September 1960; the establishment of *Citizenship Service Committees* to obtain attractive party candidates; the formation of *To the People Committees* to hold public forums on issues and the need for political action; the use of *Regional Training Conferences* to school the new recruits for the 1960 campaign; the creation of *survey teams* to analyze county organizations; and the development of *apprentice programs* to train young Republicans in party leadership roles.

Some of these proposals were not new. In 1950, for example, the national committee had sponsored one-day regional training conferences with the "faculty members" of these "political schools" (as they were then designated) drawn from the more experienced campaign directors in various state headquarters and in unusually successful congressional candidacies. The curriculum for these schools had included instruction in political tactics, organizational improvements, publicity techniques, and current issues.

A second Alcorn suggestion, the nationwide recruitment drive, had been given an unusual twist in 1954 when just such an activity was organized under the title of Poll Takers of America. Devised by the national committee's Women's Division, it sought both to gauge the reaction of the public to the first two years of the Eisenhower administration and to add as many precinct workers to the party rolls as could be recruited from among the persons polled.

An important difference between these two national-committee efforts is worthy of note. The 1950 regional training conferences resulted from the joint efforts of the national-committee staff and the staffs of the Congressional and Senatorial Campaign Committees. The 1954 poll-takers project, was, on the other hand, undertaken by only one division at the national committee.

This latter approach was precisely what Alcorn wanted to avoid insofar as major organizational-improvement programs were concerned. Either all divisions should pull together on these priority programs or a separate Division of Political Organization should be created. The Democrats, indeed, had three years earlier formed a separate division devoted to political organization.

The Republican National Committee, however, decided to continue its policy of program development within the separate divisions of the committee staff. Thus it was that during the 1960 presidential campaign the so-called training and liaison activities were carried on essentially through three divisions: the Women's Division, the Young Republicans, and the Campaign Division.

It is interesting to note that in 1960 no section in the national headquarters was delegated the major responsibility of liaison with state organizations, in contrast to 1952 and 1956. Rather this task was apparently conceived as a basic concern of all of the headquarters divisions.

The Women's Division attempted to help prepare state and local women Republican leaders for the coming campaign through two preconvention programs in 1960. The first was a four-day conference called Campaign Countdown. The far-ranging agenda included sessions on national security, our nation's resources, party organization in rural areas, party organization in urban areas, party organization in the South, and other topics. It also included instruction in publicity techniques, operation of a speakers' bureau, utilization of radio and television, fund raising, and winning of the farm, labor, and nationality-group vote. Time was given to a general consideration of the major issues in the 1960 congressional and presidential elections.

The second training activity by the Women's Division was a Campaign Correspondence Course consisting of a series of monthly "chapters" which ultimately formed a textbook on practical politics. Geared to the developments of the 1960 campaign, these monthly assignments were designed to lead the student worker into an active and effective role in her precinct organization. The topics covered in the textbook were generally the same as those featured during the four-day conference in April.

The Young Republicans have for ten years conducted a national conference of their own which, not so strangely, closely resembles the Women's Division conference in scope and method. The standard topics of finance, publicity, issues, organization, and the like are thoroughly covered and, in recent years, these schools have emphasized the *training* function of Young Republican leadership. In 1960, for example, the YGOP national conference gave considerable attention to the Chamber of Commerce Action Course in Practical Politics as a model for training courses to be conducted by Young Republican leaders at the local-club level.

One very tangible effort to establish a link between the national committee and state and local YGOP groups began with the brief schooling of twelve young men at the committee in the rudiments of political organization and campaigning. They were then sent to various states to help coordinate state-organization activities and individual club activities with the national YGOP campaign program for the national ticket.

The Campaign Division, under the direction of Albert B. "Ab" Hermann, developed for the 1960 campaign a "training package" designed to put at the disposal of the average county chairman and candidate for Congress or the state legislature the skill, experience, and thinking of the best leadership in the Republican Party.

The approach was at once unique in its conception and sweeping in its scope. The training aids included materials on campaign organization methods and the use of campaign volunteers, a series of illustrative charts, and filmed presentations by the President, the Vice President, and leading Republican Congressmen. The "package" even made provisions for the inclusion of filmed presentations by incumbent state legislators and Congressmen (or candidates for these offices) from the constituency in which the films were being shown.

The entire project was titled the Republican Roundup and Refresher Workshop. In the words of the author of the package, J. J. Weurthner:

. . . This . . . workshop can be a useful tool for the local GOP Chairman. It gives him the opportunity to bring together in one meeting his committee organization, women, volunteers, Young Republicans, finance people, graduates of business practical politics courses—anybody and everybody who wants to be a part of the campaign effort.

The Republican Roundup and Refresher Workshop was more involved, however, than a simple set of tailor-made films and the application of some group-work theories. It involved the hiring of a field man or field woman to travel with these workshops and handle the arrangements for their presentation. The field men were hired through the state committees by the state chairmen to work only within one state.

The role of the field man in the management of the Republican

Roundup and Refresher Workshop was twofold. He was to move from county to county, presenting the workshop sessions to as many Republican groups as he reasonably could. But he was also charged with the responsibility of developing a complete list of any graduates of practical-politics courses in each locality, and of helping the Republican organization in each community to develop ways and means by which these recent graduates of practical-politics courses could be successfully drawn into the campaign plans for the November elections.

This latter responsibility had much to commend it as a potentially significant activity since a conservative estimate placed the number of such graduates in the United States at well over 200,000 by September of 1960. (These were graduates from courses sponsored by a wide variety of organizations such as the National Association of Manufacturers, the AFL-CIO, the Ford Motor Company, chambers of commerce, and others.)

It was expected that personnel from the state organizations would work with these field men to make effective use of particularly promising recruits. From the standpoint of control and support, then, the Republican Roundup and Refresher Workshop was a state program, but the materials and the method were national in origin and, in a sense, national in orientation.

Less heralded than the national conferences and the packaged-deal training innovations were the relationships which developed between the functional sections of the Campaign Division and similar divisions at certain of the larger state headquarters. Since the majority of state headquarters just do not have the kind of budget to support functioning division personnel in the fields of labor, agriculture, nationalities, and the like, such liaison activities were limited.

A majority of Republican state headquarters do have at least one man functioning in the general area of public relations and publicity. In 1960 most state headquarters sent a representative to a week-long conference in Washington. There, these representatives were acquainted with the services of the national committee and of the congressional and senatorial committees, and were offered suggestions as to how best to utilize these services, particularly with reference to the presidential campaign.

The programs and procedures which have been briefly examined thus far were attempts to bridge the gap between the national party organization and the state and local organizations. But they were not, for the most part, designed specifically for the presidential campaign.

Before the Nixon-Lodge campaign programs are considered, brief mention should be made of one event in which both national-committee and Nixon-Lodge organizations went to the grass roots looking for support under one banner. The occasion was "Pat for First Lady Week," October 3-8, 1960.

Four high-level women leaders (Mrs. Clare B. Williams, assistant chairman of the Republican National Committee; Mrs. Peter Gibson, president of the National Federation of Republican Women; Mrs. Carol Arth, national director of Women's Activities, Volunteers for Nixon-Lodge; and Mrs. David G. Fernald, cochairman of Young Republican National Federation) issued joint statements setting forth the role of their individual groups in the week's activities.

Mrs. Williams suggested the regular Republican state vice chairman and each county vice chairman initiate a vigorous effort in "Pat's Precincts," with a "Pat's Parade" to kick off the whole affair. Mrs. Gibson stressed the need to intensify the Neighbors for Nixon meetings during Pat Week. Mrs. Arth urged a concentration of coffee caucuses and shopping-center programs during Pat Week. Mrs. Fernald announced the expediting of "Projects for Pat" during the October 3-8 period. This effort to unite all womenpower for Nixon behind one drive apparently, was quite successful and was one of very few such united efforts during the entire campaign.

REPUBLICAN EFFORTS AT THE GRASS ROOTS IN 1960

Shortly after nominees Nixon and Lodge had returned to Washington, their official citizens organization was named. It became the National Volunteers for Nixon-Lodge. The chairman of the organization was Charles S. Rhyne of Washington, D.C., a former president of the American Bar Association. Rhyne's major field of interest was international law. He had been for some time a leader in the World Peace Through Law program. Although the new chairman planned to devote full time to his Nixon-Lodge duties, he did turn over the administrative management to a young New York businessman, Peter M. Flanigan. Assisting Flanigan was E. H. "Ned" Harding, a New York public-relations man.

Several members of the Vice President's campaign staff were put to work on a chairman's manual; others were sent into the field to organize.

By September 15 Chairman Rhyne announced that 41 states had been organized. In some, the organization was mostly paper. In others, paid professionals took charge and began to develop extensive operations.

Meanwhile the Volunteers for Nixon-Lodge *Chairman's Manual* had been completed and issued. The purpose of organizing state and local Nixon-Lodge clubs and committees, in the words of the manual, was:

. . . To mobilize broad Nixon support for effective action . . . While the Nixon candidacy will, of course, be supported by the Republican organization, many of your neighbors will prefer to work solely for the election of Dick Nixon and to carry on their activity through an independent organization. Your club is that independent organization.

The staff office for the volunteers in Washington under Flanigan's direction supplied the local clubs with "launching kits" (including research and promotion materials) and with special-interest items (such as feature films on the Vice President). It also attempted to furnish a measure of coordination with other volunteer activities in the immediate area and gave to each club a direct contact with the Nixon campaign headquarters.

The *Chairman's Manual* explicitly instructed the local clubs "never to attempt to replace nor compete with the Republican Party in your state or community."

Although the regular Party organization will gear its efforts to the election of candidates at all levels, the presidential race . . . which is our *single objective* . . . still is of *primary importance* to the overall Republican campaign.

This makes it inevitable, and essential, that we work together harmoniously and effectively.

In its desire to elect Richard Nixon, the Party recognizes the vital importance of broadening the effort beyond Party lines. And this is where the Nixon Volunteers and your Club come in.

Our job is to enlist, stimulate and activate Independents and Democrats, as well as Republicans, in the Nixon campaign. The Republican Party, of course, will focus its main attention toward turning out the Republican vote.

Moving independently and forcefully toward the same objective, Nixon Volunteers and the Republican Party together can develop the mighty momentum necessary for victory in November.

Your role, then, is to supplement and broaden the Republican effort, cooperating with the Party, but working independently and autonomously.

The manual had much to say about how to handle public relations, suggested a wide variety of campaign activities (including coffee caucuses, first-voters parties, television and radio parties, smokers, library parties, fair booths, parades, and rallies).

Headquarters specifications and finance came in for substantial treatment as well. The manual made very clear that every Nixon club operated on an autonomous and self-sustaining basis and that the local clubs had no direct financial obligation to the national campaign organization.

A still more direct approach was made by the volunteers organization to individuals who evinced some interest in the Nixon candidacy. It was called Operation SNAP (Support Nixon At the Polls). SNAP packs, consisting of buttons, literature, sign-up postcards, and a request for financial support, were mailed to all persons who responded to various mass mailings (doctors, lawyers, professors, and other categories). The recipients of the SNAP packs were assumed not to be members of Nixon clubs and hence were given suggestions similar to those for club members, involving the recruitment of at least six friends for Nixon, mailing postcards, holding parties, writing "letters to the editor," distributing campaign literature, canvassing, and getting out the vote on Election Day.

It is difficult to assess the effect of the volunteers organization. Undoubtedly the impact varied from state to state. In Ohio, where the volunteers were successfully integrated into the total campaign effort under the direction of Republican state chairman Ray C. Bliss, support for the Vice President and Ambassador Lodge was unquestionably broadened without organizational conflict or duplication. And the overwhelming Nixon victory in Ohio strongly supported Chairman Bliss's views about tying citizens organizations into the total campaign strategy designed by the regular party organization in a given state.

But there are very few men in American political life with Bliss's skill at resolving conflict and with his understanding of effective campaign organization. In some states, where volunteer organizations insisted on a status completely separate from the regular party, there may well have been merit in their case.

REPUBLICAN NATIONAL-COMMITTEE EFFORTS IN 1964

Aside from the always important job of developing campaign literature for use at the grass roots, the national committee's role in assisting the presidential campaign at the state and local level in 1964 was mainly coordinative.

The men recruited as regional directors to handle intraparty difficulties as well as the touchy problems arising out of contacts between regular party officials and citizens leaders were men of considerable experience in politics.

Wayne Hood, former Wisconsin party chairman and former executive director of the national committee during the Eisenhower campaign in 1952, was assigned the key states of Ohio, Pennsylvania, Texas, New York, and California. This assignment was in addition to his other duties as director of campaign organizations at the national committee.

The Middle Atlantic states were under the jurisdiction of Fred C. Scribner, general counsel for the national committee, who had been a prominent figure in both the Eisenhower administration and the 1960 Nixon presidential campaign.

The New England states were assigned to David A. Nichols, state Republican chairman of Maine and an early leader in the Draft Goldwater movement.

Sam Hay, Milwaukee County's Republican chairman, was responsible for the Great Lakes region, while Richard L. Herman, president of an Omaha trucking firm, became director of the Great Plains states.

The southern states were made the responsibility of Sam V. Claiborne, a member of the Tennessee House of Representatives, and the western states were assigned to Goldwater's close friend, Stephen Shadegg of Phoenix.

In various operational manuals, regional directors of both the national committee and the citizens group were urged to cooperate and coordinate wherever and whenever possible. In the event of irrepressible conflicts, the problem was to be submitted to Clif White and Wayne Hood for ultimate disposition.

Only the southern region was supported by national-committee literature designed specifically for regional use. In the case of the so-called Southern Division, publications were issued and distributed without the benefit of headquarters, organizational structure, or staff.

Traditional efforts were made by the Women's Division and the Political Education and Training Division to assist state and local party workers in canvassing techniques, use of the telephone, and getting out the vote through such programs as VIP (Voters In your Precinct or Very Important People), which dealt with the whole problem of personal visits and telephone canvassing; GROW, which was a more extensive and educationally oriented recruitment program for party workers; and MORE, a program designed to register more Republicans through an exhaustive survey and sign-up of potential support at the precinct level.

These programs were helpful where they were used, but they were not always enthusiastically received by those new workers who wanted immediate and dramatic conversion to the conservative cause. There the traditional, long-range national-committee programs were separated by a wide angle from the short-range, evangelistic programs suggested by much of the citizens activity. The final paragraph in a MORE pamphlet stated:

Bear in mind that for purposes of registration there is no such thing as a "good" Republican or a "bad" Republican; a "liberal" Republican or a "conservative" Republican. A Republican is a Republican, period.

In the end the difference between the win-oriented approach of traditional American politics and the no-compromise, ideological approach characterized by the army of citizen volunteers was often the difference between a vote for or a vote against the Republican national ticket in 1964.

REPUBLICAN EFFORTS AT THE GRASS ROOTS IN 1964

One of the major effects of the 1960 defeat was to direct the attention of Republican leadership once again to the problems of state and local party organizations. Attention was focused particularly on one area of chronic Republican weakness—the big cities in the industrialized and populous states of the Northeast: Detroit, Philadelphia, Newark, Boston, New York, Chicago, St. Louis, Pittsburgh, Cleveland, and Baltimore. The margins by which Kennedy carried the states of New York, Pennsylvania, Michigan, Illinois, Minnesota, Missouri, Maryland, and New Jersey were provided by one large city in each state. In the 13 cities of more than 300,000 inhabitants located in these eight states, Kennedy amassed a plurality of 2,400,000 votes.

This figure was a surprise to some Republicans, for the most striking aspect of the 1956 presidential election was the erosion of the Democratic Party in these same cities. Eisenhower had carried 10 of the 20 largest northeastern cities and received more than 40 per cent of the vote in all but two—Detroit and St. Louis. His success led political analyst Samuel Lubell, writing in 1957, to conclude that the Democratic majorities in the cities had been slashed so drastically the Republicans must be rated as favorites to win the White House in 1960.

The breakthrough in 1956 was not followed by the organizational effort which might have solidified some of these gains. Except for Nelson Rockefeller's strong showing in New York City, the 1958 elections indicated the Republican beachhead established in these cities in 1956 had been lost.

Because of the sizable losses in the big cities for the Republicans, analysts freely stated that it was here that the presidential election of 1960 was indeed won for Kennedy and lost for Nixon. Senator Thruston B. Morton, well aware of the 1960 voting statistics, appointed a Committee on Big City Politics to study the problem. State party chairman Ray C. Bliss of Ohio was appointed its chairman.

The studies of the Bliss committee brought to light the fact that is manifest during presidential election years—that in most states there is basically no organization at the grass roots worthy of the name. It found, for example, that in only 8 of 27 of our largest cities are all precincts manned by Republican Party workers. From this survey came a series of recommendations by special subcommittees on party organization and candidate recruitment; labor, business, professional, and independent groups; nationalities and minorities; public relations; use of surveys and educational methods. The subcommittee reports were thorough and realistic, yet imaginative.

Following the issuance of the Bliss report, some regular Republican state and local organizations made every effort they could afford to implement its suggestions. In some areas, extraparty organizations which had formed even before the committee had studied the big-city problem appeared determined to move with or without the official party blessing.

In Illinois, for example, the Republican Citizens League was formed in 1961 to build a broader and stronger grass-roots organization. The initial emphasis was upon recruitment and training of a force of workers in the Chicago metropolitan area. The league stated from the outset that its purpose was to do the jobs which the formal party organization had not successfully performed: to provide workers where the party organization had none, to take care of the difficult areas in which representatives of the Republican Party are captives of the Democratic machine, to establish contact with voters who are untouched by or unresponsive to the organization. The league established a harmonious relationship with the formal party hierarchy and had several high-ranking party leaders on its governing board.

The Republican Alliance, a similar group established in Philadelphia early in 1961, also undertook basic organizational activity. It was independent of the Republican city organization, and, unlike its Chicago counterpart, it did not initially enjoy cordial relations with regular party leaders in Philadelphia.

These extraparty organization groups can perhaps improve party strength at the precinct level and perhaps are needed in special circumstances. But they are ordinarily short-lived and quite. limited in scope. A more promising development that has occurred since 1962 may have great long-range significance for the improvement of American political parties at the state and local levels.

In December 1962, Republican National Committee Chairman William Miller appointed Ohio Republican State Chairman Ray C. Bliss to head a Republican State Chairmen's Advisory Committee. The purpose of this group (which included all Republican state chairmen) was to generally advise the national committee on developments within the various states and to direct the thinking of the national committee to the perennial problems of state and local party organization. Under the leadership of Bliss, this association of state chairmen has met quarterly to examine various programs carefully and to share interpretations of the reasons for individual successes and failures.

The significant innovation here is that the actual "line officers" involved in campaign direction and organizational improvement are talking with one another rather than being talked at by a staff man who may not be exposed, regularly, to their day-to-day problems.

In January 1964, 46 of the 51 (the District of Columbia is included) state chairmen or their executive directors attended a three-day workshop. The esprit de corps of this particular association was, at that time, extremely high and there was a universal feeling that finally a realistic starting point had been found from which to build more responsible and more responsive state and local party organizations, not only for the 1964 presidential election but for many years to come.

CITIZENS FOR GOLDWATER-MILLER

While the state party leaders were discussing ways and means through which they could strengthen their organizations for the upcoming 1964 elections, a number of party conservatives were planning a presidential campaign with an ideological thrust.

Some groups were formed in various parts of the country as early as mid-1961 to advance the candidacy of Senator Barry

Goldwater for the Republican presidential nomination. By far the most important group, however, to advance a program for turning the national Republican Party to the right was a group of 22 men who first met in Chicago on October 8, 1961, to explore the status and future of the Republican Party.

Steve Shadegg, a long-time Goldwater aide and friend, said:

In a very real sense, Senator Barry Goldwater was nominated for President by the men who met in Chicago thirty-three months in advance of the Republican Convention.[1]

Clif White, one of the leaders of the Chicago meeting to whom Shadegg refers, responded to the Shadegg analysis by saying:

I prefer to think that all we did was give direction and focus to a great grassroots movement.[2]

Actually these men who were later to form the Draft Goldwater Committee gathered originally to discuss the need to "re-establish the Republican Party as an effective conservative force in American politics." In the words of Clif White:

At this meeting in Chicago, I presided as chairman and presented a preliminary blueprint of the plan Ashbrook, Rusher and I had conceived. There was a completely free and open discussion, and very early in the game everyone agreed that our principal goal should be to re-establish the Republican Party as an effective conservative force in American politics. Some of us felt that to a considerable degree the party had performed that function all through the eight Eisenhower years. But we all recognized that the Republican emphasis had been shifting more and more away from traditional American principles. We all felt that if this trend was permitted to continue it would eventually bring about the end of any meaningful two-party system in the United States. In its place there would ultimately be established a monolithic state, with at best two factions, erroneously labeled Republican and Democrat, going through the motions of fighting a rubberstamp election every four years for control of an all-powerful federal government. . . . I repeated what I had previously said to Bill Rusher, that it was still much too early to tie ourselves and our program to any specific candidate. In the end, everyone concurred.[3]

---

[1] Stephen Shadegg, *What Happened to Goldwater?* (New York: Holt, 1965), p. 44.

[2] F. Clifton White, *Suite 3505* (New Rochelle, N.Y.: Arlington House, 1967), p. 37.

[3] *Ibid.,* p. 40.

Subsequently, the conveners of this meeting, F. Clifton White and William Rusher of New York, and Congressman John Ashbrook of Ohio, called two additional meetings in New York and Washington to discuss the potential support for a Goldwater bid for the Republican presidential nomination. Goldwater, it appeared to them, was best suited to carry the banner for their "ideological" campaign.

On April 8, 1963, at a press conference in Washington, D.C., Peter O'Donnell, Texas state Republican chairman, acting as chairman of the group, made a formal announcement concerning the formation of the Draft Goldwater Committee.

After establishing a budget and securing a national headquarters in Washington, O'Donnell and his committee launched their drive for state and local leadership. In O'Donnell's words:

This was crucial and we had to work with great delicacy. I think we did the job successfully because we finally got 42 or 43 states organized and we had people working even in the states where we didn't have a full-time organization.[4]

The plan was to build an organization roughly paralleling the regular party organization, with a state chairman, congressional-district chairman, and county and precinct leaders. The immediate purpose of this grass-roots effort was to line up delegate support. As O'Donnell said:

In one State we'd be off and running almost immediately for delegates. Then we'd hit another State where it was a ferocious job just to get a State Chairman.[5]

When the Draft Goldwater Committee had demonstrated to Goldwater that there was substantial support for his candidacy across the country, the Senator accepted the draft and announced his candidacy for the 1964 Republican presidential nomination on January 1, 1964. With that announcement the usefulness of the Draft Goldwater Committee came to an end. Most of the committee staff was absorbed by the new Goldwater for President organization which had formed overnight and which was housed scarcely

---

[4] Quoted in James M. Perry, *Barry Goldwater* (Silver Springs, Md.: National Observer, 1964), p. 76.

[5] *Ibid.,* p. 77.

100 feet from the headquarters of the former Draft Goldwater offices.

Along with a good share of the Draft Goldwater staff went detailed information on all delegate contacts, mailing lists, and the remarkable roster from every state of workers who had proved they were willing and able to labor zealously for the Arizona Senator and the conservative cause.

These were the people who, following the Republican National Convention, waited in the hustings for their marching orders, and in large part they were the flesh and blood around which the skeleton called the Citizens Committee for Goldwater-Miller was built.

These tried and true veterans of the campaign for the Republican nomination, who constituted the hard core of the Citizens for Goldwater-Miller, were a different breed of amateur politicians from the individuals drawn into the Citizens for Eisenhower or the Volunteers for Nixon-Lodge. For the most part they were dedicated conservatives and their cause-consciousness gave them a militancy seldom equaled in volunteer political organizations. It was that same ideological thrust, however, that frequently narrowed rather than broadened the support they sought.

To officially head the citizens, Lieutenant General James H. Doolittle (USAF, retired) was named chairman, and Mrs. Clare Boothe Luce (former congresswoman from Connecticut and ambassador to Italy) was named cochairman.

The driving force behind the organization was F. Clifton White, the New York Republican leader who had been so deeply involved in the Draft Goldwater Committee and later in the Goldwater for President organization. Other officers were Wiley T. Buchanan (former U.S. ambassador and State Department Chief of Protocol), treasurer; Mrs. Ione Harrington (former Republican National Committeewoman from Indiana and assistant director of the Goldwater for President Committee), director of women's activities; Rus Walton (on leave as executive director of the United Republicans of California), director of public relations and public information; Travis Cross (on leave as press aide to Governor Mark Hatfield), special assistant to Walton; and Tom R. Van Sickle (Kansas state senator), coordinator for the six regional directors and state chairmen.

Chairmen for the state citizens organizations were, as a rule, decided upon by the national citizens leaders only after consultation with regular state party chairmen. The citizens chairmen were expected to develop their own organization with minimum staff and financial assistance from Washington headquarters. The major help forthcoming from national citizens headquarters was campaign literature (during the campaign more than 30 million pieces were distributed through the citizens organization), limited financial support, and assistance with the special-interest appeals for which the state and local citizens organizations were held responsible.

Lateral communications with the regular party organizations varied from state to state. In several southern states the citizens and regular party organization were virtually one and the same. In the Midwest and West, the citizens and regular party organizations, though separate, worked closely together. In certain states, notably in New England, little communication existed between the citizens and regular party organizations.

Although the Ohio citizens organization was not typical, a brief look at one of its final reports illustrates how extensive an organization was developed in some states to support the national ticket. The preelection statistical summary from the executive director of the Ohio Citizens for Goldwater-Miller indicated on October 30, 1964, that all 88 Ohio counties had active organizations, that 62 counties had central headquarters manned by 1,735 volunteers, that 25 counties had 113 additional neighborhood or community headquarters staffed by 1,673 volunteers, that 19,743 volunteers were actively engaged in campaign efforts outside of citizens headquarters, and that on an average 6,701 persons visited the various citizens headquarters daily to make inquiries and to pick up literature.

An interview with the Delaware County (Ohio) citizens-committee chairman revealed that the citizens county group was financially independent, supporting its activities from the sale of literature, a kickoff banquet, and some direct contributions. The campaign functions of these county and local groups were the usual party organizational functions of neighborhood canvassing, coffee parties, providing transportation to the polls on Election Day, conducting polls, assisting absentee voters, and so on.

STATE AND LOCAL ORGANIZATIONS

Support for the national Republican ticket from state and local Republican organizations and from candidates for public office varied within each state and across the nation. Three patterns of support were discernible.

First were those party organizations and state and local candidates who tied their efforts tightly to the Goldwater-Miller campaign. In the southern states this was the usual pattern. Campaign literature there invariably featured the national ticket, with the state and local candidates receiving subordinate attention. Examples of states in this category were Arizona, Florida, Texas, New Mexico, and Tennessee.

A second pattern was seen in the regular party organizations and candidates who cooperated fully with the national ticket but who spent a greater-than-normal share of their efforts on state and local races. If an active citizens organization existed, much of the aggressive campaigning for the national ticket was frequently left to, or taken over by, the Citizens for Goldwater-Miller. Examples of this dual campaign approach were to be found in Wisconsin, Washington, Montana, Iowa, Illinois, Vermont, Virginia, New Jersey, and Ohio. There were variations, of course, from state to state. Ohio's organization, for example, gave headline attention to the national campaign in the widely read weekly *Ohio Republican News* and urged county and local organizations repeatedly to give all possible help to the national ticket. Chairman Bliss personally planned and arranged an extensive train tour for candidate Goldwater throughout the state and even though painfully ill at the time, insisted on accompanying the tour to make certain that every detail was properly taken care of.

The third pattern was seen in the approach taken by those candidates and organizations who largely ignored the national ticket or, as in some well-known cases, publicly disassociated themselves from the Goldwater-Miller campaign. In Michigan and New York, though both state party organizations distributed some Goldwater-Miller literature, the lion's share of their efforts was concentrated on their own state and local candidates—with their most prominent candidates, like Governor Romney and Senator

Keating, refusing to appear on the same dais with the Republican presidential candidate.

THE DEMOCRATIC PATTERN IN 1964

In 1964, the Johnson campaign depended heavily on the regular Democratic state and local party organizations. No new or separate state or local organizational structure to promote the national ticket was either necessary or desirable outside of the deep South. So clear-cut was the ideological conflict between Johnson and Goldwater and so delightful the prospect of unchallenged Democratic occupancy of the political stage from right of center to the far left that virtually all Democratic candidates and organizations could find their own immediate campaign interests consistent with the objectives of the national campaign.

The need for internal party unity also dictated the policy of no separate citizens organizations in the states. At the Democratic National Committee meeting in January 1964, the regular Democratic state and local party organizations, through their national committeemen, expressly urged that no separate system of state and local citizens committees for Johnson and his running mate be established. In 1960, many regular state and local Democratic central committees found that the separate Citizens for Kennedy-Johnson Committees became rivals both for contact with the national leadership and for local political power. They were anxious to prevent a repetition of such conflicts, and the national party leadership was equally ready to accede to their wishes.

Lawrence O'Brien, who had developed the hard-working national political organization of the 1960 campaign, was detached from his White House staff duties during the summer and fall to lead the drive to round up the proffered state and local support. His trips about the North, Middle West, and West produced encouraging reports about both the sincerity of regular organization efforts and the likelihood of victory for the national ticket. By October, with national victory no longer in doubt, attention turned to the prospective Democratic majority in Congress and in state legislatures. This change still further reenforced cordial relations between the national committee and the regular state and local party organizations, but also sowed the seeds of national-committee ineffectiveness for the 1966 congressional campaign.

To foster close cooperation with the regular party organizations, O'Brien appointed a state coordinator in all but Alabama, where Mr. Johnson was not on the ballot. Thirteen were Democratic state chairmen, one a state vice chairman, four Democratic national committeemen, and three members of Congress. In the deep South, especially in South Carolina, Georgia, Mississippi, and Florida, however, O'Brien turned largely to other than state party organization leaders for his coordinators.

Seven regional coordinators managed the effort in the field: H. William Brawley, former Deputy Postmaster General, for the eight southeastern states; John V. Singleton, a Houston attorney, for seven southwestern states; Irvin A. Hoff, former administrative assistant to Senator Warren G. Magnuson of Washington, eight far-western states; State Senator Culp Krueger of Texas for eight Mountain and upper-midwestern states; Ivan Nestingen, former Under Secretary of Health, Education, and Welfare, and Mayor of Madison, Wisconsin, for seven Lakes states; Blair Lee III, former Maryland state legislator, for five Middle Atlantic states and the District of Columbia; and William Dunfey, former national committeeman from New Hampshire and regional coordinator in New England for the Democratic National Committee in the late 1950's, the six New England states and New York.

In states where intraparty rivalry threatened party success, O'Brien made special adjustments. Bowing to the traditional north-south rivalry in California, he appointed two state coordinators: Don Bradley in Los Angeles for southern California, and Tom Saunders in San Francisco for northern California. To unite party efforts in Ohio, the national committee sent United States Representative Edward P. Boland of Massachusetts. In the Washington office, the committee used two men, one each from the 1960 Johnson and Kennedy teams.

To respond to the state and local calls for ammunition, the Democratic National Committee mounted "Operation Support." Headed by David L. Chewning, an economist and a senior associate with Robert R. Nathan Associates, this unit drew heavily on the resources of the Democratic women's clubs to put out pamphlets, information kits, and brochures on the issues of the campaign. It also worked with the speakers' bureau of the national committee to supply state and local meetings with issues-oriented speakers. By early October, activities were under way in 35 states. Six regional coordinators assisted the effort. Local participation took many forms. In Delaware, for example, a decorated Operation Support bus toured the state, dispensing materials and enlisting organizational support.

The national committee's most important organizational effort, however, was the voter-registration drive. Based on the theory that it is easier to get nonvoters of Democratic persuasion to the polls than to convert Republicans, the drive was headed by Matthew Reese, architect of Kennedy's West Virginia primary victory in 1960. By October, when registration books closed across the nation, the drive claimed substantial success, especially in 50 key counties where efforts had centered. In New York City, for example, 151,000 new voters were registered, 4 to 1 Democratic; in Toledo, 37,000; in Cleveland, 166,472; in Indianapolis, 36,600. State totals were even more impressive. Texas reported 400,000 new voters; New Jersey, 500,000; Pennsylvania, 400,000.[6] All recorded lopsided Democratic preferences, reflecting the temper of the times and the economic status of the previous nonvoters. As part of the registration drive, the committee launched a "4 for 64" program to use volunteers to find potential Democratic voters and to aid them in registering and voting.

THE DEMOCRATIC PATTERN IN 1960

The Kennedy campaign of 1960, unable to offer the prospect of certain victory and facing the religious issue beneath the surface in many areas, had to accept offers of help and to organize a national effort. Emerging from a vigorously contested primary campaign to take over a national committee which had alienated many regular state and local party organizations, the Kennedy managers moved promptly both to restore good relations between the national committee and the state and local committees and to mount their own campaign programs.

To please the state and local organizations, the Kennedys moved

[6] See *The Democrat,* October 5, 1964, p. 1.

directly to eliminate those organizational elements of the old national-committee staff which had been the most prominent arms
of Paul Butler's ideological efforts. First to fall were the Democratic Advisory Council and the Division of Political Organization.
Staff to the advisory council was assigned to assist Sargent Shriver,
a Kennedy brother-in-law, to organize special-interest groups for
Kennedy and Johnson, and was later discharged. Staff members for
the Division of Political Organization were relegated to organizing
"Educators for Kennedy" and to the voter-registration drive. They,
too, were later fired. Regional coordinators for the division were
reassigned to help the Kennedy state coordinators during the campaign, then discharged.

Many regular organizations, especially those in the big cities,
were pleased—for the time being. The party as a whole, however,
is paying a high price for this symbolic repudiation of Paul Butler's
efforts to make the Democratic Party a "responsible" liberal party.
The Division of Political Organization had been far from a tool in
the hands of Chairman Butler. It had, rather, been engaged primarily in a comprehensive program to train precinct workers, county
organization people, and state party leaders. Calling upon the
talents of several of the nation's outstanding adult educators, the
program had applied the latest group-work techniques to teach
practical political skills, to develop leadership ability, and to stimulate cohesive local-group action. Although no official count was
ever assembled, an estimated 25,000 persons were trained by the
new techniques over a four-year period. Many would have been
available to man the precincts in an orderly way in the 1960
campaign, but none of them was used unless, in the words of the
former assistant director, they walked in and volunteered for duty.

Initiated in 1955 by the establishment of a Committee on Political Organization headed by Neil Staebler, Michigan state chairman, the effort had developed by the summer of 1960 into four
major training programs:

The Precinct-Worker Training Program. Precinct needs were
met first. The adult educators promptly prepared an instructor's
manual which outlined an eight-hour precinct-worker course divided into two instructional sessions of three hours each and a

two-hour field exercise. Modern group-work techniques were encouraged in the training sessions, which used films, buzz sessions, panels, questions and discussion, role playing, field work and reports thereon, and listening groups. Formal lecturing was held to a minimum. A precinct worker's handbook also was prepared to serve as a textbook for each trainee.

The first step in implementation was to train instructors capable of presenting the precinct program. Beginning in November 1957, fifty-six instructors' courses were held in 36 states, with the bulk of the sessions coming in the first year of the program. Approximately 1,500 instructors were graduated. Hundreds of precinct-worker training courses were given by the graduates, but no record exists of how many. Some 30,000 precinct handbooks were sent out, most of them for use in training courses.

The County-Leader Workshop Program. In August 1959, a program to train county leaders was inaugurated. A county leader's handbook had been previously prepared to serve as a textbook for the course. A carefully prepared manual for workshop leaders was issued September 15, 1959. Again a six-hour course using group-work techniques was programed to cover such topics as problem analysis, how to conduct effective meetings, how to get good press, how to finance your party, candidate recruitment, and campaign planning. The program, operating on a do-it-yourself basis, went over well.

The Leadership-Conference Program. Beginning in the summer of 1959 and continuing through the spring of 1960, state party leaders in each of five different regions were invited to a three-day conference at a central city. No training manual was used and no textbook prepared. Instead, three people experienced in adult leadership were sent to conduct each conference. Basic group-work techniques were followed. Each party leader was given a looseleaf notebook with index tabs for the major topics so that he could jot down the ideas he wanted to keep. Discussions centered on the many duties of a party leader, how to get people into politics, what makes an organization effective, understanding people—the leader's job, how to share leadership, improving party relations, and simple steps in solving political problems. State leaders themselves played the roles in problem scenes which showed how one might deal with a labor organization or how to placate a dissident party faction.

The "You Decide" Program. At the 1960 national convention a new neighborhood discussion program was launched. Seven elaborate "flip charts," designed to stimulate discussion, were prepared and more were planned. Accompanying each flip chart was material to enable any interested party member to lead a discussion of the facts and problems raised. Emphasis was placed upon participation in small groups rather than speech making by a discussion leader. Adult educators again were called in to help prepare materials and to help train those who volunteered as discussion leaders.

Although some scoffed at these efforts and others even argued that they were a waste of money, no one could actually claim offense. The outcome of the 1958 election, the success of the 1958 and 1959 Dollars for Democrats Drives, and the creation of sparkling new volunteer political organizations in many states which long had been Republican strongholds soon muffled the doubters.

To insure state and local support for the national ticket, the Kennedy managers promptly mounted three direct efforts of their own. Regular Democratic organizations were stimulated through the Democratic National Committee by state coordinators selected from preconvention Kennedy supporters. Independents, pro-Kennedy Republicans, and antiorganization Democrats were rounded up by Citizens for Kennedy-Johnson. Nonvoters were made eligible to participate by a slam-bang voter-registration drive in cooperation with state and local party organizations.

Heading up the system of state coordinators at the Democratic National Committee was Lawrence O'Brien, who reported immediately to Robert Kennedy. O'Brien conducted much of his work through two lieutenants, Ralph Dungan and Richard Donohue, who provided central staff services to the state coordinators and received information from them about the progress of the campaign. State coordinators dealt not only with state central committees but also directly with county central committees, when appropriate.

Dungan and Donohue sought as much political intelligence as possible. From their gleanings, they advised upon campaign scheduling, policy emphasis, and special-group appeals. In general, Don-ohue kept track of the North and East, Dungan the South, upper Middle West, and Far West. However, they worked closely to-gether, as a team, and each knew much of the situation in all states. In the West, particularly, where Kennedy lacked a strong base and close political advisers, they both kept touch with developments.

In the last few weeks of the campaign, the scheduling and speech-writing teams depended heavily on the intelligence reports of the O'Brien operation to establish where the candidate should go, how much time he should spend, and what he should empha-size in his speeches. O'Brien himself joined the tour group one day a week to make an oral report on how the campaign was faring in each state and to check personally on the information he was receiving. The information and the organization team's analysis of it proved to be reassuringly accurate.

Citizens for Kennedy-Johnson. Citizens for Kennedy-Johnson was thoroughly independent of the Democratic National Commit-tee. Quartered across Washington, D.C., in the preconvention Ken-nedy headquarters in the Esso Building, it had its own funds, its own organizational structure, and its own program.

Three main assignments fell to Citizens for Kennedy-Johnson. They provided an independent organization for people who wanted to help elect Kennedy President but who couldn't or wouldn't work with a regular local Democratic organization. They raised funds and, after mid-October, paid the campaign bills.[7] They established several special auxiliary committees to woo the votes of veterans, young people, senior citizens, businessmen, and nationality groups.[8]

Byron L. "Whizzer" White of Colorado, Rhodes Scholar, All-American football player, and a close friend of John F. Kennedy, served as national chairman of the citizens organization. His prin-cipal lieutenant for general organization work was Fred Dutton of California.

White personally reported to Robert Kennedy and for all practi-cal purposes operated as a sixth male member of the Kennedy family team. Occasionally, Dutton provided needed liaison.

[7] See Chapter X, "Financing the Campaign," for details.
[8] See Chapter VII, "Attracting the Special-Interest Groups," for details.

Throughout the campaign, coordination with the Kennedys was kept informal and depended upon very frequent telephone and face-to-face contacts. However, the citizens committee maintained no contact with the office of Chairman Henry M. Jackson of the Democratic National Committee and felt no obligation to do so.

White promptly set up an organization parallel to the Democratic National Committee in all states except in the South, where the citizens activities were handled through the regular Democratic organizations. A state chairman was appointed and usually a woman cochairman. County chairmen were designated in urban and semiurban counties, but no attempt was made to organize citizens committees in most small rural counties. Some states organized thoroughly anyway. In California, a Citizens Committee for Kennedy-Johnson was established in every county.

Special emphasis was given to women's roles in the campaign, for White and Dutton felt that women in general needed greater recognition in politics and wanted to identify with Senator Kennedy. Many women were appointed local chairmen. Special events for women were featured. News stories were prepared aimed at the women's pages in the newspapers. A particular effort was made to enlist women from middle-income families who were likely to have had a good education and to be able to spare time from household chores to help win the election. Assignments were even divided to create additional spots for women volunteers.

Taking a leaf from Larry O'Brien's book, White selected coordinators for each region to stimulate the state citizens committees and to provide political intelligence. He also set up a press section and a speakers' bureau to service his state organizations.

State citizens-committee chairmen were urged to work closely with the regular party organizations and were asked to accept the plans of the Democratic state chairmen. Unfortunately, such pleas were sometimes ignored. Effective and energetic state chairmen, as in California and Michigan, welcomed the citizens organizations as useful extensions of their influence. Where a Democratic organization was divided, even crumbling, as in New York, the citizens committee had to carry the principal burden of campaign organization. In some states, especially if the state chairman was weak or inexperienced, rivalry developed.

Although White and his men conscientiously sought real independents to fill their ranks, a great many citizens-committee leaders turned out to be well-known Democrats. In Philadelphia, for example, the citizens chairman was Mayor Dilworth! The weaker the regular Democratic organization or leadership and the stronger and more effective the citizens effort, the greater the opportunity became for clashes between them. In some places volunteer citizens leaders turned out to be leaders of rival Democratic factions who used the new Kennedy organizations to rally their followers, raise funds, and stage a revival of their power. The rise of such problems of local rivalry was, however, regarded as the price of having a citizens movement. Despite its impact on the health of some local Democratic organizations, Robert Kennedy viewed the effort as an over-all gain, for he was anxious to get as many campaign activities going as possible.

Smaller than the Democratic National Committee, more cohesive, and single-purpose, Citizens for Kennedy-Johnson was able to launch telephoning campaigns, prepare and distribute pamphlets, get out news releases, and supply films directly to state committees with much greater expectation of their being placed in the hands of local units and actually being used than could the national committee.

The Voter-Registration Drive. A separate, but closely related emergency activity involving the state and local party organizations was the voter-registration drive, led by United States Representative Frank Thompson of New Jersey. Organization was informal and lines of authority fluid. Thompson did not believe in organizational charts and staff meetings, so had neither. Housed with Citizens for Kennedy-Johnson, the drive's leaders maintained close personal liaison with White and Dutton, but reported directly to Robert Kennedy. Late in the campaign, the registration drive's staff merged with citizens to get the newly registered voters to the polls.

The registration drive started with a rush and kept its momentum. Congressman Thompson was appointed drive leader on July 21 and was given until October 5 to get the job done. Assembling a talented and experienced crew to assist him, he promptly appointed drive chairmen in all states except poll-tax states where registration was already closed. By July 29, with chairmen in nearly all states and local chairmen in the major metropolitan areas, Thompson was able to hold a meeting in Washington attended by representatives of 20 states and 35 cities. There he explained the problem, provided basic information, and told what he wanted.

The problem was simple. Forty million Americans, eligible to vote, had not bothered to register. Public-opinion polls repeatedly had demonstrated that the bulk of these nonvoters were poor, ill-educated, and uninterested. But the Kennedys reasoned, and the polls confirmed, that the vast majority of them would vote Democratic if they could be brought to the voting booths. Thompson set a goal of 10 million new registrations by October 5.

Beginning August 1, Thompson set out for a series of regional registration meetings. The first, in Philadelphia, brought in drive chairmen from Delaware, Maryland, New Jersey, Pennsylvania, and West Virginia. The program was reviewed in detail and the need for haste emphasized. Boston was next; then Thompson went on across the nation, returning to New York City on August 9 for the final meeting.

Next, on August 19, to prove the merit of the registration effort, Thompson launched a pilot project in Baltimore, Maryland. Forty college students and recent college graduates were recruited. Top specialists were brought in from Washington to train them. Agreement was reached with local Democratic leaders to concentrate on 60 key precincts which were known to have a large potential Democratic registration. Canvassers were told to register Democrats, not to bother with Republicans. The results were sensational. In one day 2,600 people were registered in the drive, all but 39 of them as Democrats!

Training teams promptly fanned out to use the technique and to equip others to train canvassers. Kansas City, St. Louis, Syracuse, Utica, Rochester, New York City, and other centers heard the word.

Funding was minimal for so crucial an effort, an estimated $500,000. The registration team raised $35,000 and received an additional $100,000 from the Democratic National Committee. Local funds were made available where needed. For example, in

New York, Syracuse supplied $5,000. Fortunately, the American Heritage Foundation and the National Advertising Council engaged in a very extensive advertising campaign to promote voter registration. Much of the cost of a mass-media appeal was thus shifted from the Democratic registration committee.

By the day registration books closed in the last state, Thompson's estimates showed 9,750,000 more Americans registered to vote than ever before. How many the Democratic effort added could never be determined. But in so close an election, the voter-registration drive, like several other factors, could easily have made the difference.

Bibliography

Flinn, Thomas A. "How Mr. Nixon Took Ohio: A Short Reply to Senator Kennedy's Question," *Western Political Quarterly,* XV (June 1962), 275-279.

Shadegg, Stephen. *What Happened to Goldwater?* New York: Holt, 1965.

White, F. Clifton. *Suite 3505.* New Rochelle, N.Y.: Arlington House, 1967.

Chapter VII

Attracting the Special-Interest Groups

 The United States has been populated by immigrants. Its 200 million inhabitants have come from nearly every nation in the world. As a symbol of welcome to the "huddled masses yearning to breathe free," the Statue of Liberty stands in New York Harbor.

THE PATTERNS OF GROUP POLITICAL GEOGRAPHY

Successive waves of immigration, the concentration of various groups of immigrants in different localities, the ways the newcomers have made a living, and the varied reasons for their coming have greatly shaped American politics. No brief portrait can adequately describe the complexity.

The majority pattern of American politics was set by the first, largest, and longest continuing wave of immigrants—the white Protestants from England and Scotland. Still a near majority of the population, they gave the United States the English language, the English common law, the English traditions of politics and government, and a new concept of their own: the separation of church and state. They drafted the Constitution and basic laws and they have provided most of the nation's leaders. Their reasons for coming and their convictions about the basic organization and purpose of government have set the perimeter of political debate throughout American history.

The original British immigration had two basic motives: to obtain religious freedom and to improve individual economic opportunities. Thus the New England and Middle Atlantic states, even colonial New York, were peopled by religious dissenters—Congregationalists in New England, Dutch Reform in New York, Quakers in Pennsylvania, Roman Catholics in Maryland. In the South, where Episcopalians predominated in the lowland areas, the Scotch-Irish brought the Presbyterian faith to the Piedmont and the highlands. Later came the Baptists and Methodists, who now are dominant there.

Religion has always been important in American politics. The nation is deeply committed to the separation of church and state and to the Protestant concept that every person has the inalienable right to worship or not to worship as he pleases. Religion, then, is a private matter in the United States. More than one-third of the population belongs to no church at all. Thus no religious group has had either the numerical strength or the moral basis to seek special support from the government, and Americans have come to regard the existence of many different and completely private religious groups as a characteristic of freedom and democracy.

Next on the scene were the Negro slaves, virtually all imported from Africa before the War of Independence. Kept in bondage until the Civil War, this group of some 19 million has proved the most difficult to assimilate. Concentrated heavily in the South until the 1940's and still largely centered there, the Negroes have acquired the English language and the Protestant faith (largely Baptist and Methodist) of their former owners, but have been confined chiefly to minor roles both economically and socially. Inheriting a matriarchal society from their two hundred years of slavery, dwelling apart and, in some states, receiving their schooling apart from white society, the Negro community has developed its own social standards and strong ingroup feelings which are having significant political impact.

The third major wave of immigrants was the northern Europeans, chiefly Germans, Swedes, Norwegians, and Danes, and mostly of Lutheran faith. Triggered by the failure of the liberal

German revolt of 1848 and by faltering economic opportunity in the north country, the immigration had two important features: it came before the American Civil War; and it settled in the rich farming country of the upper Middle West, chiefly in Illinois, Wisconsin, Iowa, Minnesota, and North and South Dakota. At the same time, the potato famine and political and religious strife in Ireland induced still another wave of movement: the Irish Catholics, who flocked in great numbers to the mill towns of New England and to New York until that city had more Irish than Dublin.

Just before and after the Civil War another and minor wave of immigration came from the Orient, when Chinese and Japanese laborers were induced to work in the construction of the transcontinental railroads. Never a significant number on the mainland, they did become the most numerous group in Hawaii.

The last great wave of immigrants was from southern and eastern Europe and came principally in the last decades of the nineteenth century and the early years of the twentieth century, before World War I. From that time until 1965, immigration was strictly controlled on a national-origins quota basis. Led by Italians, this wave also brought in large numbers of Poles, and some Greeks, Russians, and people from the smaller Balkan states. Attracted by the opportunities in industrial development, these people flocked to the cities of the East and to the mining and steel towns of the Appalachian highlands and the Great Lakes: Pittsburgh, Scranton, Cleveland, Toledo, Detroit, Gary, and Chicago. Few ventured to the Far West and virtually none to the South.

The Far West, as a result, was in the main peopled by eastern Americans, many looking for new land and better economic opportunity, although the Mormons settled Utah in search of religious freedom. A mixture of the eastern settlement pattern, the Far West's northern states were settled largely from New England and the upper Middle West, its southern tier from the South.

The politics of the incoming peoples were greatly influenced by the economic opportunities they found and by the domestic issues of the times. Opposed to slavery and favoring the principle of the Homestead Act, the northern European farming immigrants were strongly pro-Union during the Civil War and as a result became overwhelmingly Republican in politics. On the other hand, the Irish immigrants, working in the mills and homes of the dominant English group in the Northeast, found themselves unwelcome in the party of Lincoln and rallied around the Democratic banner as the Knights of St. Tammany. The southern European immigrants, also working for wages in the cities and also Catholic, therefore found common cause easier to make with their Irish brethren than with the northern European farmers. With the formation of labor unions in the 1890's and the early decades of the twentieth century, these Democratic groups became a major component of the labor movement.

The Civil War, however, also divided the original English stock. The North, defending the Union, became overwhelmingly Republican. The South sought refuge in the Democratic Party, which it was to dominate for two generations. Postwar alliance between the southern white leaders, virtually all Protestants, and the northern big-city immigrant forces, mostly Catholic, was not long in coming. Alliance clearly was to their mutual advantage for they had a common opponent and a common interest in changing the pattern of political power.

The Republican alliance of the Protestant British and the northern Europeans in the northern states was a solid one, however, and controlled national politics for nearly 70 years. Its demise was heralded in the early 1900's when the farmers of the upper Middle West and Plains states began to find that their interests—in controlling business monopolies, in the development of natural resources, and in the regulation of railroads and utilities—were in conflict with the interests of their eastern Republican colleagues, who were dominated by manufacturing and trading interests. First the farmers organized, particularly in the Farmers Union, to protect the small farmer and to provide cooperative marketing and buying. Turning to politics, they became Populists, Progressives, Farmer-Laborites, some of them even Socialists. After a generation of groping, many of their sons joined the Democrats in 1932 to establish the New Deal and remake that party into the present-day majority.

Shifting with them were the Negroes. After the Civil War, those few Negroes who voted generally were Republican, for Lincoln had freed the slaves. But the party of Lincoln seemed to do little more in their behalf and appeared to some to espouse the cause of the employer and business more than the aspirations of the workingmen. Accordingly, many defected. Franklin Roosevelt's New Deal captured the Negro people en masse. Today, only the Jews are more strongly Democratic.[1]

The New Deal also captured the bulk of the labor movement, which originally had been heavily Republican, when the rise of the industrial-union movement brought new leaders and millions of new union members in steel, automobiles, electrical appliances, textiles, rubber goods, and other mass-production industries. Thus the new majority coalition of the 1930's was a union of big-city immigrant groups, organized labor, the traditional leaders of the South, Negroes, small farmers of the upper Middle West, and western conservationists.

History, then, made the two parties what they are and dictated the patterns of appeals which the two candidates would make in 1960. John F. Kennedy, the grandson of an Irish immigrant, symbolized in a very special way the aspirations of all the more recent immigrant groups which had become the backbone of the working class. Yet he knew enough not to emphasize his religion. Kennedy himself had been raised in the mainstream American schools and understood the concept of separation of church and state. He also understood very well that within his party only the Irish, Italian, and Polish groups in large numbers shared his religious faith. The northern Europeans, the white voters in the South, the Negroes, and the ideological liberals from the northern British stock were overwhelmingly Protestant and were a substantial majority in his own party. And he could not overlook the very influential Jewish community. Kennedy, then, needed the support of a very heterogeneous collection of minority groups which he somehow had to weld together behind him.

Richard M. Nixon, on the other hand, was operating from the relatively homogeneous base of Protestant British and northern European stock which comprises a near majority of the population. Composed of the majority of business and professional men and

[1] Angus Campbell *et al., The American Voter* (New York: Wiley, 1960), pp. 159-160.

including a good proportion of the farm owners, his party represented the bulk of those families who had found America a place of economic reward and who wished to keep it so. His basic problem was to keep these conservatives behind him while converting to his cause enough of those who wanted change to enable him to win the presidency. The obvious source of new strength for him was the dominant Protestant British stock of the South, which theoretically should have common ideological cause with their brethren in the North. But in 1960, such realignment was foreclosed by the economic aftermath of the Civil War, still felt in the South; by considerations of party advantage; and by the desire of southern congressmen to keep the advantages of seniority. Yet, in part because he shared the religious faith of the South and of many of the disadvantaged groups, Nixon very nearly won anyway.

The election of 1964, on the other hand, was an aberration in American politics and offers at best a negative illustration of the principle of coalition politics. The Republican candidate, Senator Barry Goldwater of Arizona, acted as though American political parties are vehicles for the promotion of ideological causes. Having gained the presidential nomination as the candidate of the conservative wing of his party, he apparently set out to convert his party from a broadly based coalition of interests to a vehicle for the promotion of conservative ideological goals. In his acceptance speech at the Republican National Convention, he even invited liberals to leave the Republican party.

The Democratic candidate, President Lyndon B. Johnson of Texas, a believer in the politics of consensus, promptly seized his opportunity. Preempting the middle of the road and spreading the tent of the Democratic Party wide, he offered something for everyone and invited everyone to support him. Simultaneously he cleverly exploited several ill-chosen remarks by his opponent, particularly on foreign policy and control of nuclear weapons, which enabled him to brand Goldwater as irresponsible and "trigger-happy."

There followed a political upheaval in American politics which, if permanent, would have destroyed the Republican Party. Mr. Goldwater commanded only a portion of the regular Republican vote and could win from the Democrats only the extreme conservative segregationists of the South. Mr. Johnson kept all normally Democratic groups outside the deep South and won many of the liberal and moderate Republicans. Especially marked was the shift of businessmen and farmers to the President.

The outcome was a highly unstable, record political triumph for the Democrats and a monumental political disaster for the Republicans. Senator Goldwater carried only six states—his own and five in the deep South (only one of which had gone Republican in modern times).

The defection of Republican businessmen and farmers to Johnson and of Southerners to Goldwater were both short-lived. The dominant groups in the traditional Democratic coalition proved both unable and unwilling to accommodate the major demands of business and the goals of the similarly oriented large farm owners.

In the southern states, the traditional power holders soon returned to office under the Democratic label. There the Republican party is the party of the Union which crushed the War for Southern Independence and imposed Reconstruction. Lasting unity of southern conservatives with their fellows elsewhere must await either the lifting of a new banner which bears no stain of fratricide and vindictive punishment or the rise of a new generation of Southerners who are willing to forget the Civil War.

The rebuilding of the Republican coalition and its successes in the 1966 congressional and state elections in the North and West demonstrated both the durability of traditional American political loyalties and the realistic hard work done by pragmatic Republican leaders to reestablish their party as a broadly based arena of compromise. The return of traditional southern Democrats to Congress in the states of the deep South, especially in Alabama, offered similar testimony to the instability of the 1964 alignments.

THE DEMOCRATIC APPEALS IN 1964

The 1964 campaign offered Democrats an opportunity to make the widest possible range of special-group appeals. Not even in the depths of the Depression had their potential coalition been so broad. They hastened to make the most of the opportunity.

Ideologically, the President and Senator Humphrey welcomed the support of all citizens. "L.B.J. for the U.S.A." was their slogan, and L.B.J. himself sounded the theme in his acceptance speech at the Democratic National Convention:

> Tonight we offer ourselves—on our record and by our platform—as a party for all Americans. This prosperous people—this land of reasonable men—has no place for petty partisanship or peevish prejudice.
>
> The needs of all cannot be met by parties of the few—
>
> —Not by a business party or a labor party
> —Not by a war party or a peace party
> —Not by a Southern party or a Northern party.
>
> Our deeds will meet our needs only if we are served by a party which serves all our people.
>
> We are members, together, of such a party, the Democratic Party of 1964.

Organizationally, the search for special-group support took two forms. The Democratic National Committee extended its traditional minority-group efforts, and a national Citizens for Johnson and Humphrey Committee organized at least 11 specialized subgroups.

For many years the national committee had maintained on paper a Minorities Division, usually chaired by a prominent Democratic office holder and staffed by a Negro. In 1964, as in earlier campaigns, this division was again activated, primarily to register Negroes. Ailing Representative William L. Dawson of Illinois left the real work to Louis Martin, who had left the Chicago *Daily Defender,* a Negro newspaper, to join the Kennedy campaign in 1960. With Goldwater's prominent and consistent record against civil-rights legislation, Martin had only to deliver the votes, not change the minds, of his fellow Negroes. As one Democratic leader enthusiastically put it, "If any Negro votes for Goldwater, it will be by mistake."

Taking a leaf from the successful 1960 Kennedy drive for ethnic-group votes, the national committee also established an "All Americans Council," chaired by New York Mayor Robert F. Wagner. Seventeen separate ethnic groups were activated or reactivated to appeal to special immigrant groups. Among them were the highly successful Spanish-language group, relabeled "Viva Johnson," and the Polish, Italian, German, and Greek units.

Citizen groups, drawing on the lesson of 1960, centered their efforts on publicizing support from prominent liberal Republicans who were willing to support Johnson but who preferred not to be identified with Democratic candidates for lesser offices. Some, like Robert B. Anderson, who served as Secretary of the Treasury and Secretary of the Navy for former President Eisenhower, and Mrs. Oveta Culp Hobby, who was President Eisenhower's Secretary of Health, Education, and Welfare, joined generalized citizen efforts for Johnson. Others, like Dr. George Kistiakowsky, President Eisenhower's science adviser, preferred to work with their own occupational groups.

One such bipartisan group, the Committee for Responsible Leadership, chaired by John L. Loeb, ran large ads supporting the President. For example, its ad of October 22, entitled "A statement concerning the character of Lyndon B. Johnson and his qualifications as President of the United States," was signed by former Secretary of the Treasury Robert Anderson. Its message included a typical statement:

In recent weeks I have become increasingly concerned by the direction and the tenor of the campaign. I had earlier, after many quiet and searching hours, made a personal decision. I had determined, despite my regular affiliation, that I would cast my vote for Lyndon B. Johnson. It was a choice to be exercised in the silence and secrecy of a voting booth. It had not been in my mind to make my decision public.

However, as I followed the course of the campaign, I felt I must speak out.

State citizens committees centered their activities on publicizing the breadth of group support for Johnson and Humphrey and on naming prominent state Republican leaders who were backing their candidacy. In Florida, for example, the state citizens group was led by former Republican United States Senator Harry P. Cain of Washington state. In Utah, the Citizens for Johnson Committee took out full-page ads saying, "Sorry Senator Goldwater, In Our Hearts We Feel You're Wrong."

The citizens effort, then, early took on the 1960 pattern of setting up specialized subgroups, but avoided the 1960 method of establishing grass-roots organizations which would compete with the regular Democratic committees.

Appeals to special occupational groupings were handled as subcommittees of the citizens committee. Some were basically efforts to advertise bipartisan support for the President. Others were efforts to shape the campaign message to a special audience.

Chief among the bipartisan advertising types was a group called Scientists and Engineers for Johnson-Humphrey. Its essential appeal was the use of the names of its many prominent members rather than the use of ordinary political propaganda. Its cochairmen were Dr. Detlev W. Bronk, president of Rockefeller Institute, and Dr. Laurence A. Hyland, vice president of Hughes Aircraft. In addition to Dr. Kistiakowsky, the group included such famous figures as Dr. Paul Dudley White, the heart specialist who treated President Eisenhower, and Dr. Jerome Weisner of the Massachusetts Institute of Technology. Appeals to veterans, headed by John W. Mahan, former National Commander of the Veterans of Foreign Wars, carried a similar bipartisan flavor.

Channeling the campaign message were Rural Americans for Johnson and Humphrey; Educators for Johnson and Humphrey; Senior Citizens for Johnson and Humphrey, who used Senator Pat McNamara and Representative John Fogarty as cochairmen; Lawyers; District Attorneys; Overseas Citizens; Artists and Entertainers; Mayors; Professors; and Young Citizens for Johnson and Humphrey. All were staffed by experienced Democrats. For example, Rural Americans was handled by Kenneth Birkhead, long-time Democratic national-committee staff member who after 1961 was assistant to the Secretary of Agriculture. Senior Citizens leaned on Charles O'Dell of the United Automobile Workers and Sidney Spector, who had handled a similar group for Kennedy in 1960. Organizationally, the Young Citizens and the Scientists and Engineers were independent of the national citizens group.

Groups channeling the campaign message typically issued pamphlets and newsletters which they mailed to selected lists of people. Taking advantage of Senator Goldwater's long record of conservative voting, each of the groups was able to assemble a formidable list of major legislation of primary interest to its specialized audience which Goldwater had opposed.

Educators for Johnson and Humphrey, for example, issued a pamphlet entitled "In These Hands, the Hope of America's Children and Youth." Its inside pages consisted of a list of recent education legislation the President had supported or signed into law on one side and a list of Goldwater's votes opposing education legislation on the other. Choice Goldwater quotes accompanied the list of "no" votes, in this instance, "The child has no right to an education. In most cases the children will get along very well without it."

Still other special efforts were undertaken separately. The National Committee Faculty Fellow, Dr. Paul Smith, headed a College Faculty Program to enlist the professional aid of campus specialists, particularly in studies of electoral behavior for the campaign and in combating the propaganda being issued by rightist groups backing Goldwater. A group calling itself "Industrial Relations Committee for Johnson and Humphrey," composed principally of arbitrators for labor-management disputes and industrial-relations specialists for management and unions, set up headquarters at 1001 Connecticut Avenue, N.W., in Washington and sponsored ads saying, "We support Johnson and Humphrey to encourage industrial peace."

Special appeals to women were particularly useful to the Democrats primarily because Mrs. Lyndon B. Johnson proved to be an able campaigner in her own right. A "Lady Bird" special toured the South, and Mrs. Johnson dedicated recreation areas, visited Indian reservations, and even took a float trip down the Snake River in Grand Teton National Park to express her interest in conservation and natural beauty. A separate speakers' bureau for women was set up under Peggy Mann and Florence Hoff to fill requests from women's groups.

To retain the special appeal to the academic community which had marked all three preceding Democratic presidential campaigns, President Johnson announced on September 30, 1964, that eleven groups of distinguished intellectuals and administrators had been asked to study major policy areas and to recommend what actions the administration should pursue, including legislative proposals. Operating in secrecy, the groups were to make their recommendations to the President a week after the election. Their reports were never made public.

The groups and their leaders indicate the breadth of appeal: Agriculture, Charles D. Murphy, Under Secretary of Agriculture;

Education, John W. Gardner, president of the Carnegie Foundation; Foreign Economic Policy, Carl Kaysen, professor of economics at Harvard; Government Reorganization, Don K. Price, dean of the Littauer School of Public Administration at Harvard; Metropolitan Affairs, Robert C. Wood, professor of political science at the Massachusetts Institute of Technology; Intergovernmental Fiscal Relations, Joseph A. Pechman, Brookings Institution; Natural Beauty, Charles M. Haar, professor of law at Harvard; Natural Resources, Joseph A. Fisher, president of Resources for the Future; Sustaining Prosperity, Paul A. Samuelson, professor of economics at the Massachusetts Institute of Technology; Transportation, George W. Hilton, professor at the University of California; and Reducing Costs, chaired by a Princeton University economist who was unnamed.[2]

THE DEMOCRATIC APPEALS IN 1960

John F. Kennedy faced a more difficult organizing task in 1960. Few Republicans were flocking to his cause and these were mainly Catholic Republicans who saw in the Senator from Massachusetts a vindication for their religious faith.[3] Some Democrats, however, especially in the South, were deserting him because of his religion.

Kennedy's special-group appeal therefore centered on laying to rest the religious issue and attracting minority groups normally identified with the Democratic Party. The religious issue he handled himself, then used a special Community Relations Division to disseminate his statements. The organization of minority groups he left to his brother-in-law, R. Sargent Shriver. He also took advantage of a special family tie with Polish Americans in the person of Prince Stanislaw Radziwill, husband of Mrs. Kennedy's sister. The Prince traveled widely to Polish gatherings and won many votes to the Kennedy cause.

No special-group issue was more pervasive in the 1960 campaign than the religious affiliation of the Democratic nominee. The

[2] *New York Times,* October 1, 1964, p. 25.
[3] Philip E. Converse and associates found that 4.3 per cent more Catholics voted for Kennedy than a Democratic candidate normally can expect. See Philip E. Converse *et al.,* "Stability and Change in 1960: A Reinstating Election," *American Political Science Review,* LV (June 1961), 269-280.

only other Catholic nominated by a major political party had been Alfred E. Smith, the Democratic candidate in 1928. He had become the butt of scurrilous anti-Catholic propaganda. Although memories of the Civil War were then still much stronger in the South, Protestant Southerners fearing "the Pope in the White House" voted heavily for Hoover, the Republican nominee and a Quaker.

Kennedy had set the strategy of his appeal on the religious issue during his primary campaign in West Virginia, where he had opposed Congregationalist Hubert Humphrey in a heavily Protestant state. He stated unequivocally that he was dedicated to the separation of church and state. He reiterated the constitutional principle that no man should be denied high office because of his religious beliefs. And he implied that a vote for Kennedy was a vote for tolerance.

Kennedy's appeal was aimed entirely at the electorate. Two more religiously tolerant opponents than Senator Humphrey or, in the general election, Quaker Richard Nixon, could hardly have been found. Yet both were by such strategy forced to accept religion as an issue and were virtually compelled to endorse the Kennedy position.

Kennedy's key move in handling the religious issue was his statement to the Greater Houston Ministerial Association on Monday, September 12. In one crisp paragraph he stated his case, earnestly and sincerely:

I believe in an America where the separation of church and state is absolute—where no Catholic prelate would tell the President (should he be Catholic) how to act, and no Protestant minister would tell his parishioners for whom to vote—where no church or church school is granted any public funds or political preference—and where no man is denied public office merely because his religion differs from the President who might appoint him or the people who might elect him.[4]

Followed by an open question-and-answer period, the talk was well received. The Community Relations Division promptly, adroitly, and quietly proceeded to exploit the candidate's position

[4] U.S. Congress, Senate, *Freedom of Communications,* Vol. I (Washington: Government Printing Office, 1961), p. 208.

to the full. Film clips and tape recordings of the talk were widely circulated to television and radio stations. Pamphlets reproducing the speech were printed in large quantities and widely distributed.

Using contacts which had been built up by the Democratic Advisory Council, Sargent Shriver established at least a dozen units to appeal to special segments of the electorate. Organizationally, the special units fell into three categories: divisions of the Democratic National Committee, independent citizen organizations which raised their own funds and technically were independent of the committee, and divisions of Citizens for Kennedy-Johnson. In practice, all kept in touch with Sargent Shriver and all but two or three cleared their expenses through Ralph Dungan or Richard Donohue in Lawrence O'Brien's office at the national committee.

The Nationalities Division developed by far the most complex machinery, partly because of the variety of appeals it tried to make and partly to adjust to a sister organization, the Nationalities Division of Citizens for Kennedy-Johnson. Fortunately, the latter organization was set up principally to use the services of John T. R. Godlewski, who had headed the Polish section of the Republican National Committee in 1956 and who preferred to operate through a citizens committee. It concentrated almost entirely upon winning the Polish-American vote.

The Nationalities Division proper had four major sections—the German, Italian, Polish, and Spanish—and set up 26 special committees to make appeals, for example, to the Greek, Croatian, Czech, Slovak, Hungarian, Lithuanian, Chinese, Syrian-Lebanese, Armenian, Romanian, Bulgarian, American Indian, and Jewish vote.

Operating principally from a national headquarters in New York, it focused on six objectives in the key states of California, Illinois, Michigan, Minnesota, New Jersey, New York, Ohio, Pennsylvania, Texas, and Wisconsin: (1) voter registration of nationality groups; (2) personal actions by Senator Kennedy to demonstrate interest in nationality groups, consisting of a press conference with editors and publishers of foreign-language publications, a meeting in Hyannis Port with leaders of the principal nationality groups, and his appearance at a few large gatherings of nationality groups; (3) speaking engagements by leading Democrats before such groups;

(4) radio tapes by Senator and Mrs. Kennedy; (5) press releases and statements to the foreign-language press and radio; (6) distribution of eight-page two-color illustrated folders in Spanish, Polish, Italian, and German. In addition, efforts were made to appoint state and local nationalities chairmen, to provide background materials on the availability of campaign materials, to supply sample speeches aimed at the interests of special nationality groups, and to get prominent leaders of nationality groups to endorse Mr. Kennedy. Some sections operated more widely than others—the German, for example, in 31 states.

An independent Spanish-language operation stimulated the formation of 200 local-level Viva Kennedy clubs in the 21 states which have concentrations of Spanish-speaking citizens. Its principal activities were registration drives, particularly successful in New York and California; the distribution of literature, buttons, automobile bumper stickers, and banners in Spanish; the recruitment of eight major platform speakers who were fluent in Spanish to address rallies; the preparation of press releases for Spanish-language newspapers; and the distribution of Spanish-language radio tapes.

Businessmen for Kennedy were organized as two independent groups and a division of the national committee. The key unit was the National Committee of Business and Professional Men and Women for Kennedy-Johnson. Working closely with it was the Businessmen for Kennedy Division of the Democratic National Committee and the Greater Washington Committee of Business and Professional Men and Women for Kennedy-Johnson. Technically, the businessmen's national committee headquartered in Chicago and was chaired by Governor Luther Hodges of North Carolina. Its Washington affairs were handled by Herbert Klotz, who served as the staff director for the entire program.

Unlike most of the committees, the businessmen's group was an important source of funds. At least $500,000 was collected by the national businessmen's committee, $34,800 by the Greater Washington group alone. In addition to covering its own expenses, the committee was able to pick up several large campaign bills, at least one for television time.

Labor's Committee for the Election of Kennedy and Johnson made no attempt to form a mass citizens movement. Its purpose instead was to stimulate the regular Committees on Political Education of the AFL-CIO and other labor units to get out the vote in the campaign.

Operating on a labor-supplied budget of $45,000, most of which dribbled in after the campaign was over, labor's committee distributed two million pieces of literature; circulated prints of a film, "Kennedy Speaks to Labor"; pressed a national get-out-the-vote campaign complete with prizes for communities and districts making the best increase over 1956; channeled requests for automobile bumper strips, pictures, and signs to the Democratic National Committee; prepared 1,500 copies of a long-playing record of political songs,. "Ballads for Ballots"; and placed "Don't Miss the Bus" car cards in street cars and buses in 18 of the nation's largest industrial centers.

Farmers for Kennedy-Johnson set up units in as many states as possible and used an elaborate system of regional directors to coordinate activities and to provide special advice in particular commodity areas. The state and local organizations stimulated farm rallies for Kennedy, participated in local arrangements for his visits, and encouraged turnouts of local citizens. Local groups also inserted paid advertising in weekly newspapers, distributed Farmers for Kennedy-Johnson literature, supplied speakers for local groups, raised funds, and talked up Kennedy for President—a very important technique in rural areas.

A series of printed and mimeographed pamphlets and statements on many farm problems was prepared and mailed to a rather extensive list of farmers and persons interested in agriculture. The central staff also handled heavy correspondence on farm problems which flowed into the national committee and prepared farm speeches and statements for Senator Kennedy, for clearance through Myer Feldman.

Senior Citizens for Kennedy was designed to rally the supporters of Medicare to the Kennedy bandwagon. Its chairman was Representative Aime J. Forand, sponsor of the bill to provide medical care for the aged through the social-security system, and its staff director was Dr. Blue Carstenson.

State organizations of Senior Citizens for Kennedy were formed in 40 states and special efforts were made in 5 more. Many local clubs were formed so that 490 state and local chairmen served during the campaign and more than 35,000 senior citizens joined local Kennedy clubs.

Senior Citizens turned up one special asset: many of its members had time to give to the campaign. Carstenson was able to recruit full-time volunteers of top quality in Washington, including a retired Congressman. State and local committees had similar experiences where members of Senior Citizens Clubs proved available to man Democratic Party campaign headquarters during daytime hours, stuff envelopes, do telephoning, and render other services. An estimated 17,500 retired citizens contributed volunteer services at all levels during the campaign.

To convert the older voters, who traditionally tend to vote Republican, more than 3,500,000 pieces of literature were distributed, of which 700,000 went in direct mailings to them. Drop-in centers were established. Eighty-one social-security rallies attracted 64,000 senior citizens. Congressman Forand made 22 radio and television appearances. These efforts, plus paid advertising in three states, especially California, led Carstenson to estimate that 5 million older Americans heard their message.

Shooting for 80 per cent of the Negro vote, Shriver set up a Civil Rights Division under his personal direction. Its continuing assignment was to identify Kennedy with Negro aspirations by beaming two main themes to Negro voters through pamphlets and the Negro press. The anti-Catholic attacks on Senator Kennedy were identified as stemming from the same sources as anti-Negro attacks. Kennedy was portrayed as being in the Roosevelt tradition.

The major contribution by the Civil Rights Division, however, proved to be a single dramatic idea which may have tipped the scales in the close 1960 presidential contest.[5] Ten days before the election, a Georgia court sentenced the Reverend Martin Luther King to four months' hard labor in the Reidsville State Penitentiary for his participation in a sit-in demonstration in a department-store restaurant in Atlanta. Harris Wofford, campaign coordinator for the Civil Rights Division, suggested that Senator Kennedy call Mrs. King and express his concern.

Senator Kennedy's call and Robert Kennedy's follow-up call to

---

[5] See Theodore H. White, *The Making of the President, 1960* (New York: Atheneum, 1961), pp. 385-387, for a detailed narrative of the incident and an analysis of its political significance.

presiding Judge Mitchell appear to have helped bring about Reverend King's prompt release. The Reverend's father, a highly influential Negro leader in his own right, immediately switched his support to Kennedy. Louis Martin and the Civil Rights Division promptly followed up with a million pieces of literature and personal telegrams to Negro party workers across the nation in the last week of the campaign. They believe this one act "triggered a new wave of pro-Kennedy sentiment among Negroes" and did more than any one thing to identify Kennedy with Negro aspirations.

Young Citizens for Kennedy-Johnson and Students for Kennedy-Johnson operated jointly as adjuncts of Citizens for Kennedy-Johnson but in close cooperation with the regular Young Democrats Division of the national committee. Richard Murphy, permanent staff director for the Young Democrats, coordinated the entire youth effort.

The Women's Division of the Democratic National Committee, with a permanent staff in being, handled women's activities without the establishment of any special campaign units. The scheduling of appearances by women in the Kennedy family and by Mrs. Lyndon Johnson was handled separately but in close cooperation with the Women's Division.

Five smaller groups rendered limited assistance in appeals to other special interests: the Kennedy-Johnson Natural Resources Advisory Committee, Educators for Kennedy-Johnson, the Urban Affairs Division, Special Projects, and Veterans for Kennedy-Johnson.

In both the 1960 and 1964 campaigns, as in previous presidential campaigns, all such special groups were disbanded following the election. At each succeeding election, the efforts had to be established anew. Few records were kept and those which were prepared were soon discarded. Thus appeals to special groups probably will continue to be organized almost entirely on an ad-hoc basis at the beginning of each campaign and will be as effective as the budget and the ingenuity of the staff permit.

THE REPUBLICAN APPEALS IN 1960

From 1860 to 1932 the Republican Party was clearly the majority party in American politics. During this period, its party leadership did not concern itself, in the main, with particular programs to woo the so-called special-interest groups. The party base was broad; it could count on the support of a good portion of the farm population, the academic community, small business and large business, and even a sizable segment of the labor vote.

But with the coming of the Great Depression and the New Deal in the 1930's, the Republican Party lost its position of preponderance; it became the minority party. Although the presidential elections of 1952 and 1956 gave an unprecedented majority to the Republican national standard-bearer, Dwight D. Eisenhower, congressional, statehouse, and courthouse election returns indicated that the Democratic Party was, at mid-century, still the stronger of the two major parties.

Republican Party leaders realized that attempts to enlist the support of voters in special groups must be improved and enlarged in areas where rudimentary programs existed and initiated where necessary.

The Republican National Committee's organization chart for the Eisenhower reelection campaign demonstrates the breadth of the appeals to special-interest groups which were extant at the committee in 1956: a Special Activities Board, under the direction of the assistant to the chairman, Miss Bertha S. Adkins, included a Minority Division, a Veterans Division, an Ethnic Division, the Young Republicans, and the Women's Division. The Campaign Division, under Robert Humphries, sponsored programs in the fields of agriculture, nationalities, labor, and healing arts.

By 1960 the national committee had developed additional interest-group programs for Senior Republicans, the academic community, and business (particularly those who had received instruction in practical-politics courses in their home community).

The pattern for most of these special activities was identical. First came the identification phase, then the recruitment, the programing, and finally the attempt to involve the members of these groups in productive campaign work. Some of the programs stressed assistance to congressional candidates in "marginal districts" as well as assistance to the national ticket. The assumption was made throughout all of these programs that the state and local organizations would benefit, too, from the broadening of the party base.

Most of the special-interest divisions were year-round, continuous activities at the national committee. In 1960 these were Agriculture, Labor, Nationalities, Minorities, Arts and Sciences, and Senior Republicans. The Veterans Division, on the other hand, was resurrected only for the 1960 campaign. It is true that the Women's Division is a kind of special-interest division also, but since it services such a large and broad constituency its role and approach are somewhat different from the smaller "auxiliaries" or special-interest groups mentioned above. The same thing applies to the Young Republicans and the National Federation of Republican Women's Clubs. Strictly speaking, these latter two organizations are not an integral part of the national-committee staff. They are separate from the committee staff but are housed in the same offices.

The report of the 1956 Republican National Committee's labor program illustrates the usual pattern of approach taken by the special-interest divisions. This report reveals that months before the actual initiation of the campaign, the Labor Division's personnel had been occupied with the identification of Republican labor leaders and union members. Much to the surprise of some, they had found a considerable number actually active as Republican Party leaders.

Labor committees were then organized for the 1956 campaign on the county and city levels in 25 states. These labor committees ranged from 20 to 5,000 members. In some of the highly industrialized states as many as fifty such committees were formed. Other states had no local labor committees but did organize state-wide committees and, according to the report, a "minimum state labor campaign" to develop strength among laboring men and women for the national Republican ticket.

After identification and recruitment, the third step was program development, consisting, for the labor committees, of meetings, banquets, television and radio debates, the use of sound trucks and rank-and-file labor endorsements for the Republican ticket, all of which were organized and supported by the labor committees.

In conjunction with program development, campaign materials were created stressing the candidate's concern and accomplishments in the labor field.

Appropriate pictures of the candidates with prominent interest-group members are standard. It should be noted that to accomplish the recruitment phase of their general programs, special-interest divisions are often authorized to employ a number of men for field organization and operations. Thus a special-interest group can be a very expensive campaign item for a national committee during a presidential year.

As the 1960 campaign drew nearer, it appeared that the special-interest divisions at the national committee would be asked to function as they had in 1956. But because the campaign was not directed from the national committee, the special-interest organizations in the committee headquarters tended to be overlooked or bypassed in the actual conduct of the campaign.

Although appeals to specialized groups constituted an important part of the Nixon-Lodge campaign plan, the special-interest divisions at the national committee played a minor role in this plan. The farm group at the Republican National Committee appeared to be the only group, other than the Young Republicans, which was able to maintain a field staff in the 1960 presidential election. The Minorities Division and the Labor Division were not allocated funds, and the directors of these divisions were thus unable to activate their own divisional campaign plans and to employ the extensive contacts they had developed in the minority community and in major labor organizations.

Certainly this neglect was not the intent. It undoubtedly resulted from the organizational problems mentioned earlier in Chapter V. The costly effect of poor organization in this field is seen in a convention incident. A good deal of effort had gone into preparation for a dinner honoring a large number of labor leaders and union-member delegates to the national convention. Nixon had been invited, along with other prominent party leaders who would be in Chicago at that time. Some top party leaders did appear. Governor Rockefeller, for example, came early and stayed late. The Vice President, however, was too busy with an overloaded convention schedule. He was unable to make even a brief appearance at this important labor dinner.

Those responsible for special-interest appeals at the national Volunteers for Nixon-Lodge headquarters decided on a direct-mail campaign. Consequently, mailing lists were purchased for a wide variety of interest groups, and letters requesting support for the Nixon-Lodge campaign went to vast numbers of individuals within these groups.

Such letters of invitation, for example, were mailed to 232,000 doctors, 19,000 civic leaders, 100,000 scholars, 100,000 retired service officers, 200,000 veterans, 232,000 lawyers, and even to several thousand certified public accountants.

As affirmative responses were received, SNAP packs (mentioned in Chapter VI) were mailed to each respondent with the hope that the campaign material contained therein would be distributed and that the Nixon-Lodge treasury would benefit from contributions sent by the pack recipients. A report to Nixon-Lodge Volunteers division heads on the accumulative donations and the replies received from these various interest groups was issued daily by the Nixon-Lodge headquarters. Late in the campaign the volunteers had tallied up roughly 18,000 replies from doctors, 1,500 from civic leaders, slightly fewer than 3,000 from scholars, a like number from retired service officers, over 5,000 from lawyers, and roughly 1,000 from the accountants.

This direct-mail approach, however, was not the only effort expended by the Nixon-Lodge Volunteers headquarters to develop support from various interest groups. The volunteers also had organizers in the field to strengthen support among farmers and entered into some joint programing with national-committee personnel in the fields of nationalities, veterans, and arts and sciences.

It should be pointed out that there were two distinct phases to the direct-mail campaign among special-interest groups. First, the direct person-to-person follow-through as a result of the receipt of a SNAP pack and, second, an attempt to form state and local special-interest organizations throughout the country.

Thus the names of the nearly 3,000 academicians who had responded affirmatively to the direct mailing were supplied to state leaders of Scholars for Nixon-Lodge where such clubs existed. The clubs would then invite these interested persons to participate in their activities. A letter from the Southern California Scholars for Nixon and Lodge illustrates the kind of program these special-interest groups developed and how they used individuals suggested

September 9, 1960

Dear Colleague:

Many scholars throughout the nation are uniting behind Richard M. Nixon and Henry Cabot Lodge for the offices of President and Vice-President of the United States. We hope that you are or will become an active participant in this movement, without regard for your present or past political party preference.

We believe that the Nixon-Lodge team is particularly well-qualified to serve our nation:

    1. Their experience in international affairs best equips them to deal with the wide-ranging aspects of American foreign relations.

    2. Their record of firmness in dealing with the threat of Russian Communism is heartening and inspiring.

    3. Their philosophy of individual freedom is in keeping with our free academic tenets and sense of personal responsibility.

    4. They are at home intellectually in an academic environment, and will be attentive to the view of scholars.

    5. Their dedication to individual liberty is combined with their high sense of social responsibility.

    6. We can have confidence in these candidates because of what they have done, because of what they are, and because of the purposeful leadership we know they will provide.

If you share our confidence, we hope you will discuss this letter with your colleagues, many of whom are receiving a copy, and with the members of your family. As an important and respected member of the community you are charged with a clear responsibility to make known your judgements on this subject.

                           Yours sincerely,

        Carl Q. Cristol   George C. S. Benson

                     Co-Chairmen

A letter from Southern California Scholars for Nixon and Lodge. The margin carried a warning in solid capitals: "Please Remember: You can not vote if you are not presently registered. The last date for registration is September 15."

to them by the national Nixon-Lodge Volunteers headquarters. In some cases the corresponding national-committee division supplied names as well.

A memo to one of the authors from E. H. "Ned" Harding illustrates the conceptualization of the utilization of interested scholars, doctors, veterans, and other categories by the Nixon-Lodge staff.

> With our other committees we have been referring all those who want to participate in volunteer activities or to work on Mr. Nixon's behalf to the Volunteers chairman or to state representatives in their own state. Please don't hesitate to refer any of your people to organizational men in their state. Their job is to put all interested persons either in an advisory capacity at the state level or in a more active capacity in their local communities.

Where there were strong and extensive Nixon-Lodge state organizations and where respected and energetic leaders could be found to head up the various state volunteers auxiliaries, the direct-mail approach proved effective. Unfortunately, such state organizations were the exception rather than the rule, and the hurried attempt to recruit prominent leaders of special-interest groups was not always successful. What happened in too many states was that thousands of persons interested in assisting the campaign never were called upon to help.

This shortcoming points to a basic problem in the development of political auxiliary groups. Ostensibly the purpose of the groups is to broaden the base of party support. But more is required than simply identifying known Republicans among these groups and then flooding them with literature.

If a doctor, lawyer, scholar, or labor leader goes so far as to commit himself to work for a candidate or a party, he then expects that opportunities will be offered him which will employ effectively his energy and talents. Failure to offer opportunities for service in the campaign has been one of the major weaknesses in all auxiliary-group organizations at the national level.

THE REPUBLICAN APPEALS IN 1964

Unlike the Democratic National Committee, the Republicans maintained at least token forces in most of their special-interest divisions from 1960 to 1964. The work of the Agriculture, Labor, Minorities, and Arts and Sciences Divisions continued unabated, and even though the Nationalities Division was not staffed continuously, volunteer and intermittent staffing made possible the continuation of the program in that field.

The Women's Division approached 1964 with a particular interest in the recruitment of support from special-interest groups. A program called GROW (Grass Roots Organization of Women) had been designed to direct previously uncommitted women to such appropriate party special-interest groups as did exist. The Women's Division program had divided its work into six special activities: Women in Minority Groups; Women in Nationality Groups; Farm Women; Women in Education; Women in the Labor Force; and Women in Business and the Professions.

The root problem remained, however. After identification and referral, what were these people going to do that would make them feel that they were really involved in worthwhile party-building efforts? This question became critical as the 1964 campaign design became apparent, for the very essence of the GROW program was "to grow" through enlarging the Republican Party's base and this was not necessarily consistent with an ideological approach.

Local and state organizations which had been working on the same problem of expanding party support were caught in the same 1964 organizational vise as the national Women's Division. The big-city (Bliss) report made particular mention of ways in which to improve the Republican position with respect to special-interest groups. These suggestions, along with extensive workshop sessions on these same topics at the State Chairmen's Association, forecast considerable involvement of volunteers from special-interest groups in the metropolitan areas.

Finally, the Republican workshops, supported by Republicans of such diverse outlooks as Nelson Rockefeller and Barry Goldwater, had successfully appealed to issues-oriented community leaders in more than 20 states. They had drawn large numbers of leaders from minority and nationality groups into active party roles and were making significant inroads into some big-city Democratic precincts. In many cities they were conducted jointly with women's Republican groups; in others they operated as separate auxiliaries.

But all of these efforts—Republican National Committee Campaign Division programs, the Women's Division's GROW program, the Bliss big-city report, the state chairmen's workshop sessions, and the Republican workshop appeals—were predicated on two assumptions: (1) that the Republican Party could win only if it directed its attention and efforts where the votes were—the nation's major metropolitan areas; and (2) that the Republican Party should appeal to all voters in terms of their particular life style and interests.

The architects of the 1964 campaign did not accept those two assumptions. From the beginning, leaders of the Draft Goldwater Committee developed their strategy around sectional appeals in the South, the Midwest, and the Mountain states. The major metropolitan areas—New York, Chicago, Los Angeles—were not counted in. And the traditional specific appeals to special-interest groups gave way to general philosophic pronouncements.

An illustration of the abstract approach of the Goldwater campaign is seen clearly in a student report of an interview in October 1964 with an intelligent, idealistic, young Goldwater campaign leader from the Midwest who responded to the question of Goldwater special-interest appeals as follows:

People from all over the world seek to come to this land of opportunity in order to break away from their ethnic origins, to free themselves of their ethnic shackles. When this conglomeration of individuals reach America, they become equal—all assuming the new characteristic of a larger whole American. The Republican Party *is not* and *will not* specifically appeal to special-interest groups.[6]

Shadegg says:

The decision to avoid lowering the candidate by making a direct appeal for votes focused on local problems or special interests was made in the "think tank."[7]

Goldwater, indeed, was to be a national candidate and above such segmented appeals.

[6] From a student report on presidential politics, Ohio Wesleyan University, January 1964.
[7] Stephen Shadegg, *What Happened to Goldwater?* (New York: Holt, 1965), p. 212.

Thus it was that during the campaign the presidential candidate did not mention lumber or fishing while campaigning in Oregon though lumber and fishing support the economy of that state. In Idaho, a bitter controversy was raging in 1964 between the public and the private power interests. Goldwater did not mention this controversy. And though the agricultural states of Idaho, Montana, and Minnesota were vitally concerned with a variety of farm problems, Goldwater said nothing about agriculture during his visits to those states.

The general campaign philosophy concerning special-interest group appeals is clearly revealed in the national committee's Reorganization Plan. Special-interest divisions were, with three exceptions, deactivated. Only the Nationalities Division continued within the Campaign Division. The Arts and Sciences Division was transferred to the Research Division, and the Southern Division actually became part of the operation of the new Southern Regional Office.

In terms of special-interest publications, only the Nationalities Division continued its periodical, "The National Reporter." The Arts and Sciences Division temporarily suspended its "Republican Report," and the Southern Division's monthly newsletter, "Southern Challenge," ceased publication. It was later replaced, however, by several publications from the new southern regional campaign office, all of which stressed the message that the Republican Party was conservative. One, urging a strong two-party system for the South, was entitled "Something Is Missing." And a second pamphlet, inviting all conservative voters to affiliate under one roof—the Republican Party—was entitled "You Are the Balance of Power."

A special all-media attack on the South's one-party system designed in conjunction with registration canvasses was called "The Big Snooze." It included a pamphlet, newspaper ads, and radio commercials, each with a basically conservative ideological thrust.

Pamphlets developed for senior citizens and newly naturalized citizens were also available through the national-committee catalogue of materials, but they had been developed prior to the 1964 campaign and were given only small circulation.

Some items developed by the public-relations department for

general distribution were aimed directly or tangentially at special-interest groups. The pamphlets on "Barry Goldwater and Social Security" obviously were aimed primarily at the votes of senior citizens and relatives and close friends.

The problem here was a major one for Goldwater. Because of statements made before and during the nomination campaign suggesting that the social-security program be made voluntary, Goldwater was immediately on the defensive on this issue even before the campaign began in earnest. To counteract the argument that a Goldwater administration would work toward a weakening of the social-security system, a variety of literature from the national committee and from national and state citizens groups quoted the 1964 Republican platform pledge to support "a strong, sound system of Social Security with improved benefits to our people." Goldwater's speech of August 21, 1964, on the floor of the United States Senate was also reproduced for wide distribution. It stated, in part:

I favor a sound Social Security System and I want to see it strengthened. I have voted for genuine improvements in the system since I have been in the Senate and I plan to do so now. I supported the 1956 amendments to the Social Security Act, and, in 1950, I voted to raise benefits so that their value in terms of purchasing power would be preserved.[8]

At the same time, however, Goldwater seriously questioned the validity of the proposed Medicare program:

We shall not preserve the Social Security program if we saddle it with unnecessary burdens such as Medicare. We penalize every senior citizen if we thus bankrupt the system that protects him.[9]

Goldwater's heavily publicized questions and doubts about social security were too much to overcome and the Republican standard-bearers suffered heavily at the polls at the hands of the senior citizens. Normally Republican in their voting habits, this increasingly large block of voters constituted the most serious defection for the Republican Party in 1964.

[8] Quoted in Republican National Committee Pamphlet on Social Security, 1964.
[9] *Ibid.*

As Theodore H. White has pointed out, the Democrats chose wisely to "hook and hang" Goldwater on an issue that affected personally more than 109,000,000 people. (By 1964, 19,000,000 were recipients of the old-age or disability benefits of social security, and another 90,000,000 were insured with the system.) To quote White's analysis:

To attack Social Security is, in the highest political sense, dangerous. Nor did Goldwater ever attack it—just as he never demanded war. What he did instead was to ruminate aloud about what might be done with it.[10]

Although his final campaign statement on the subject of social security clearly stated that he favored the system and wanted it strengthened, it was Goldwater's earlier spoken thoughts, particularly those during the primary contest in New Hampshire, that were continually brought to the attention of the voters and that frightened them.

The Goldwater strategy called for heavy support from the nation's farmers, particularly in the Midwest. And early in the campaign it appeared that there was reason to be optimistic about that support. In the spring of 1964, wheat farmers had rejected the wheat proposal of Secretary Freeman in a national referendum. Discontent was widespread, particularly among dairy farmers and cattlemen.

To nail down this support it was necessary to go to the farmers and demonstrate a specific interest in them and their problems. Early in the campaign, however, the "antipolitics" of the "think tank" intervened. According to Shadegg, Kitchel and Baroody announced that Goldwater would not attend the annual national plowing contest at Fargo, North Dakota. Apparently, it took Republican Senators Karl E. Mundt and Milton R. Young to persuade Kitchel and Baroody that Goldwater's appearance at Fargo was imperative.

It was necessary, they felt, for Goldwater to clarify his stand on the farm issue—to state forthrightly that although his goal for the

---

[10] Theodore H. White, *The Making of the President, 1964* (New York: Atheneum, 1965), p. 361.

farmer was an ultimate return to the free market, he recognized such a transition from a government-dominated agrarian economy would require a number of years coupled with the development of workable free-market program alternatives.

Claude P. Streeter, a friendly editor of the Philadelphia *Farm Journal,* was concerned about Goldwater's failure to exploit the weaknesses in the administration's farm position and to state vigorously his own position on this issue. In a memorandum to his publisher, Richard Babcock, Streeter carefully defined Goldwater's problem as he saw it:

Mr. Goldwater is allowing the impression to get around that he would wreck all farm programs forthwith. A lot of farmers are afraid he would. Mr. Goldwater needs to state forthrightly that (a) farm income is too low, (b) that he intends to do something about it, (c) that he favors support prices for price stabilization purposes, but low enough not to aggravate the surplus problem, (d) that he favors encouraging more industries located throughout rural America to offer good jobs to those who want to or have to leave farming, (e) that he favors the continuation of the Rural Electrification program with some changes, (g) that he is compassionate toward those having a hard struggle, and (h) that he intends to decrease the role of government in agriculture and turn more of the control of farming back to the farmers.[11]

In response to the prodding by Senators Mundt and Young and to the suggestions made by friendly farm experts like Streeter, some changes were made in the Fargo farm speech. But Goldwater was not specific enough about his own program, and he again condemned the administration's farm program by reminding his audience that 77 per cent of the farm income, $2.1 billion, represented a national government subsidy.

As with social security, Goldwater late in the campaign became more clear in his pledge on agricultural policy. He said he would

. . . honor commitments already made by the Federal Government [and] would not propose a change in the farm program until something better has been developed that could gradually be substituted for it.[12]

[11] Shadegg, *What Happened to Goldwater?,* p. 233.
[12] *Ibid.,* p. 237.

In an effort to develop support for Goldwater among the farmers, the Citizens for Goldwater-Miller established a national Farm Division, out of which flowed extensive campaign material to state Goldwater-Miller farm groups. Although the national and state farm groups had little apparent success in building the widespread support they sought among farmers, they did succeed in raising substantial financial support for the Goldwater campaign through a Bushels for Barry program. According to *Farm Roundup,* the Citizens for Goldwater-Miller Farm Division newsletter, this program was initiated by irate wheat farmers in North Dakota and Montana in a movement against administration farm policies. By filling a self-imposed quota of 200 bushels of wheat, a sizable number of farmers did participate in helping to fund the Goldwater campaign. Some Republican farm groups attempted to use the same idea with producers of corn, soybeans, livestock, and other farm commodities. The success in other fields, however, was not as substantial as it was with the wheat farmers.

Civil rights involved two special-interest groups in the 1964 campaign—the Negro voter and the southern white voter. It has already been pointed out that the newly created Southern Division at the national committee (another name for the Southern Region of the campaign organization) published materials (1) stressing the conservative philosophy of the Republican Party and its candidates and (2) urging southern citizens to vote Republican to bring all conservatives under one tent and to thus strengthen the two-party system in the South. But it was Goldwater's own civil-rights record and position that framed the issue in more dramatic terms for both the Negro and the southern white voter.

In an appeal to the Negro voter in the District of Columbia, Goldwater-Miller campaign headquarters there issued the strongest procivil-rights literature of the Republican campaign. Entitled *What About Civil Rights and Barry Goldwater,* this pamphlet quoted Goldwater's statements in the Senate, in his book *The Conscience of a Conservative,* and in campaign speeches to the effect that he "was unalterably opposed to discrimination or segregation on the basis of race, color or creed."[13]

---

[13] Speech in U.S. Senate, June 18, 1964.

It so happens that . . . I believe it is both wise and just for Negro children to attend the same schools as whites, and that to deny them this opportunity carries with it strong implications of inferiority.[14]

I believe completely in vigorous enforcement of the Civil Rights Bill, for I believe in majority rule.[15]

To emphasize Goldwater's civil-rights record, the pamphlet compared the Republican presidential candidate's support of civil-rights programs at the city, state, and national level with the record of President Johnson. So strong was the pamphlet in pointing out Goldwater's procivil-rights disposition that Democratic headquarters in several southern states distributed it as prima-facie evidence that Goldwater was, after all, a traditional Republican and not to be trusted on the civil-rights issues.

On the other hand, there was more than ample opportunity for the Democrats to attack Goldwater on the civil-rights issue from the anticivil-rights viewpoint. He had voted against the 1964 civil-rights act, charging on the Senate floor that its sections on public accommodations and equal employment were unconstitutional. The Goldwater-controlled platform committee had resisted moderate and liberal Republican efforts to write into the platform a liberal civil-rights plank, and Goldwater delegates on the convention floor had projected this intransigence to a nationwide audience. Even during the campaign, while pledging to execute the civil-rights act, if elected, Goldwater's penchant for philosophic rumination on this issue led him to question repeatedly the wisdom and the possible unconstitutionality of the 1964 act.

One series of publications by the Republican National Committee was entitled *The Debate That Never Was,* an apt title particularly for the pamphlet *Civil Rights and Responsibilities.* Neither Goldwater nor Johnson ever did hit head-on the larger questions relating to civil rights—jobs, housing, and education. Regardless of this fact, the general posturing of the candidates on the issue was speedily accomplished through the oversimplification of the issue by the press, the skillful exploitation of the Democratic campaign

[14] Barry M. Goldwater, *The Conscience of a Conservative* (Shepherdsville, Ky.: Victor Publishing Co., 1960), p. 37.
[15] *What About Civil Rights and Barry Goldwater* (pamphlet by Washington, D.C., Citizens for Goldwater-Miller), p. 1.

leaders, and the stubborn adherence of the Goldwater campaign architects to at least part of the so-called southern strategy.

The southern strategy, based on economic conservatism, did indeed succeed in gaining the support of a majority of voters in the five states of the deep South. But the civil-rights overtones of this strategy were an important factor also in the disastrous Republican loss in 44 other states.

The most traditional of the 1964 Republican special-interest-group appeals was made in the nationalities field. The Nationalities Division was the one special-interest division remaining active and within the framework of the Campaign Division under Wayne Hood's direction.

A newsletter entitled *The Nationalities Reporter* was published biweekly during the campaign and stressed Goldwater and Miller's close relationship to and understanding of nationality groups and their problems. Goldwater bumper strips in 26 languages were available as reinforcement devices for those individuals committed to his candidacy. Goldwater addressed himself primarily to the "captive-nations" theme when he appeared before various East European ethnic groups, pledging his every effort, if elected, to free the captive peoples now behind the Iron Curtain.

No significant programs in the field of attracting support from academic, labor, healing arts, and veterans groups were launched by the national committee. Special-interest-group programs of this type were the province of the Citizens Committee for Goldwater-Miller.

Organizational activity in this field by the national and state Citizens for Goldwater-Miller was directed toward the development of voter support and of financial assistance. Under the direction of James M. Day, individual special-interest organizations were formed by the citizens national organization, for senior citizens, pilots, businessmen, Democrats, builders, diplomats, celebrities, Americans abroad, labor, doctors, dentists, a wide variety of nationality groups, veterans, scientists, engineers, architects, educators, and Mothers for a Moral America. An appeal was made even to Goldwater's fraternity brothers of Sigma Chi.

Clifton White states that more than 30 million campaign pieces were distributed by the national citizens offices, much of which was special-interest literature.[16] Shadegg states that state organizations, using the national citizens plates printed an additional 20 million pamphlets, brochures, bumper stickers, and posters.[17]

In some states, Citizens for Goldwater-Miller special-interest-group organizations were quite extensive. In Ohio, for example, separate statewide Rumanian, Bulgarian, Cossack, Georgian, Greek, Lithuanian, Serbian, Byelorussian, Estonian, German, Hungarian, and Ukrainian Goldwater for President clubs were formed.

The effectiveness of these statewide groups in changing Johnson supporters into Goldwater voters can be questioned. One thing is certain, however, the Goldwater-Miller special-interest groups did contribute substantially to the 1964 campaign coffers. The conservative-cause-conscious citizens recruited for leadership of the special-interest groups were militant about their beliefs, and they backed up that militancy with generous donations. Even though the militant leadership was there, as was adequate financial support, the in-depth support for the Goldwater-Miller team from among the special-interst constituencies was missing.

Bibliography

McClosky, Herbert, and Harold E. Dahlgren. "Primary Group Influence on Party Loyalty," *American Political Science Review,* LIII (September 1959), 757-776.

Sorensen, Theodore C. *Kennedy*. New York: Harper, 1965. See especially pp. 175-177 and 188-195.

[16] F. Clifton White, *Suite 3505* (New Rochelle, N.Y.: Arlington House, 1967), p. 417.

[17] Shadegg, *What Happened to Goldwater?,* p. 188.

Chapter VIII

Presenting the Candidate

 A candidate's image can make him or break him. If he can convince the people that he understands and will respond to their wishes—as Dwight D. Eisenhower and Franklin D. Roosevelt were able to do—he can be unbeatable. If instead he appears aloof and cannot communicate with the citizens, he is headed for defeat.

THE STRATEGY OF IMAGE MAKING
AND NAME FAMILIARITY

What is "image" anyway? "Image" has a special meaning to political professionals. It refers to the impressions a candidate leaves with the public about his personality and his philosophy of government.

Personality can be all-important. The American people expect their President to be warm, outgoing, "human." He must enjoy people and be sensitive to their desires, concerns, and needs. This quality of empathy has marked all recent Presidents.

Next, a candidate for President must be virtuous. One major mark of virtue is having a happy family life, with an adoring wife and children, and even grandchildren. Honesty, trustworthiness, and a record of having opposed "machine" politicians are all substantial pluses in the background of a would-be presidential candidate. The virtue of a candidate is suspect if he has stooped to mudslinging or has accepted large sums of money or other substantial gifts.

Third, a candidate must be "big enough for the job." As some eastern politicians put it, he must have "heft." Fundamentally, being big means having experience, competence, wisdom, and understanding equal to the job. The candidate should have discharged some very important assignments with distinction. His personal actions should reveal maturity, and he should appear as an alert, adroit, and sensible person in his public appearances. Name-dropping, parading his achievements before others, being condescending to those whom he regards as beneath him, seeking honors and rewards beyond his merits are all negative traits to candidate connoisseurs and can be detrimental to the presidential aspirant. On the other hand, humility, modesty, concern, and sympathy for the problems of even the weakest of his fellowmen are traits generally respected in candidates for high political office.

A candidate's philosophy of government can also seal his fate. He must fit the times. If the times change (as they did for Herbert Hoover) and he does not change (as Hoover did not), defeat may follow.

Generally in American politics the moderate center has been the path to victory. Candidates of clearly liberal or conservative hue, like William Jennings Bryan and Alf Landon, have mounted interesting but disastrous campaigns. Yet, when the time is ripe, a candidate can take a bold position and lead the nation, as Lincoln did against secession and as Franklin D. Roosevelt did against depression.

Once a major candidate has created a firm public image of his public philosophy, he usually must live with it. This was true for Governor Nelson Rockefeller in his two efforts to obtain the Republican presidential nomination and equally important for Senator Goldwater during his preconvention and postconvention campaign in 1964.

"Name familiarity" is professional jargon used to describe the extent to which the general public knows even a candidate's name, let alone anything he stands for. It rests on the simple logic that a voter has to know at least the candidate's name before he can decide to vote for him.

Name familiarity is acquired by repetition. The more often a voter sees or hears a candidate's name, the more likely he is to remember it. The more he remembers the candidate's name, the more likely he is to remember other things about the candidate and, hopefully, the more likely he is to vote for him.

The psychological importance of repetition in making a name familiar to large numbers of people and the psychological importance of such familiarity with a name as a condition for an individual's identifying with it in some way have been well demonstrated by brand-name advertising. Nationally advertised products will be purchased, even at a higher price, by people who sincerely believe these products are better than unadvertised alternatives of higher quality.

The lessons of repetition in brand-name advertising have been given practical application by professional politicians. For the price of one 30-minute telecast which may attract but a limited viewing audience, a candidate can flash his name on the screen many times for many days in 20-second spot announcements which the viewing audience will be far more likely to see. All recent presidential candidates have used numerous spot announcements and have avoided formal 30-minute studio programs to present their names and views.

THE USE OF ADVERTISING AND THE MASS MEDIA

No presidential candidate can meet all the people. He must depend on advertising and the mass media to carry his name and his image to most of his fellow citizens.

Presidential candidates use the mass media to establish a public image in two main ways. They appear on television and radio, and they make news and buy advertising space in the press.

In 1960, the Republican National Committee employed Campaign Associates and the Democratic National Committee retained Guild, Bascom, and Bonfigli to handle national advertising for the presidential campaign. Both firms handled most of the time- and space-buying for their clients. Each party paid nearly a quarter of all its campaign expenditures to its advertising agency. The Republican National Committee paid out $2,269,578 while the Democratic National Committee spent $2,413,227.[1]

[1] Herbert E. Alexander, *Financing the 1960 Election* (Princeton, N.J.: Citizens' Research Foundation, 1962), p. 31.

Nevertheless, advertising agencies do not run national presidential campaigns. Some agencies do, however, suggest advertising programs which become a basic part of presidential campaigns.

In 1952, for example, Rosser Reeves, a representative of a small New York advertising firm, strongly recommended a television campaign for General Eisenhower featuring maximum penetration through the use of numerous short spot announcements. The General himself was to appear in each announcement.

Three basic arguments were advanced for such an innovation. The cost would be low per thousand homes reached. Spots, unlike full-length programs, would reach people not already for a candidate. Spots would allow concentrated efforts in the relatively few critical states which could not be counted in either candidate's column.

Reeves, a volunteer, got agreement on his plan from Walter Williams, the national chairman of Citizens for Eisenhower, and from John Hay Whitney, the chief fund raiser for the Eisenhower organization. Ultimately, 50 spot announcements of 20 seconds each were prepared, and approximately $1.5 million was spent on their presentation. The contents of the spots were statements of concern and general promises, each of which helped reinforce the favorable image of experience, kindliness, and sincerity which Eisenhower enjoyed as a result of his command positions during World War II.

Today, New York advertising agencies continue to remind political leaders who are interested of the fact that television can play a crucial role in any major election. Speaking to the Republican National Committee in January 1962, Carroll Newton, vice president of Batten, Barton, Durstine and Osborn, said:

It is estimated that 9 out of 10 homes in the United States will have television this fall, and that the average one of the homes will have a set tuned in with someone looking at it more than 5 hours every average day.

During the evening hours 6 out of 10 families are watching, with about 1.7 adults at the TV set at any given moment.

Assume there are three television stations in the city in which you reside, and assume that your candidate is on television at a particular minute between 8 and 9 in the evening on each of these stations. In that one television appearance, your candidate has shown himself—practically in the flesh—to more than half of the potential voters in his constituency.

And people seen on television are living, breathing, alive individuals to the viewers, even though the candidates themselves find that hard to believe as they look at that unwinking eye of the TV camera.

Television represents the sole opportunity of presenting a flesh-and-blood candidate to *all* the voters who will or will not elect him.

While it is not true that TV is the deciding factor in all elections, it *is* true that TV *can* make the difference in a close election.

In the first week of October, 1956, a national sample of 2,400 eligible voters was asked where they learned most about the campaign. The survey showed that TV was the most important source of information by a rather wide margin—49 per cent vs. 38 per cent for newspapers.

On the farm—it was TV by a substantial margin. 56 per cent of the farmers said they learned most about the campaign from TV. A significant breakdown was made by income groups. This indicated that as incomes decrease people rely more heavily on TV—and it is in lower income areas where the Republican party has traditionally had greater difficulty in attracting voters. Television was the major source of campaign information to 58 per cent of the people with average incomes.

At the time this study was made 37.7 million U.S. families had TV sets. It is estimated that more than 49 million families will have TV sets in October, 1962, and the importance of TV will be about 25% greater than these figures show.

These surveys strongly suggest that you cannot afford to allow your candidate to be seen at his best less often than his opponent.

The fact that television does exert a tremendous influence over voter choice may not be questioned by many today. But should it? Consider Washington, with his ill-fitting false teeth and smallpox scars; Lincoln, with his heavy features and warts; or Jefferson, often described as having "shifty eyes"—would they do well in a modern television-centered campaign? Was John Kennedy's handsome young face more important in his victory than his articulation of views on crucial issues? Or did Nixon's appearance on television detract from the content of his expositions?

Answers differ. But some reporters have recorded the fact that interviews with voters in the crucial Wisconsin and West Virginia primaries indicated a universally favorable reaction to John Kennedy's television appearances even if that reaction were grudging.

Certainly television imposes new demands and offers new opportunities to the individual politician. For the political party it means that it, too, has new responsibilities as well as opportunities.

Before the turn of the century, every effort was made to secure a candidate who was at ease in small groups of powerful political leaders and who also could be eloquently persuasive when facing a crowd of twelve to fifteen thousand people, many of whom would commit themselves following the speech or debate. In the 1960's, a party looks for a man who is at ease, articulate, and attractive when facing the television cameras and who likewise can spark the massive gatherings of a purely partisan nature. He must be an expositor as well as an orator.

Television is unquestionably extremely important in projecting the *symbolic* image of a candidate. Another kind of image, however, is of major concern to influential community leaders and hence to party strategists: the candidate's *instrumental* qualities. The symbolic image of a candidate is the voter's inference as to what kind of President the aspirant would make in general: his basic social and intellectual qualities. The instrumental image is the voter's inference as to what the candidate, as President, will do in certain substantive fields under various conditions.

The importance of the instrumental image has grown with the ever expanding number and variety of interest groups. While television exalts the factor of personality, the interest-group leader wants to know a candidate's views in a given area of political concern. The candidate must, then, from time to time eschew the capsule comment and the deliberate dodge. He must endeavor, instead, to spell out his over-all philosophy for a particular constituency. The occasion may come when the candidate speaks to the national convention of an interest group, or it may be made by the preparation and dissemination of policy statements.

THE GOLDWATER IMAGE PROBLEM IN 1964

There are two basic concepts of representation in modern democratic theory. One holds that public officials should represent their constituencies' thoughts and desires insofar as these can be ascertained. The second theory holds that elected officials represent their constituencies best by doing what they, the officials, feel is right and proper and in the interest of the citizens in their jurisdiction. The first view is generally associated with the French political philosopher Jean Jacques Rousseau (1712-1778) and his somewhat ambiguous theory of the "general will." The second theory was most forcefully presented by the English conservative, Edmund Burke (1729-1797).

The Rousseauistic philosophy can be said to characterize the American view of representation, even though for many public servants it may be only an inarticulate premise underlying their public acts. Such an approach fits the American pragmatic, win-oriented, arena-of-compromise party system. Hence it has become the modus operandi of most American political leaders. The question of a proper, popular image is critical to the elected official who accepts this Rousseauistic view. Hence the contemporary penchant for political-opinion polls and the constant desire on the part of office holders for a variety of indicators of the changing views of the electorate.

In 1962, when Ohio State Republican Chairman Ray Bliss conducted an in-depth study of what the voters wanted most in their candidates, the top-ranking requirement was an office holder who responded to the voters' needs and wishes. In their response to the Bliss poll, then, the voters gave support to their Rousseauistic views: Let the "general will" be known to and felt by the public official, and let him reflect that view in his public acts.

Senator Goldwater, however, did not accept this approach to public leadership. From the beginning of his political career he had stuck tenaciously to a Burkean conservatism, and this conflict between his personal philosophy of public leadership and the opposite view held by most American voters became a part of every issue and played a prominent role in Goldwater's personal campaign strategy and tactics.

Many commentators and political analysts have missed the significance of this point even though Goldwater acted out his concept of political leadership clearly and consistently during the entire campaign. He believed he must first examine the serious questions of the day, then attempt to instruct the voters on his answers to them, and finally, if elected, propose to direct the government as he saw fit until the electorate had an opportunity to assess his performance at the polls four years later.

Though this personal political philosophy was never really explicated as such, it was Goldwater's stubborn adherence to such a view of public leadership which inevitably placed him in a most difficult situation in the eyes of the press, made him an extremely vulnerable target for the Democrats, and finally ended in his great personal disappointment in the American electorate.

In short, Goldwater not only attempted to run a presidential campaign as if an ideological party system obtained in America; he also introduced into his campaign a theory of public leadership which ran counter to the views of most Americans.

Early manifestations of his Burkean approach were to be seen in Goldwater's preconvention sorties across the country. He felt it his obligation to inform, educate, and reform, rather than to listen, learn about, and reflect the views of the voters on major public issues. Hence his startling ruminations about social security among the aged in New Hampshire, his frank and negative appraisal of the Tennessee Valley Authority in the Tennessee Valley, and his blunt analysis of the war effort in Vietnam to a nation frustrated, frightened, and confused about international conflict in the nuclear age.

It was such a philosophy, too, which underlay his personal refusal to accept compromise at San Francisco on the attempts by moderate Republicans to amend the platform in the areas of civil rights and extremism. In his view the platform committee had studied the issues, stated its (and his) position, and given the American voter "a choice, not an echo." This, as he saw it, was honest, forthright politics and was consistent with his personal approach to public leadership.

Much can be said to defend the Goldwater-Burkean brand of conservatism. As developed by Goldwater it was evolutionary, in favor of the traditional liberties of American life as he understood them and believed in them, constitutionalist, and parliamentary.

Unfortunately for Goldwater, all of the conservatives in his camp were not Burkeans. Although sharing some of his views, they departed from the Burkean approach to political life in several important areas. In terms of historical political thought many of his supporters were closer to the more extreme brand of conservatism most often linked to Joseph de Maistre (1753-1821). This type of conservatism, like Burke's, favors tradition as against innovation. But the Burkean fights innovation for the sake of traditional liberties; those of the de Maistre school, for the sake of traditional authority. The latter group tends away from constitutionalism and toward authoritarianism, although to cast this philosophy in a totalitarian light is to go much too far.

In any case it was from this group of de Maistre conservatives that Goldwater's public image of intransigence and political polarity received additional support. Furthermore, it was from the activities of members of this group that the public began to raise additional doubts about the Senator's suitability for the American presidency.

What Goldwater's image projection represents, in American political life, was not a new "privatization" of politics, as some political scientists have suggested.[2] The explanation is a simpler one. It is an example, par excellence, of a Burkean running for the highest executive office in a country where Burkean principles when practiced at all, are practiced successfully only at the congressional, state-legislative, county-board, or city-council level. In short, Goldwater was attempting to apply to an American presidential campaign the same theory of representation which had served him well in elective legislative positions but which was highly inappropriate for a national executive office.

Consequently, out of his adherence to this philosophy came an entirely different kind of image from the image Goldwater had as a local and national legislator. That image, however unfortunate, was an accurate characterization of the Burkean spirit which lay behind each campaign utterance and act. Like Burke, he had written numerous statements covering his positions on various issues of the day. This meant of course that his flexibility in response to the changing dimensions of contemporary problems was considerably diminished. But, far from attempting to escape these earlier position statements, he brought them to the attention of his nationwide audience again and again throughout the campaign.

[2] Aaron Wildavsky, quoted in *Ripon Society Report* (Cambridge, Mass.: Ripon Society, 1965), p. 13.

Theodore White's statement that "the fundamental Goldwater problem was himself"[3] was thus not without its truth. There were other problems, however, which created an unfavorable image for Goldwater. The working reporters, for example, did not, in the main, understand Goldwater or the philosophic premises underlying his campaign. As a result, he was subjected to an unusual amount of harsh treatment in the press. White has stated:

. . . never in any campaign had I seen the candidate so heckled, so provoked by opposition demonstrations . . . so cruelly bill-boarded and tagged . . . for the fact was that Goldwater was running not so much against Johnson as against himself—or the Barry Goldwater the image-makers had created. Rockefeller and Scranton had drawn up the indictment. Lyndon Johnson was the prosecutor. Goldwater was cast as defendant. He was like a dog with a can tied to his tail—the faster he ran, the more the can clattered.[4]

The *Cincinnati Enquirer,* in its statement of endorsement for Goldwater, blamed the Democratic Party for an unfair image of Goldwater:

Barry Goldwater has become the most slandered man in American political history . . . he is portrayed as a poisoner of children, as a creature of the nightriders, as a pawn of the militarists and the warmongers.[5]

Beyond his Burkean philosophy, the treatment of the press, and the effective job of negative image building done by the opposition party, Goldwater suffered yet a fourth major problem in image projection. He had surrendered the initiative, the offensive, to the opposition on every major issue of the day. Even the campaign slogan was defensive, "In Your Heart You Know He's Right." It was as if the advertising agency itself, which created the slogan, sought justification for their connection with the campaign. This defensive posture assumed by Goldwater was ironic in that he had always insisted that one could never win a defensive battle.

But why could not an image of an irresponsible, callous, anti-

---

[3] Theodore H. White, *The Making of the President, 1964* (New York: Atheneum, 1965), p. 328.
[4] *Ibid.*
[5] *Cincinnati Enquirer,* editorial page, September 29, 1964.

civil-rights militarist whose political bedfellows were mainly from the radical right be corrected? Surely he had answers to give and the funds to disseminate these answers, and surely the nation waited for an explication of his side of the campaign story.

Even though Goldwater had evoked deep concern when he had suggested possible use of low-yield tactical bombs in the Vietnam conflict and when he had suggested that the use of such tactical aid weapons be put at the disposal of field commanders, he was not without recourse, in kind, when a Democratic television advertisement strongly suggested his election could bring the death of little girls picking daisies.

He could have explained more effectively his questioning of the social-security funding and dissipated the fear that had developed from his earlier remarks about the sale of the Tennessee Valley Authority. And if Goldwater had vacillated in his support of various civil-rights programs over the years, his over-all record in this field was at least as impressive as that of Johnson.

The accusation that he was a creature of the radical right could have been partially refuted by revealing his order to exclude every member of the John Birch Society from leadership positions in the Goldwater campaign.[6]

His response to each of these major issues was amazingly bland—bland, that is, if his candidacy is viewed from the usual philosophic orientation of an American presidential candidate. His response is understandable from a Burkean viewpoint.

It is true that once a public figure has been stereotyped, it is difficult for him to change his instrumental image. Yet it is not impossible. Truman did it. Johnson himself obliterated a negative civil-rights voting record and image by becoming the champion of civil-rights legislation during his presidential tenure in 1963-1964.

Indeed, modern mass communications has made image changing relatively easy for the skilled manipulator of public opinion. But the image makers cannot remake the image of a person who does not desire, or at least acquiesce in, an image change. Goldwater, then, was not really running against himself. He was running

[6] Stephen Shadegg, *What Happened to Goldwater?* (New York: Holt, 1965), p. 105.

against a whole American tradition which is contrary to the aloofness, the detachment, the objectivity of a Burkean conservative.

During the heat of the campaign he continued to state his position on Medicare and social security, to question governmental ownership of TVA, and to express doubt over the farm price-support system. When Goldwater attempted to take the offensive by outlining the basic difference between his position and Johnson's on such issues as the draft, taxation, the Supreme Court, national defense, and civil rights, the press had already determined what he was going to say and that is the way they reported it.

It was as if the press who saw Goldwater go into the campaign as a Burkean wanted him to remain one. And Goldwater was indeed happiest when he remained what he was. In fact, time and time again he refused to be otherwise. In a major television show on September 27, 1964, Eisenhower and Goldwater talked of the question of nuclear war and the allegation that Goldwater wished to use the A-bomb in Vietnam. But it was an academic, casual discussion, not a political, polemic, hard-hitting effort to set the American voter's mind at rest on this crucial issue.

On occasion after occasion Goldwater had lectured—even scolded—audiences on their attitude toward the American presidency. In city after city Goldwater had refused to touch the highly explosive civil-rights question, though many argued he should exploit the unrest and dissatisfaction with the way in which the civil-rights program was being handled. Theodore White called it a "highly responsible position."[7]

Indeed, much in the tradition of an ideologue and a Burkean, Goldwater was happiest when he spoke of abstract things. He felt at home in extended discussions about freedom and about governmental incursions upon that freedom. He was not comfortable advancing some of the programs, such as the abolition of the draft, and thus seldom repeated this plan which had, in fact, caused some favorable reaction where it had been suggested. As White has put it, "Here was no ordinary politician itching for votes. He was on a crusade to free America from enslavement."[8]

[7] White, *The Making of the President, 1964,* p. 390.
[8] *Ibid.,* p. 391.

But his crusade went beyond the freedom argument. Much in the manner of a religious leader, he was concerned with the deterioration of the quality of American life, and he spoke at length about these concerns to audiences wanting answers to immediate, basic economic and political problems.

Though Goldwater can be credited with being a Burkean conservative in an alien political environment, this does not mean that he was an effective Burkean leader. Had he been a true Burkean, he would have taken the offensive on many of these issues and developed constructive alternatives to the Democratic administration's programs. This Goldwater did not do. He did not effectively explicate the strong conservative case which could have been made.

More damaging, however, was the fact that even though he and his immediate staff made every effort to avoid extremist tactics and associations, some of both occurred and were well publicized. And even though these were not of his making, they added credence to the charges of irresponsibility and unresponsiveness upon which the Democrats had pegged their entire campaign against him.

Most writers, even those friendly to Goldwater, admit also that Goldwater's press relations were not the best. F. Clifton White, the director of the citizens organization, states:

In fairness to the working press, however, it must be noted that neither the candidate nor his staff went out of their way to endear themselves to reporters. Towards the end, the Senator unbent a bit and on occasion, succeeded in re-establishing the old easy camaraderie he had once enjoyed with the press. But many members of his staff remained arrogantly standoffish towards newsmen till the bitter end. Perhaps they just gave up when they saw that no matter what they or the Senator did, he would be violently gored by the media men.[9]

Goldwater's efforts to attempt to improve his image through television were well planned and well financed. The Goldwater television plan seemed, in September, to be well organized. The Republicans had employed Lou Guylay as their public-relations director, and Guylay in turn had retained the services of the

[9] F. Clifton White, *Suite 3505* (New Rochelle, N.Y.: Arlington House, 1967), p. 412.

mammoth Interpublic Group public-relations firm of New York. A special task force was set up with the most sophisticated techniques available to analyze the last three national campaigns and to design the most effective television campaign possible based on the information that could be fed into and extracted from the computer. Theodore White says that "1,700,000,000 bits of information were fed through the computers in this effort."[10] In order to bring the candidate and the issues to the people, five major half-hour television shows on national networks were scheduled: two, on October 6 and October 13, on NBC; and three, on October 20, October 29, and November 2, on CBS. Each of these was to be a key television appearance addressing itself to one of the major issues of the campaign.

In a memorandum to interested campaign personnel, Guylay suggested that political rallies should be organized around these television programs in various cities in the country. There was a suggestion that each of the television speeches be made live from a political rally for Goldwater. The "think tank," however, objected to this procedure, and this approach was not used. In the end, television programs reached relatively small audiences. Whereas the television debates between Nixon and Kennedy had drawn more than 100 million listeners, the Goldwater television presentations never topped the 7-million mark, and it was suspected that these listeners were mostly those already committed to the Goldwater candidacy.

The problem for Goldwater was indeed an image problem—not that he could not remake the image, but that in some respects he did not want to be other than he had always been in political life. Even when he tried, toward the end of the campaign, to respond to the new challenges and demands of a national campaign for executive office, many of his close followers and supporters did not allow him to depart from the Burkean tradition which he had so long embraced. Nor did the press, which saddled him throughout the campaign with his earlier pronouncements and positions. The result was not the image of a successful presidential candidate. The results reflected the difficulty for a working conservative to run in a Rousseauistic, win-oriented party environment.

[10] White, *The Making of the President, 1964*, p. 383.

PRESENTING RICHARD NIXON IN 1960

As Richard M. Nixon prepared for the 1960 presidential campaign, his image was a matter of major concern. There were many favorable aspects. Among them were his impassioned rebuttal to Premier Khrushchev, in the famous Moscow "kitchen debate"; his unflinching courage in the face of a barrage of rocks, sticks, and human spit during his tour of Latin America; his intelligent handling of the affairs of state during President Eisenhower's illnesses; his stubborn insistence on following through on every lead given him in the famous Hiss case. Nixon's advisors felt that these aspects of his image should be reinforced.

But another side was negative. It reflected the strong reactions to some of the tactics Nixon employed during his first campaigns for the House and for the Senate, the charge of having used unfair accusations against opponents in both campaigns. He had been labeled by some as the "parlor McCarthy," and the label and the image stuck.

Nixon's biographers have pointed out that the complete story of his House and Senate campaigns is involved and two-sided. There was no denying, however, that Nixon's campaign tactics in those races had antagonized a sizable proportion of the so-called community-thought leaders across the nation—people Nixon wished to win over to his side. The problem, as characterized by a popular song, became one of "accentuating the positive and eliminating the negative." Several tactical steps were involved.

The first, taken long before the convention, was the issuance from the Volunteers for Nixon offices of a set of question-and-answer sheets on the following topics: civil rights, economic policy and philosophy, Africa, social welfare, labor, Latin America, education, national defense and security, international Communism, agriculture, economic growth through freedom, why we should study Communism, national resources, the steel-strike settlement, politics, and some "off-the-record" comments. The tone of these succinct statements (five to twelve pages each) is scholarly, and the political position—insofar as one can be inferred from such a variety of topics—is what might best be described as

"moderate liberal" or what some have termed "liberal conservative."

These papers were released in a packet entitled *Become Better
Acquainted with Richard Nixon.* Their chief purpose was to impress thought leaders in particular with the Vice President's
breadth and depth of vision and to reveal his concern over the
major issues of the day and his reasonable position on them.

The second step was Nixon's choice of his running mate. Although the selection of the vice-presidential candidate is usually a
matter of "balancing the ticket" geographically and ideologically, it
was more than that for Nixon in 1960. His personal choice of
Henry Cabot Lodge reflected how deeply he felt about conveying
an image of ethical responsibility. Nixon knew that community
leaders saw in Lodge not only a respected internationalist but also
the Republican on the 1950 Tydings subcommittee investigating
Senator McCarthy's charges of Communists in government who
had filed a strong minority report critical both of Democratic
laxness and of his Republican colleague's unfounded accusations.
Thus the selection of Lodge can be interpreted as another action
calculated to help improve Nixon's position with certain groups
whose support was in question.

The third step was Nixon's decision to develop a dual campaign
organization. Impressed with his need for a strong showing among
the independents and the need to capture a sizable Democratic
vote in addition to maintaining virtually all of the Republican
support, the Vice President had determined to call his campaign
signals from the Nixon-Lodge Volunteers headquarters rather than
from the national committee (see Chapter V). He made this
decision in part because he felt that many independents and many
Democrats were anxious to work for his election but that most of
these volunteers would refuse to work out of a regular Republican
headquarters. Perhaps he felt that a campaign planned and administered by professional partisans would be less helpful to the creation of a strong image as a candidate of all the people than would a
campaign planned and administered by relative amateurs representing independents and Democrats as well as his own party.

A fourth tactical step, aimed like the first at improving his instrumental image, was the issuance of a series of what were called "position papers" on the major issues of the day. The first of these was published on August 31, 1960, and the last about the middle of October. These policy statements were prepared essentially for the nation's thought leaders and, according to the field of interest, were dispatched promptly to interested respondents of the mass mailings to special-interest groups.

Although the ideological position taken in these papers represented the thinking of the Vice President, members of an impressive Policy Advisory Board went over the content of these statements with Nixon. The board consisted in part of such academic notables as Henry Ahlgren, director of Wisconsin's Agricultural Extension School; John Burchard, dean of M.I.T.'s School of Humanities and Social Sciences; Arthur Burns, economist from Columbia; Paul Cherrington of the Harvard School of Business Administration; William Y. Elliot, professor of government at Harvard; Lon Fuller, Harvard Law School; John Hannah, president of Michigan State University; Joseph Kaplan, professor of physics at the University of California, Los Angeles; Lawrence Kimpton, chancellor at the University of Chicago; and Philip Thayer, dean of the School of Advanced Studies at Johns Hopkins University. Industry and applied science contributed Marion Folsom, former president of Eastman Kodak; John Heller, director of the New England Institute of Medical Research; Charles Percy, president of Bell and Howell; David Sarnoff, board chairman of the Radio Corporation of America; Leonard Scheele, former U.S. Surgeon General; and Robert Sprague, president of Sprague Electric.[11]

The papers issued were not as numerous as originally planned.

---

[11] This list of advisors necessitates taking note of the perennial question about presidential politics: Who were the speech writers? Although several people in, around, and outside the Republican National Committee and the Nixon campaign headquarters wrote speeches, no complete speeches were ever written for the Vice President. He wrote his own.

That is not to deny that there were trusted lieutenants who did basic research and even turned a phrase or two. Some of the personalities assigned to this task in the 1960 campaign were well-known writers; others were not. Charles Lichtenstein, a young political scientist from Notre Dame, was said by some to have been the phrasemaker in the Nixon research inner circle. Dr. George Grassmuck, an international-relations expert from the

The pamphlets which were produced covered the meaning of communism to Americans, national purpose, education, the scientific revolution, housing, and medical research. The composition of the policy board itself and the scholarly approach to these topics gave additional proof that these were not only policy papers; they were papers designed to convince the recipients that the Republican candidate was thoughtful and well informed and that if he were to become President he would surely be advised by highly qualified leaders from American academic and business life.

Image-building considerations contributed to Nixon's decision to carry his campaign to each of the 50 states and fitted with his strong compulsion to present himself personally to as many people as possible. Perhaps this compulsion was also an important element in his decision to debate Senator Kennedy.

It is impossible, of course, to say that the above steps were taken wholly for the purpose of strengthening Nixon's instrumental image and chipping off the rough edges of his symbolic image. Similarly, the steps taken to reinforce his areas of strength were undoubtedly informational as well as image-centered.

The general campaign literature clearly reflects image orientation, as indeed does most campaign literature. The most elaborate mailing piece, for example, was thirty-two pages on newsprint in the *Life-Look* type of magazine format. On the cover appeared a warm and friendly Nixon. Eisenhower's letter of endorsement and a picture of the two in serious conversation followed. Then came a

---

University of Michigan, was director of research, with the assistance of James Shepley from the *Time-Life* organization and John Hamlin from the White House.

Dr. William Peterson, a New York University economist; Charles Kline, a New York political publicist; John Franklin Carter, a newspaperman; and Dr. John Hiller, a Rockefeller Foundation medical researcher, along with Lichtenstein, were the basic drafters of the position papers and of many of the press releases which emanated from the Nixon-Lodge brain trust.

At the national committee, research assignments received from the Nixon-Lodge headquarters were handled by Dr. William Prendergast, then newly appointed to the research directorship of the national-committee staff. Additional assistance was given by Oliver Gale, former assistant to the Secretary of Defense, who was formally assigned to the "answer desk" at the committee but whose actual duties ranged far afield.

It must be iterated, however, that despite all of this talent, the speeches were finally fashioned by the candidate himself.

pictorial history of Nixon's family, his boyhood, his service in the Navy, as a member of the House of Representatives, as a Senator, and as the nation's most active Vice President. Thirteen of the remaining sixteen pages were devoted to Nixon's experiences in both domestic affairs and international relations. Finally, three pages were devoted to the Nixon-Lodge team and the campaign itself.

Republican and Nixon special-interest-group organizations geared their campaign propaganda to the Vice President's record and to his statements of position in their field. Basic explications which had been prepared for the questions-and-answers packet were woven into special August and September publications for veterans, farmers, laborers, new voters, senior citizens, academicians, Negroes, businessmen, scientists, and nationality groups. Film clips, too, which showed the Vice President debating Khrushchev, touring Latin America, or serving in Eisenhower's absence, were made a part of longer motion-picture presentations for special-interest audiences. These efforts were essentially designed for instrumental-image purposes, whereas the general materials were basically symbolic in nature.

Did Nixon succeed in his extensive efforts to "accentuate the positive and eliminate the negative"? It is true that he lost the election. Many would insist, however, that despite his organizational shortcomings, the basic conceptualization of image projection employed by the Vice President was appropriate to his needs and to the time. It must be remembered when looking back at 1960 and looking forward to 1968 that the methods employed by Nixon brought him within a hair's breadth of winning the presidency.

PRESENTING PRESIDENT JOHNSON IN 1964

President Lyndon B. Johnson entered the 1964 campaign with overwhelming political advantages. So great, indeed, were his advantages that no candidate the Republican Party could have named could have hoped to defeat him in the election.

Sympathy was his basic asset. The nation still mourned the tragic loss of its young President less than a year before, and Johnson, as his chosen heir, drew to himself the emotional response of the American people. Kennedy had been struck down in his prime, before his dreams could be realized. Johnson immediately had promised to make them come true; the public's reply was to give him that chance.

Yet he had many other major assets of his own—enough to have been a most formidable candidate without the sympathy vote. No other name was better known to the American electorate. Senate Majority Leader since 1955, Vice President since 1961, and then Chief Executive, he had kept his name a household word for a decade.

In political experience he had few peers. Twenty-four years in Congress, eight as the extraordinarily successful leader of the Democratic Party in the Senate, and three years as Vice President had afforded him maturity and experience which his opponent could not begin to match.

He was a Protestant who had loyally supported a Catholic President. He faced no religious issue.

Ideologically, he was a moderate who often had voted with the conservative South, but who also had been a staunch New Dealer in the 1930's and who still carried the torch of progressivism and reform. Thus he could appeal to business as could few national Democratic leaders, and yet he could aspire to lead the entirety of his party.

To solve any problem of his ideological image, Johnson adroitly selected Senator Hubert Humphrey as his running mate. As the leader of the liberal wing of the Democratic Party, Humphrey was the unquestioned champion of all the causes which had moved the liberal Democrats since World War II. With Humphrey as his chosen heir, who could doubt Johnson's dedication to action for change?

As a platform speaker and a television personality, however, the President proved ineffective. His style and presentation came through flat, almost dull. Yet for these liabilities he was pardoned by the voters, who were more concerned about matters of substance.

Johnson's sole significant problem of image was his sectional background. Despite his Senate leadership and despite his service as Vice President and as President, he still appeared to the American people as a Southerner. And no Southerner had been elected President since the Civil War.[12]

To build an image as a national leader, President Johnson had to show real concern for national problems and especially for the problems of the industrial Northeast, the agricultural Midwest, and the natural-resources-conscious Far West.

In the months before the national convention, he sought first to prove the sincerity of his promise to make the Kennedy dreams come true and the breadth of his own concerns for the nation as a whole by using his unquestioned skills as a legislative leader to win from Congress as much of the Kennedy domestic program as he could. A major tax reduction to spur economic growth sailed through Congress in the first six weeks of the 1964 session. Business was pleased. The civil-rights bill followed after a bitter fight in the Senate. He declared war on poverty and appointed Sargent Shriver to lead the crusade. Congress responded with the Economic Opportunity Act. An urban mass-transit program amounting to $375 million became law. The North and especially its city dwellers and its minority groups were delighted. Then, to the pleasure of the West and of conservationists nationwide, he secured two long-sought measures, the wilderness act and the land and water conservation fund act. As frosting for the conservation cake, Congress added the Canyonlands National Park and the Fire Island National Seashore. All 51 Kennedy priority measures passed the Senate.

Two key proposals eluded Johnson's grasp in the House of Representatives, but afforded him strong appeals to the national electorate: federal aid to education and medicare. "Give me an increased majority," he could say, "and I will deliver these, too." And he did.

Second, he presented a challenging new national goal for America in the twentieth century—the Great Society. Addressing a

[12] The only other citizen of a Confederate state to hold the presidency, Andrew Johnson, was a Union Democrat fom eastern Tennessee who was Lincoln's running mate in 1864 and who served out Lincoln's term after the assassination.

University of Michigan audience at Ann Arbor on May 20, 1964, he declared:

The challenge of the next half century is whether we have the wisdom to use wealth to enrich and elevate our national life—and to advance the quality of American civilization—for in your time we have the opportunity to move not only toward the rich society and the powerful society but upward to the Great Society.

. . . The Great Society rests on abundance and liberty for all. It demands an end to poverty and racial injustice—to which we are totally committed in our time, but that is just the beginning. The Great Society is a place where every child can find knowledge to enrich his mind and enlarge his talents. It is a place where leisure is a welcome chance to build and reflect, not a feared cause of boredom and restlessness. It is a place where the city of man serves not only the needs of the body and the demands of commerce, but the desire for beauty and the hunger for community. It is a place where man can renew contact with nature. It is a place which honors creation for its own sake, and for what it adds to the understanding of the race. It is a place where men are more concerned with the quality of their goals than the quantity of their goods. But most of all, the Great Society is not a safe harbor, a resting place, a final objective, a finished work. It is a challenge constantly renewed, beckoning us toward a destiny where the meaning of our lives matches the marvelous products of our labor.

Third, with the convention, the President turned to a new central theme: consensus. Exploiting his opponent's narrow ideological commitment, Johnson welcomed all Americans to his banner and spoke of united action to meet the varied problems of all Americans. That, he said at Madison Square Garden in New York City, "is the Great Society—concern for the quality of the life of each person in America." All across the land he sounded the unity theme. On October 11, at Washington Square in San Francisco, he said:

The meaning of America for us all is opportunity. When divisions arise, when suspicions flourish, when hatred flowers, opportunity perishes and passes away. On this day, when we honor our heritage as free men and a peaceful nation, I ask of you, I ask of all of you as Americans, that we pledge ourselves to stand up and be counted for the best in America, because when you do what is best for America, you do what is best for yourselves.

So I hope you will always remember, I pray you will never forget, that we should stand together for an America that knows no hate, that condones no division, that remembers no North or no South, or no East or no West, but steers its course only by the fixed stars of peace, of freedom, and of justice to all people.[13]

Fourth, the President capitalized upon his responsibility for foreign policy. Intrinsically a national matter, the complex international situation offered Johnson an ideal medium to assert national leadership. Not only on the coasts, but also in the traditionally isolationist heartland of America, he spoke of peace and international relations. At Casper, Wyoming, for example, he declared:

The most important single thing in your life is peace, peace at home, peace in the world. In the 10 months since I have been President, I have conferred with 85 of the world's leaders. I have tried to reason with them. I have tried to plan with them . . . I am . . . willing to go anywhere, see anyone, talk any time to try to bring peace to this world so these mothers will not have to give up their boys and have them wiped out in a nuclear holocaust.[14]

On October 15 he celebrated the first anniversary of the nuclear test-ban treaty in a nationwide telecast.

Fifth, in its publicity and publications, the national committee portrayed the President as a national leader. Its slogans were "L.B.J. for the U.S.A." and "Johnson and Humphrey for the U.S.A." It took advantage, for example, of the swing to Johnson among the leading newspapers by issuing *The Nation Speaks Out for the President,* a collection of editorial endorsements of the Johnson-Humphrey ticket. Across the photocopied editorials of newspapers which had backed the Republican nominee four years earlier, the committee overprinted "Nixon-60." The key quotation, from the *New York Herald Tribune,* told the story:

So far as these two candidates are concerned, our inescapable choice—as a newspaper that was Republican before there was a Re-

---

[13] *The President Speaks to the People,* Vol. II (Washington: Democratic National Committee, 1964), p. 60.

[14] *Ibid.,* pp. 67-68.

publican party, has been Republican ever since and will remain Republican—is Lyndon B. Johnson.

The committee also emphasized Johnson's fitness for national office: "Can-do leadership for strength, responsibility, compassion" was its theme.

More convincing to the rest of the nation, perhaps, than anything Johnson or the Democratic Party did was his rejection by the deep South. To the segregationists, Johnson was a heretic—one of their own who had foresaken the southern cause. Their embrace of Goldwater confirmed the national basis of Johnson's leadership.

Thus did Lyndon B. Johnson shed his sectional label and become the first southern political leader to win the presidency since the Civil War.

THE JENKINS INCIDENT

Only once during the campaign was Johnson's image seriously threatened. On Tuesday evening, October 13, the President's top personal staff advisor, Walter W. Jenkins, was arrested on a morals charge in the men's room at the downtown Washington YMCA. The next morning, Washington newspapers picked up the story on a tip from an unidentified caller and verified the facts. Several hours passed while discussions were held between attorneys for Jenkins and Washington newspapers. Jenkins was sent to the hospital suffering from exhaustion, and the President was finally notified, sometime between 5 and 7 p.m. In midevening the 14th, the story was carried on the press wires.

The next morning found gloom spread thickly over the Democratic National Committee. Goldwater obviously had been handed the headlines for days to come to press his issue of "corruption in the highest circles." Bobby Baker was now second-rate stuff.[15]

Fate, however, had other designs. Three major international events were to occur in the next 24 hours which were to toss the headlines to the President and wipe the Jenkins story out of the campaign.

---

[15] Baker, a long-time aide to the Senate Majority Leader, had resigned under fire amid accusations that he had misused his office for personal gain. In 1967 he was convicted on seven counts, among them larceny and income-tax evasion.

First came the Russians. Early Thursday the Communist Party replaced Prime Minister Khrushchev in the most dramatic change of dictators in its entire history.

Next came the British. That same day they elected a Labor Government, turning the Conservatives out of office after 13 years in power.

Then, on Friday, the Chinese Communists set off their first atomic explosion.

Johnson, buoyed by cheering New York City crowds numbering in the millions, seized the initiative. On Sunday evening, October 18, at 8:30—when the greatest possible viewing audience would be available—he made a dramatic nationwide television report on the meaning to the United States of these great international events. Warning Peking that the United States would defend any nonnuclear nation against atomic blackmail from Communist China, Johnson stole all headlines on Monday.

Monday morning, Republican Chairman Dean Burch demanded "equal time," only to receive a firm denial from the Federal Communications Commission, which ruled that, as President Eisenhower had done during the 1956 campaign, the President was entitled to report to the nation on major international developments.

Then, on Tuesday, Herbert Hoover passed away in his ninetieth year. When Goldwater stole his own headlines on Wednesday by scrapping a highly controversial "morality" film, *Choice,* the Jenkins case was already a matter for an FBI report. Mrs. Johnson further smoothed the waters with a well-received expression of great personal sympathy for the Jenkins family. Released from the hospital, Jenkins quietly resigned. By Election Day he and his case had been forgotten.

THE ATTACK ON GOLDWATER

Presidential candidates rarely attack their opponents. Repeated studies have shown that the American people prefer to believe that any man who can win a major-party nomination for President is worthy of that office. Thus an attack on the competence or judgment of an opponent risks backfire.

In 1964 however, Senator Goldwater presented a target too

inviting to pass up. His many ill-chosen statements and the intemperance of many of his supporters offered ample opportunity to question his capacity to lead the nation.

Both President Johnson and the Democratic National Committee therefore decided that Mr. Goldwater was vulnerable—that direct attack on his judgment and his competence would be believable by the voters.

The Democratic attack took three themes: First, Goldwater was "trigger-happy"; he would lead the nation into nuclear war. Second, Goldwater was reactionary; he would try to undo the social and economic legislation of the New Deal and later. Third, Goldwater was irresponsible, welcomed the support of irresponsible extremists, and would be extreme himself. As ammunition, the Democrats used Goldwater's own statements and pamphlets, which proved a goldmine for political dynamiters.

The "trigger-happy" charge was easily built up from two basic Goldwater quotations. Most-used was a statement reported in the *New Republic* of July 25, 1964:

I would not use atomic weapons when conventional weapons will do the job. But I would leave it up to the commanders.

Democrats also widely quoted from an official Goldwater release:

The Supreme Commander of the North Atlantic Treaty Organization . . . should have direct command over a NATO nuclear force . . . A nuclear NATO could meet local invasions on the spot, with local tactical nuclear weapons.[16]

The Democratic National Committee exploited the issue with pamphlets[17] and a television spot announcement showing a nuclear cloud rising from a test explosion accompanied by a voice suggesting that the President, not a field commander, should decide when the weapon should be used.

Goldwater had no ready defense against such attack. The more

[16] Citizens for Goldwater-Miller Committee, *Barry Goldwater Speaks Out on the Issues*, pp. 4-5. See, for example, the use of the quotation in Scientists and Engineers for Johnson and Humphrey, *The Alternative Is Frightening*, pp. 7-8.

[17] See *A Goldwater Primer* (Washington: Democratic National Committee, 1964). The parts were "Goldwater Inconsistencies, Goldwater Votes, Barry the Bomber, Ye Good Old Dayes, Goldwater Domestic Record."

he tried to answer, the deeper he entangled himself in the issue.

Once the "trigger-happy" charge was widely believed, the President himself used it. At Madison Square Garden in New York, for example, he declared:

> But peace at home will be of little value if an impulsive thumb moves up toward the button that can destroy 300 million people in a matter of moments. Peace at home and prosperity among our people will get us nowhere if we have a government by ultimatum, and we bluff about our bombs, and we rattle our rockets around until we get into a destructive war.

The "reactionary" issue used many threads. Lyndon Johnson himself wove them together. On October 8, at Cleveland, Ohio, he described the sharp contrast of political philosophy in the campaign:

> So, the domestic issue is whether we are going to wipe out, and throw away, that program of 30 years under five Presidents.
>
> The argument [is] to go back, to repeal the present, to veto the future . . .
>
> And what do they say they are against?
>
> —They would abolish the graduated income tax.
>
> —They would destroy the whole basis for Social Security, by making it voluntary . . .
>
> They would sell the TVA . . .
>
> They would end all foreign commodity programs.
>
> They would withdraw from our responsibilities in the United Nations.
>
> They would oppose the agreement of 105 nations to stop nuclear bomb tests.[18]

The national committee gleefully took up the refrain. Most telling of all its ads was a television spot announcement showing a pair of hands tearing up a social-security card. A spoken message told the viewer that the opposition would like to end social security, but that President Johnson would defend and extend it.

Goldwater presented the "extremism" issue to the Democrats ready-made in his acceptance speech at the Republican National Convention:

[18] *The President Speaks to the People,* p. 37.

Any who join us in all sincerity, we welcome. Those who do not care for our cause we do not expect to enter our ranks in any case.

And let our Republicanism, so focused and so dedicated, not be made fuzzy and futile by unthinking labels.

Extremism in the defense of liberty is no vice. Moderation in the pursuit of justice is no virtue.

The Democrats had only to repeat these words to scare not only their own stalwarts but moderate Republicans as well.

In summary, then, the Johnson appeal of 1964 drew upon the sympathy of the American people, presented an established political personality, invited support from a wide range of interests, demonstrated national and international leadership, and attacked a vulnerable opponent. Its success, however, was due only in part to Democratic efforts. The Goldwater campaign helped significantly.

By presenting an ultraconservative image and by inviting moderates to leave his cause, Goldwater handed Johnson the center of the political stage and consigned himself to the right wing. By injudicious attacks on established institutions like the Tennessee Valley Authority and social security, in which a great many people had a stake, he alienated votes he need not have lost. By imprudent statements on foreign affairs, especially on the use of nuclear weapons, he created an impression of rashness and inexperience. By appealing for southern support, he alienated the Negroes and other minority groups. The Johnson "landslide," then, was a combination of Johnson's use of his own advantages and the mistakes and weaknesses of his opponent. No candidate of either party is likely soon again to have so favorable a situation as did Lyndon B. Johnson in 1964.

CREATING THE KENNEDY IMAGE IN 1960

In 1960, John F. Kennedy faced two basic problems of public relations which his successor never had to meet. He had served in relative obscurity in Congress and had to become known. His youthful appearance and lack of major political assignments created an impression of immaturity and inexperience which he had to overcome.

He had, on the other hand, some very great assets. Being relatively unknown, he was free to build a national image geared to the times. His voting record was moderately liberal, and he could convincingly demand action on programs falling in the broad center of the political spectrum. He was bright and quick, able to speed-read three times as fast as the average person, and could examine and absorb a huge volume of complex position papers to lend depth to his public statements. He was handsome, had a good sense of humor, and made a warm and appealing figure on television and on the speaker's platform.

He also had a three-year-old daughter and a young and very attractive wife who was expecting their second child. History offered no clues on the use of these latter assets, however, for they are the assets of a young man and presidential candidates had never been this young. They could not barnstorm with him, however, and courtesy to his audiences soon required him to offer some explanation. Theodore White, who accompanied John Kennedy on his first western trip in September, has told the story of how Kennedy learned that his young family was a political asset:

> Out of his sense of privacy, Kennedy had omitted mentioning his wife or her pregnant condition in the early days of his campaign—and a tribute to the wife is rigidly required in American political orthodoxy. Then, one noon in the warm sun in the little park behind the gleaming color-splashed courthouse of Eugene, Oregon, he impulsively offered the courteous excuse that his wife was absent because she was "otherwise committed." A friendly ripple of laughter followed. The next morning, in northern California, he had changed it to "My wife has other responsibilities," and a warmer laugh followed. By afternoon the phrase had become a forthright "My wife is going to have a baby." In the San Joaquin valley the next day it was "My wife is going to have a boy in November." It had become a certified gag; and that afternoon in Los Angeles, it became a press-conference question that ended a tense interchange of questions on religion. "How do you know it's going to be a boy?" asked the questioner. "My wife told me," said Kennedy, and the conference ended with a laugh.[19]

Youth, then, was not his problem. Name familiarity he could gain with advertising, by barnstorming, and by debating the Vice President. His real needs were to establish that he was mature and

[19] Theodore H. White, *The Making of the President, 1960* (New York: Atheneum, 1961), pp. 306-307.

experienced and that he was a moderate liberal who wanted action.

Kennedy, of course, carried the main burden of image building himself. For support he established four major units of the national committee: the Kennedy Research Team, under Myer Feldman; the Kennedy Speech Writers' Division, under Archibald Cox; the Research Division, under Robert Oshins; and the Publicity Division, under Roger Tubby and Samuel Brightman. The entire operation was managed by two key men from the Senator's Washington office: Theodore Sorensen, his principal policy advisor, who accompanied him on the airplane, and Feldman, who stayed in Washington to provide continuous supervision over all four divisions. Feldman personally approved every statement issued by the national committee which bore the signature of John F. Kennedy.

Feldman also headed the Kennedy Research Team himself. To provide adequate help, he recruited five full-time, highly experienced men, each of whom had specialized in a different subject-matter field. The team's basic task was to do deep research for Senator Kennedy himself. Key issues, selected by the candidate, were explored in great detail, and 200 fully developed briefing memoranda were prepared for speeches and for the television debates. The team especially drew on an exhaustive series of position papers which experts outside the committee had prepared in the late summer.

In the later stages of the campaign, Feldman's research team even drafted speeches for Senator Kennedy, which were then called over the phone to the touring staff. Requests from the campaign plane came at any hour of day or night. At three one morning, Feldman was called from the Texas-bound air caravan and asked to discover by eight o'clock whether there had been any Irishmen at the Battle of the Alamo! The answer: yes.

In the early stages of the campaign, speech writing was left to Cox. He drew on a Harvard-based pool of top intellectual talent which Kennedy had established in 1958. To translate its ideas into speech drafts, he recruited a seven-man staff in Washington, D.C., and set them to work writing a full-dress speech for each evening and one or two others for daytime delivery. To bolster his efforts, Cox also established a Writers' Bureau in New York modeled after the Writers' Bureau which had been set up there in 1952 and 1956 for the Stevenson campaigns. Drawing on professional free-lance writers and regular staff writers for periodicals, the group included many distinguished authors and editors.

It soon became plain that neither of Cox's efforts was useful. No opportunities were afforded the candidate to speak to a specialized audience which would appreciate an address in depth on a special problem of public policy. Instead, Kennedy was making essentially the same speech to several small audiences every day. Different areas of policy could be emphasized as the opportunity warranted, and special local information could be used; but the formal addresses Cox was preparing were having to be rewritten, culled, or discarded.

Kennedy also found that he could not use the sorts of phrases, quips, and quotes which the Writers' Bureau had supplied so effectively to Stevenson. Their product simply didn't fit Kennedy's extemporaneous speeches, his oratorical style, or the audiences he was meeting.

In mid-October the Writers' Bureau was abandoned and the Washington speech-writing staff was sharply reduced. Some of the men left to assist Adlai Stevenson, who was campaigning hard for Kennedy. Others went on the road as advance speech writers for Kennedy.

An advance speech writer would visit a city about three days before Senator Kennedy was scheduled to speak. Working with the advance man and local Democrats, he would pick up local color and local issues which the Senator could work into his speech. Material was prepared in a form which Sorensen and Richard Goodwin could quickly screen and feed to the Senator on the plane. Rarely did an advance speech writer attempt to prepare a full speech. Ideas also were supplied by the remaining Washington staff, working through Myer Feldman.

Kennedy's speeches, then, concentrated on building his image as a moderate liberal who wanted action. Repeatedly he voiced the theme, "We need to get this country moving again." Repeatedly he labeled the Republicans as the party which prefers to "sit down, sit still, and look back." Nearly every specific issue was handled in this context.

At Fort Dodge, Iowa, to a farming and industrial audience he said:

But, if you think we can do better, if you think we can move ahead, if you think we can reverse the downward trend of agricultural prices, if you think we can build a better educational system and more security for our older people, if you think we can build a better defense, if you think that the United States should reestablish the atmosphere which existed through Latin America in the 1930's of the good neighbor, if you think the power balance in the world is turning against us, not with us, then I want you to join with us. I want you to move with us. I want you to decide in 1960 that we say "Yes" to the next decade, and not "No"; that we want to move ahead, not stand still.[20]

At New York University, in a speech devoted principally to foreign policy, he declared:

I cannot believe that any young man or woman who looks to the future can possibly decide to sit down and sit still and look back with Mr. Nixon and the Republican Party which has always opposed progress. . . .

Now, in 1960, the choice lies between the candidate who in this most revolutionary time runs on the slogan "You've never had it so good," versus the candidate and a party that runs on the slogan of the "New Frontiers" of the future. (Applause.)

On that basis, I ask your help. (Applause.) I ask your support. . . . How many of you will be willing to pick this country up and move it forward and make it shine once again? (Applause.)[21]

Why did Kennedy concentrate his image building upon demanding action in the moderate center rather than upon creating a reputation of maturity and competence? The Senator's own oratorical style and the nature of the campaign appearances seem to be part of the story. The basic reason, however, seems to be that the first of the "great debates" solved both the name-familiarity and the maturity-competence problems for John F. Kennedy.

THE GREAT DEBATES

The four debates between Vice President Richard M. Nixon and Senator John F. Kennedy in the 1960 campaign are a major landmark in world history. No greater audience has ever witnessed the discussion of public policies.

[20] U.S. Congress, Senate, *Freedom of Communications,* Part I (Washington: Government Printing Office, 1961), p. 319.

[21] *Ibid.,* p. 778.

The debates, however, proved more important to the candidates for image projection than for clarification of their stands on issues. Tactically, they were a godsend to John Kennedy. Needing name familiarity and an image of experience and maturity, he gained both overnight by a very favorable performance in the first debate.

Why did Richard Nixon debate? When the debates had been proposed, some of Nixon's advisors had counseled strongly against such a venture. Why, they argued, should the better-known Vice President admit the less-known Senator to be his equal by accepting the debate? Moreover, there was always the possibility that if Nixon had a "bad night" and if the Democratic candidate were unusually effective, substantial ground would be lost. Others thought television debates with Kennedy offered a great opportunity to demonstrate the difference between the two candidates. Those who favored the debates were confident that Nixon would easily emerge as the people's choice after such an encounter.

Nixon apparently agreed with the advocates of the debates. Partly he believed that he stood to gain from the effort. He felt he needed to dispel the notion that he was overly cold and calculating, and he was confident that his knowledge of the administration would enable him to outpoint Kennedy. Partly, however, he was caught in a train of circumstances which had been started in 1956 and by September 1960 left him little room for choice.

A debate between the major-party candidates for President had previously been practically foreclosed by section 315 of the Federal Communications Act and the interpretations of that section made by the Federal Communications Commission. If free time were offered the Republican and Democratic candidates, equal time had to be offered the Socialist, Prohibitionist, and other minor-party candidates. No network was prepared to enter such a jungle.

In 1956, Adlai E. Stevenson had initiated the idea by challenging President Eisenhower to debate. The White House rejected the proposal in early September by a brief statement that a debate would not dignify the office of President. Instead, later in the campaign, President Eisenhower appeared on a paid television broadcast to answer questions from a selected group of citizens in the studio.

After the election, Democratic National Chairman Paul M. Butler, an idealistic political reformer, would not let the idea die. Working with Frank Stanton, president of the Columbia Broadcasting System, he persuaded the other networks to undertake a joint effort to repeal the equal-time requirements of section 315 for the presidential candidates. Congress picked up the idea and in July 1960, suspended section 315 for the presidential campaign of 1960 only.

Thus Nixon found himself facing not only a challenge from Kennedy but also great pressure from the television networks and the public to use the specially granted freedom. Once the debate opportunity was publicly announced by the television networks, it was not easy for the Nixon forces to turn it down. Numerous excuses could have been offered to justify a refusal to debate, but Kennedy could easily have turned any of them to his advantage. So the Vice President accepted the challenge.

Beginning early in September, arrangements for the debates were laboriously negotiated among representatives of the two candidates and the three television networks. Kennedy, anxious to meet the Vice President, generally let his chief negotiator, J. Leonard Reinsch, accept whatever arrangements seemed reasonable. Because the networks were anxious to put on the debates and were striving hard to be fair, Reinsch found himself in the favorable position of being able to accept most of the network proposals. Nixon's negotiator, Herbert Klein, offered many suggestions on procedure, format, and arrangements. On most requests from the Nixon representatives, Reinsch went along, guided by the Kennedy policy of not letting little things forestall the debates.

On the number of debates, however, Reinsch held out for five. Nixon's managers, confident their champion would score a knock-out in the first round, bargained for one. By yielding on the fine points, and with the support of the networks which had offered the time, Reinsch managed to wangle four meetings: September 26 from Chicago; October 7 from Washington, D.C.; October 13 with Kennedy in New York and Nixon in Los Angeles; and October 21 from New York.

Pressed by the networks for a "good show," the candidates' representatives accepted a format which reduced the "debates" to hasty generalizations on a wide variety of subjects. The debates would last an hour each. The first would be limited to domestic policy, the second to foreign affairs. The third and fourth were less restricted. For the first and the last debates, each candidate was permitted an opening statement of 8 minutes. The rest of the time would be devoted to answering questions put by a panel of four distinguished newsmen. Direct answers to their questions were limited to 2½ minutes, rebuttal answers to 1½. No notes were to be used. A fifth newsman would serve as moderator, introduce the programs, and close them. All three networks would carry the programs live.

The thorniest problem in the negotiations proved to be the candidates' schedules. Only by enormous effort were travel plans juggled to bring them together on the same platform for three of the four debates. For the third debate the problems proved insurmountable and a split screen was arranged. Significantly, perhaps, many observers felt that the third debate was Mr. Nixon's best.

The opening debate cast the die. Those who heard it on radio reported that the two seemed nearly equal. Those who watched on television overwhelmingly chose Kennedy as the winner. Kennedy had achieved all he had hoped. Nixon had suffered what some of his counselors had feared.

The contrast on the crucial first debate had many facets and several causes. Yet it was less in what they said than in how they looked that made the difference. Kennedy arrived for the telecast relaxed, well briefed, confident, and fresh from a nap. Nixon arrived tense, unbriefed, and tired; and as he alighted from his car he struck his recently injured knee a severe jolt.

Each candidate had prepared for the encounter in typical fashion. John Kennedy had summoned to Chicago the leaders of his research team—Ted Sorensen, Richard Goodwin, and Myer Feldman. Feldman had brought his campaign files from Washington. For a full day the four operated almost around the clock "like young men at college cramming for an exam."[22] The effort centered upon filling Kennedy's head with all the latest figures, percentages, trends, and comparisons which would enable him to demonstrate

---

[22] White, *The Making of the President, 1960,* p. 341.

his mastery of any questions which might be asked. A brainstorming session uncovered most of the probable questions, and swift raids on the files developed answers for them. By Monday afternoon the candidate and his youthful brain trust had the key ideas on fact cards and were able to let Kennedy have a good nap; next take a last review of the cards with them, his brother Robert, and pollster Louis Harris; and then eat a relaxed dinner.

Richard Nixon spent the day alone. Dependent on his own memory and on the materials he carried with him, he prepared his opening statement and tried by himself to anticipate the coming questions. Having been forced to interrupt his campaign in early September because of his knee injury, Nixon was tired. Heavy campaigning to make up for the lost time had visibly emaciated him. Only as he drove to the studio did he take time for a hasty consultation with his television advisor on arrangements for the program and what he might expect in the debate.

On the air, the two candidates were startlingly different. Theodore White caught the picture with remarkable sympathy and understanding:

. . . the contrast of the two faces was astounding. Normally and in private, Kennedy under tension flutters his hands—he adjusts his necktie, slaps his knee, strokes his face. Tonight he was calm and nerveless in appearance. The Vice-President, by contrast, was tense, almost frightened, at turns glowering and, occasionally, haggard-looking to the point of sickness.[23]

The debate itself provided another contrast. Centered on domestic policy, it offered Kennedy the opportunity to voice his "action-now" theme and to emphasize the Democratic Party's record of liberal domestic programs. Nixon, centering upon answering his opponent instead of capturing the unseen audience, repeatedly agreed with Kennedy's goals, then disagreed with his methods and offered an alternative. Whatever its merits for formal debating, this technique was decried as "me-tooism" even by his liberal Republican supporters.

Remedial steps were promptly taken in the Nixon camp, and the remaining three debates were scored by the supporters of each

[23] *Ibid.,* p. 346.

candidate as a victory for their man. In all four debates both candidates proved themselves remarkably adaptable to this new form of presidential campaigning. It appeared that each could discuss anything within the allotted time of 2½ minutes and could rebut with equal ease for 1½. Unfortunately, the questions by the newsmen were sometimes trivial, occasionally improper, and often complex enough to be unanswerable in the allotted time.

More people watched the debates than voted for President. Estimates of the viewing audience ranged from 85 million to 120 million. Kennedy polled 34,227,096; Nixon 34,107,646.

The debates also made a major change in the use of television in the campaign. Originally the Democratic National Committee had reserved eight 30-minute periods for major nationwide television broadcasts so that the candidate could speak to the nation on the major issues of the day, as Adlai E. Stevenson had done in 1952 and 1956. When the debates were scheduled, most of that time was canceled, except for election eve. Instead, Kennedy appearances in key cities around the nation were telecast over regional networks and paid for by the participating state party organizations. Never did he offer a formal nationwide address on a major policy issue.

Did the debates help people make up their minds? Polls taken during and after the campaign indicated that enough people said they did to have altered the outcome of the election.

Did the debates help shape the course of public policy by informing the people, as so many scholars think political debate should? Some observers said no, such innovations in presidential politics are unrealistic and irrelevant—unrealistic because a President does not engage in crucial decision making in 2½-minute periods, irrelevant because skill in debate does not prove that a man will make a good President.

Some observers said yes, that the debates were spectacularly successful, though not without faults. The proponents of continued debates insisted that the portraits of the candidates given the voters were unusually accurate. Moreover, they said, the debates were never intended to be more than very useful additions to other evidence on the candidates' qualifications for the presidency.

There were no debates in 1964. Congress did not suspend

section 315 of the Federal Communications Act, and the networks accordingly could offer nothing.

There would have been no debates in any event. President Johnson had earlier made clear that he did not enjoy such encounters and probably would not have agreed to them had they been possible. Senator Goldwater publicly opposed such debates in principle, especially when an incumbent President was involved.

The 1960 debates may therefore be both the first and the last. No incumbent President is ever likely to offer his opponent an opportunity to debate him before live television cameras. Under normal conditions, every other election involves an incumbent President.

Nonincumbents may be equally reluctant to debate. The 1960 events proved that such affairs carry great political risk. Only the man who feels he is behind and has more to gain than he has to lose can really afford to debate his opponent. If the two seem nearly equal, each risks losing more than he may gain. The man who seems ahead is foolish to risk his lead in a public debate.

The debates of 1960, then, probably should not be repeated. Future debates can produce but little enlightenment to the electorate and are more likely to injure the candidates than to help them. The nation does not need a public, verbal confrontation between the champions of its major political parties in order to choose between them.

Bibliography

Benham, T. W. "Polling for a Presidential Candidate: Some Observations on the 1964 Campaign," *Public Opinion Quarterly*, XXIX (Summer 1965), 185-199.

Citizens for Goldwater-Miller Committee. *Barry Goldwater Speaks Out on the Issues.*

Democratic National Committee. *The President Speaks to the People.* 2 vols. Washington: Democratic National Committee, 1964.

Ellsworth, John W. "Rationality and Campaigning: A Content Analysis of the 1960 Presidential Campaign Debates," *Western Political Quarterly*, XVIII (December 1965), 794-802.

Shadegg, Stephen. *What Happened to Goldwater?* New York: Holt, 1965.

Sorensen, Theodore C. *Kennedy.* New York: Harper, 1965. See especially pp. 177-188 and 195-210.

Thompson, Charles A. H., and Frances M. Shattuck. *The 1956 Presidential Campaign.* Washington: Brookings Institution, 1960.

U.S. Congress, Senate. *Freedom of Communications.* 2 vols. Washington: Government Printing Office, 1961. The complete speeches of John F. Kennedy and Richard M. Nixon delivered during the 1960 presidential campaign.

White, F. Clifton. *Suite 3505.* New Rochelle, N.Y.: Arlington House, 1967.

White, Theodore H. *The Making of the President, 1960.* New York: Atheneum, 1961.

White, Theodore H. *The Making of the President, 1964.* New York: Atheneum, 1965.

Chapter IX

Meeting the People

There is no substitute for meeting the people. The candidate who goes to the people gets the people. This elementary principle of American politics stems from a small-town tradition in American behavior. Voters give their confidence to leaders whom they know. Television, radio, newspapers, advertisements, and magazine articles can acquaint them with the name and qualifications of a candidate. But getting to know him requires meeting him face to face, shaking his hand, asking him a question, and talking to other people who know him.

WHY GO TO THE PEOPLE?

What is the candidate really like? Does he shake hands firmly, with vigor, or limply like a cold fish? Does he seem really genuinely glad to meet you? Is he interested in what you have to say? Does he think your opinion is important? Or is he aloof, haughty, self-centered, "phony"?

A homely illustration of this basic search for the inner quality of a man has been offered by Senator Paul H. Douglas of Illinois. He reports that the best training he received for a career in politics was milking cows as a boy, for he thereby developed a strong and tireless grip.

These questions, trivial as they may seem to those who want a presidential campaign to be a grand debate on policy issues, are at the heart of political decision making in presidential elections. American men and women prefer to entrust their government to a man whom they would trust with their savings, their legal difficulties, and their personal problems. And they don't hesitate to write him about such matters once he is elected.

If he is to meet the people, the candidate must go to them, and in a country as large as the United States this means a grueling tour, state by state, city by city, to meet and shake hands and talk to as many people as he can. And as he does he not only seeks their confidence, he learns from them whether he is winning that confidence. Theodore White eloquently caught the candidate's need to get the people's response:

> . . . the candidate, whoever he is, sits at the center of a web of affairs so complex as to be dehumanized; his ideas, his phrases, his finances, his schedules, are all prepared for him by others; wherever he pauses to consult with staff, he must already make the detached executive decisions of a President. Thus only the personal audience, below the level of strategic calculation, can give him the one thing he needs most: the response of warmth or frost, of applause or indifference. Its laughter, its scowl, its silence, its cheers, its yearning, its measuring eyes, are the only clues in the mystic communication between the leader and the led, to tell truly whether he has reached those he seeks to lead. Becoming President is an utterly personal business between the man who offers himself as national leader and the Americans who judge him. The candidate must feel the beat of the people he hopes to lead; their heart is his target. And no public-opinion poll or analysis can tell him half so well whether he has reached that target as can the people themselves, giving him the beat of their response.[1]

Only Warren G. Harding, Republican candidate in 1920, has dared in this century to campaign from his "front porch"—to have the people come to him and see but few of them. His managers had judged that if he went to meet the people he would lose the election. So they kept him home and kept him quiet.

Television, radio, and air travel have made the campaign from

[1] Theodore H. White, *The Making of the President, 1960* (New York: Atheneum, 1961), pp. 305-306.

the front porch obsolete. Both major candidates for the presidency now must barnstorm—tour the nation as widely as possible—in their search for votes.

As they travel, the candidates reach at least four levels of audiences. The nation as a whole hears their appeals through the reports of fifty or more national press representatives who accompany each candidate. The many and frequent stops in a barnstorming campaign, however, preclude a unique and newsworthy speech each time. The traveling press soon learns to listen for something new and to ignore most of what is said. Most speeches, therefore, go unreported or command relatively slight attention in the press across the land.

The local press, television, and radio, however, see a personal appearance as front-page news or as lead-off material for newscasts. Pictures, film clips, reports of the candidate's remarks, little events which convey his personality—all are presented in volume and eagerly consumed, especially by those who saw him or attended a rally.

The face-to-face audience, the people who gather at airport rallies, in school gymnasiums, on street corners, constitute a third audience level. Having made the effort to come to see the candidate, they usually are his staunch supporters. Their reward, principally, is reinforcement and reassurance that their choice is indeed a good one, although by their enthusiasm they may help sway their fellow townsmen watching on television.

The fourth audience is a selected one, composed of those community leaders who are deemed important enough to be granted a few moments of private conversation with the candidate. In such meetings, many votes may be gained by winning the support of men and women whose judgment will shape the attitudes of others. Sometimes, when a particularly important local figure is unable to come to the candidate, the candidate visits him and thereby gains highly valuable local front-page publicity.

Both the 1960 and 1964 campaigns saw the major-party candidates visit virtually every state, some states repeatedly. Of the four, President Johnson toured least, Kennedy most. All flew to most events, and thus could undertake widely scattered appearances in a single day.

Johnson typically made two or three major appearances a day. For example, in his mid-October western swing, the President spoke at the Phoenix, Arizona, airport and at Washington Square, San Francisco, on Sunday, October 11. The following day, he campaigned at the state building in Reno, Nevada; the Natrona county courthouse in Casper, Wyoming; and the Coliseum in Denver, Colorado, before flying back to Washington, D.C., that night.[2]

Senator Goldwater was scheduled more tightly. On Thursday, October 15, for example, he left Denver, Colorado, early in the morning to invade the President's home state of Texas. Swinging along the Gulf Coast from the Mexican border to Beaumont, he made three stadium speeches, among them one at Lamar State College of Technology in Beaumont and another at the high-school stadium at Harlinger. He wound up the day with a motorcade in Houston, followed by a major evening address. Friday morning he flew to Sioux City, Iowa, for a speech, then took a tugboat up the Missouri River to celebrate the channel deepening. Next he hopped to the National Cornpicking Contest at Sioux Falls, South Dakota, where he chanced to meet Senator Humphrey, Johnson's running mate, at the airport. The evening found him addressing a $100-a-plate fund-raising dinner in Chicago.[3]

In 1960, both Kennedy and Nixon made many widely scattered appearances daily in September. By October, both changed to three or four principal appearances a day, usually in a single state.

A Kennedy September schedule is well illustrated by the two-day swing of Thursday and Friday, September 22 and 23. Starting with a talk at the stockyards in Sioux City, Iowa, just before 9 a.m. on September 22, he spoke twice at Fort Dodge, Iowa; addressed the National Plowing Contest at Sioux Falls, South Dakota; spoke at the Corn Palace in Mitchell, South Dakota; met an airport rally at Fargo, North Dakota; and gave a major speech on electric-power policy before a convention of public power groups in Billings, Montana, in the evening before flying to Denver, Colorado, for the night. The next morning found him at Frontier Park, Cheyenne, Wyoming. He was back in Denver for an address and luncheon, then made two appearances in Salt

[2] *Washington Post,* October 16, 1964, p. 6.
[3] *Ibid.,* October 17, 1964, pp. 1-2.

Lake City, Utah, one a major address on religious freedom at the Mormon Tabernacle.

Vice President Nixon started his barnstorming proper a week after Kennedy, on Monday, September 12. He spoke first that morning at Friendship Airport, Baltimore, Maryland; then at Monument Circle in Indianapolis, Indiana; at Memorial Auditorium in Dallas, Texas; and finally at Union Square in San Francisco. Swinging north the next day, September 13, he spoke in Portland, Oregon; Vancouver, Washington; and Boise, Idaho; then mounted his midwestern campaign on Wednesday, September 14, at Grand Forks, North Dakota, and Peoria, Illinois.

By contrast, October 24 and 25 found both candidates spending two full days each in the pivotal midwestern states: Nixon in Ohio, Kennedy in Illinois. Both filled man-killing schedules. Nixon spoke at Marietta, Parkersburg (across the Ohio River in West Virginia), Athens, Chillicothe, Cincinnati, Middletown, Dayton, Springfield, Columbus, Marion, Lima, Deschler, London, and Toledo. Kennedy appeared at Rockford, Champaign-Urbana, Peoria, East Peoria, Moline, Rock Island, Des Plaines, Libertyville, Carpentersville, Elgin, St. Charles, Geneva, Batavia, Aurora, and Elmhurst.

ADVANCE SCHEDULING AND PREPARATION

Barnstorming by a presidential candidate in the 1960's calls for the most elaborate and careful advance preparations.

The candidates of both major parties must now expect to travel with an entourage of nearly 100 persons, two-thirds of them representatives of the press, radio, and television. The count runs up quickly. The candidate himself must have a minimum personal party of 8 or 10 persons: an administrative assistant to handle delicate political negotiations; a press secretary to prepare news releases, negotiate with the press, set up press conferences, and provide facilities for the press; a campaign-scheduling manager to map the trips and make physical arrangements; and at least one good speech writer to assemble and draft material for public presentation. Such a personal crew also requires clerical support.

Courtesy requires the candidate to include his party's key political figures from the state he is visiting. The governor and the United States Senators and Representatives, or the party's candidates for those offices, expect to appear with the presidential candidate. Protocol also usually obliges the inclusion of the state's party chairman, possibly the national committeeman and committeewoman, and especially the state chairman of the citizens or volunteers groups for the national ticket. An incumbent President has further to include any cabinet or other key administration officer from the state. Each of the elected officers, moreover, is likely to have a key staff member of his own with him. A minimum of 8 or 10 seats for such very important people is unavoidable.

Local party organizations rarely are prepared or equipped to deal with such a deluge. Being subject to high turnover of leadership and dependent upon volunteer working personnel, they find it nearly impossible to imagine the detailed work and the expense required to prepare for the visit of a presidential candidate.

Even a simple speech at an airport demands fantastically complex arrangements. A platform must be provided in a location inside a permanent fence which can keep the crowd from mingling with the visiting party or invading the press section. A flatbed truck trailer has often proved the most economical type of platform. A second platform, fully wired with many outlets for television and movie cameras and radio broadcasters, must be provided about 30 feet in front of the rostrum and at a slightly higher elevation. The press must have tables and chairs for at least 80 persons in a restricted area immediately by the platform and requires direct access to at least two teletypewriter operators and a dozen long-distance telephones. If the President is involved, a local White House switchboard must be installed somewhere in town and a phone placed just at the foot of the steps to the platform by which he can reach any place on earth instantly.

Security precautions require a system of passes to identify those who will greet the candidate at the aircraft, those who will have seats on the platform, the press, telephone and other workmen, local committee workers, and plain-clothes guards. Police must be instructed to keep all others in the public areas and must know to whom to turn in case of an emergency that might demand an exception.

Bands and other suitable entertainment must be arranged. Since school and college bands are the most frequently used, someone must see to it that they know how to play "Hail to the Chief" or the candidate's theme song. Chairs and transportation must be provided for the bands and agreements made with their schools to excuse them from classes if necessary.

Protocol in seating, suitable decorations, and even instructions for the introduction of speakers are required. Thus, when the President is the speaker, the person introducing him, no matter what his station, is permitted to say only, "Ladies and Gentlemen, the President of the United States."

A speech away from the airport means a motorcade. The local committee will be expected to provide several open cars for the candidate, other dignitaries, and photographers; closed cars for the security personnel and communications men; and at least three buses for the press and staff. When the President is involved, special equipment is provided by the Secret Service. But routing, timing, order of march, and protection of the motorcade call for careful preparations.

If meals are to be taken by the visiting party, or an overnight stop is scheduled, hotel or motel rooms with special telephones must be provided the candidate, other dignitaries, and key staff. Press people usually do not expect individual rooms at a luncheon stop.

The local organization is expected to meet all local expenses. The candidate is at enough expense to bring his party in for the appearance. Thus, even a shoestring appearance by a presidential candidate will cost the local party organization several hundred dollars.

Advice and suggestions for the appearance of a presidential candidate, therefore, simply cannot be made by long-distance telephone or even be provided in a quick overnight visit by a traveling representative from national headquarters. The only workable solution is for the candidate to send out one of his own team as an advance man to work closely with the local party people on arrangements for his visit. A good "advance" requires the full-time night-and-day work of an experienced man for a week to ten days on the scene. The advance man must be in early enough to shape the arrangements and must stay with the show until the candidate's airplane is on its way to the next airport. For large cities, or a visit of several days which includes a variety of activities, a team of advance men may be needed. In late October 1960, John F. Kennedy had a team of 11 advance men to handle his three-day visit to Philadelphia.

BARNSTORMING WITH KENNEDY AND JOHNSON IN 1960

In 1960, campaign barnstorming by John F. Kennedy and Lyndon B. Johnson was coordinated, but each managed his own movements separately. Each candidate had his own advance-scheduling officer and each his own team of advance men.

The theory governing the sequence of appearances was to move the candidates rapidly about the country so that their presence in any locality would be top news for a considerable area. It was deemed better to make separate return appearances in three or four very important cities in one section of the nation rather than to move systematically from one to the other during a single trip. Each time he returned to a region, the reasoning ran, the candidate could expect headlines in most of the regional papers. Air travel made such scheduling possible, even if it was expensive as well as wearing on the candidates and their assistants.

Kennedy scheduling was entrusted to Kenneth O'Donnell, who accompanied the Senator on his trips. Headquarters scheduling was managed by Richard Maguire, supported by Richard O'Hare and John E. Nolan, Jr., who was Advance Chair. The Johnson schedule was entrusted to James Blundell supported by Wilson McCarthy.

The general schedules were worked out early in the campaign by top-level discussions at Democratic national headquarters, but details frequently were modified. The days to be spent in each state by each candidate were decided, and the proportionate time to be given each major city was determined. Representatives of the scheduling office called on key party leaders in the big states—men like Mayor Richard J. Daley of Chicago, the late United States Representative William Green of Philadelphia, and Governor David Lawrence of Pennsylvania—to learn their wishes before making final allocations of time.

Once the broad outlines were set, representatives of the scheduling offices worked with state party leaders to establish which less important cities would be visited and how long the candidates would spend at each. In some instances, the detailed schedule was worked out by the advance men after they arrived on the scene. For example, Byrne Litschge and Dan Ogden worked out the Kennedy Kentucky schedule with state Democratic leaders in Louisville about ten days before the Senator's arrival, then cleared it with Washington.

Whatever the requests for appearances, the scheduling offices tried to give both candidates two days' rest each week. The days were juggled, however, so that before each of the four television debates, Senator Kennedy would have two full days free of appearances so he could rest and prepare for the confrontation. Such conservative scheduling paid handsome dividends before the television cameras.

Kennedy barnstorming was conducted almost entirely by air. The Senator and his immediate party used the *Caroline,* the Senator's personal plane. The press and other members of the traveling party flew in two Douglas DC-6's, chartered from American Air Lines. Ordinarily a group of nearly 100 traveled in the three-plane air caravan.

Space aboard the *Caroline* was at a premium. Only 20 seats were available. In addition to the Senator, one of his sisters, Sorensen, Salinger, and O'Donnell, stenographic help had to be accommodated. Six to eight seats always were reserved for state dignitaries. Sometimes another key staff man might be added if he were needed for a particular appearance.

Final arrangements for each appearance were handled by an advance man who flew in about ten days before the Senator's arrival. He was especially instructed to work with the local party organization and not to do the work himself nor to run the local show.

Each advance man had four basic tasks. First, he was to generate a big crowd. To this end he was expected to promote publicity, set up phoning committees, stimulate attendance from surrounding communities, and use any other device to build interest and enthusiasm in the event. Second, he was responsible for the Senator's personal safety. No Secret Service aid was available. Inasmuch as an advance man rarely was trained in security work, he was expected to make suitable protection arrangements with local and state police. Third, he had to obtain adequate facilities for the traveling party. Specific directions were given him about housing for overnight stays and even for luncheon rest stops; about facilities and telephone and teletype requirements for the press; about the number and order of vehicles in a motorcade; about food (Senator Kennedy avoided dining in public); and even about fanfare upon the candidate's arrival—a band, decorations, buttons, and the like. Fourth, he was to work with local party people to insure united support for the Kennedy-Johnson ticket. Primary scars, local factional fights, and differences over policies and programs were to be smoothed over, especially during the candidate's appearance.

Kennedy forces recruited some 87 young men, mostly volunteers and largely from the legal profession, to be Kennedy advance men. Of this number, 45 helped in only one or two appearances. A basic crew of 23 did most of the work and handled four or more appearances each. Among this group were 13 men who set up five or more appearances and served as team captains from early October to the end of the campaign.

Johnson's advance team totaled at least 28 and leaned heavily upon congressional staff once the special session was over. On both the Kennedy and Johnson teams, those asked to do virtually full-time advance work were added to the national-committee payroll if they had no other means of support.

Training was highly informal. Unlike the Republican National Committee, the Democrats depended upon a 32-page instruction manual and the good sense of the men chosen for the advance team.

Much therefore depended upon the good judgment and practical political experience of individual advance men. Commonly a new recruit would find himself airborne within a matter of hours, headed for a strange city with his instruction manual, a cash advance of $200, the name of the local party leader, and the number of the private telephone line to the scheduling office in Washington. If local politicians chose to play games to outwit him, his life could be made miserable. If he knew enough politics to be sure he had the unreserved support of men with real power in the community where he was assigned, he usually could carry matters off with ease.

When several stops were to be made in one state, a team of advance men would be sent under a team captain. Often a captain would find himself with one or two experienced men and one or two rookies. He would distribute his men as the loads demanded. Ordinarily the inexperienced men were assigned simple jobs such as airport speeches. As a man gained know-how, he drew assignments involving motorcades, then meals, and then overnight stops.

Big teams of advance men were used in New York, Chicago, and Philadelphia. For the three days of appearances in Philadelphia and its suburbs during the next-to-last weekend before the election, a team of 11 advance men was sent in by the Kennedy forces. The team captain appointed lieutenants for each day who in turn were assigned two or three men to handle various segments of the work. On Saturday, for example, the team lieutenant and one rookie assistant ran a 12-hour motorcade through the western suburbs. One experienced advance man handled the morning appearances, another those in the afternoon and evening. Handling three or four appearances simultaneously taxed the powers even of men who had been through six weeks of rugged campaigning. In desperation, they finally had police cars carry them from shopping center to shopping center 30 minutes ahead of the candidate to permit last-minute inspections of facilities.

Each team captain was expected to go over the ground in the stops to be assigned him some five or six weeks before the appearances if possible. He thus could better guide his advance men in the final stages of their work.

Whatever the situation, Kenneth O'Donnell and Richard Maguire backed their men down the line. When the advance man made a decision, it stuck. When the traveling party arrived, the advance man was boss. No one left the planes until he gave the order, and no one changed the order of arrangements after arrival.

An advance man had to be equal to any occasion. In one city the county jailer, who was a committee chairman for the Kennedy-day rally, proposed that he serve a luncheon to the Senator and his party on the fourth floor of his "hotel." He even displayed three prime country hams he had been curing for the occasion and exhibited the facilities—four cells!

One enthusiastic rally chairman announced to a planning meeting that he had arranged to release a thousand pigeons as Senator Kennedy arrived! A firm "no" from the advance man and a conciliatory discourse on the psychological importance of centering the crowd's attention on the candidate rather than the birds dissuaded him.

Sometimes rivalry spilled over from the primary campaign to complicate the advance man's life. In one city the local Kennedy chairman was planning to exclude Humphrey supporters from the speaker's platform. He couldn't accommodate everyone and felt the workers from the primary deserved to be rewarded. The dropping of a few careful hints by the advance man enabled other local leaders to persuade the chairman that an appearance of party unity was more important for success than recognition for all the preconvention Kennedy faithful.

Sometimes plans well laid and well executed would go awry. At Fort Dodge, Iowa, Senator Kennedy arrived 45 minutes late because of an unscheduled stop in the previous city. A complicated program, involving a tumultuous ride through the city behind a long parade of floats and high-school bands, a brief address in the city park, and a second address at the airport, was run off in ten minutes less than the scheduled time. Senator Kennedy and his party were hustled back on their planes and the local rally committee congratulated themselves joyfully on a job well done as the caravan taxied for the end of the runway only 35 minutes late. Then came the blow. Clearance for takeoff would not be given by the control tower because a scheduled commercial airliner was coming in for a landing! For 30 agonizing minutes the advance man had to "sweat it out" while the planes jockeyed around on the field in an event that had been entirely disregarded in the advance planning because no conflict had been expected with the commercial schedule.

Occasionally the advance man had a stroke of good fortune. Once in the Middle West, when an exceptionally large crowd had wholly blocked Senator Kennedy's return route to the airport, the advance man obtained police permission to use a prearranged emergency back road which required crossing a farm and entering the airport by the landing strip. As the motorcade turned unexpectedly into his yard, the farmer, in overalls and battered hat, stepped out to shake hands with the Senator. The motorcade stopped, the photographers had a field day, and the advance man got special thanks for arranging a good human-interest angle which he had not planned.

Group-work techniques proved especially useful to advance men who knew them. The basic problem was to get volunteer committee chairmen to work as a group in a common enterprise from which they could not be permitted to back out at the last minute. Success turned first on the advance man's making certain that all major tasks had been assigned a responsible person who had an adequate number of helpers. Then the advance man personally visited each committee chairman to determine just what he had done, what he had left to do, and when he planned to do it. It was at this stage that judicious use of the instruction manual enabled the advance man to shape the course of planning to meet the traveling party's needs. The third step in the process was to assemble the committee chairmen, with the local leader presiding if possible, two or three nights before the candidate's arrival. After a detailed rundown of the timing, procedure on arrival, numbers of people who would be coming, and other basic facts which needed confirmation, each chairman was asked to report. All other committee chairmen were invited to ask questions as he went along to insure that their part of the activities would fit properly. The committee chairman known to be most advanced in his plans and preparations was called on first, and a logical sequence of related committees called on thereafter. By the close of the meeting, every committee chairman was fully informed and had made firm commitments of action to all his colleagues, and the group as a whole had developed confidence in the certain success of its endeavors. By such experiences advance scheduling proved its worth.

BARNSTORMING WITH JOHNSON AND HUMPHREY IN 1964

In 1964, President Johnson had to meet the people of the Northeast, Middle West, and West. They held the votes to make him President in his own right and they were suspicious of his opponent. They had liked President Kennedy and grieved over his untimely death. They were ready to listen to Johnson and to vote for him.

With the experienced Kennedy team sounding out the key states, Johnson laid his own barnstorming strategy. He would cover 44 states and visit the pivotal states at least twice.

As Democratic candidates traditionally must, the President started his campaign at a Labor Day rally in Detroit, Michigan. In mid-September he took a long swing through the Pacific Northwest, ending in California on September 17. He was back in California on October 11 and again on October 29.

The Midwest received a second swing October 7-9 when he spoke in Iowa, Illinois, Indiana, and Ohio. He was back a third time on October 30 to swing through Michigan, Wisconsin, and Illinois, ending with a huge evening rally in Chicago.

To the Northeast he journeyed September 28, stopping in all six New England states and ending with a visit to the bedside of Senator Ted Kennedy, hospitalized by an airplane accident. A successful trip through New York state from Buffalo to New York City with senatorial candidate Robert Kennedy on October 15 was followed by a trip on October 31 back to New York City and a second speech at Madison Square Garden with Kennedy at his side.

Coordinating his traveling to complement the President's schedule, vice-presidential nominee Senator Hubert Humphrey spoke in 100 cities in 40 states and campaigned 50,000 miles before winding up in Goldwater's Arizona. Like the President, he stumped primarily in the Northeast, Middle West, and Far West and concentrated on the pivotal states of California, New York, Pennsylvania, Illinois, and Ohio.[4]

In the last week of the campaign, both President Johnson and Senator Humphrey opened a concerted drive for big-city votes in the pivotal states. Starting Wednesday, October 28, in Boston, the President successively visited Pittsburgh, Los Angeles, Chicago, Philadelphia, and several intermediate points before closing the

---

[4] *Washington Post,* November 2, 1964, pp. A1 and A4.

campaign on Saturday night in New York City. Humphrey, starting in New York October 27, reversed the field to stop in Cincinnati, Chicago, intermediate points, and the northwestern states before spending the last weekend in Los Angeles. Both candidates returned to their home states to vote.

President Johnson personally set the guidelines for his campaign traveling. Arrangements for the President's movements, security, lodging, meals, and platform facilities were handled by the Secret Service. Taking a leaf from the Kennedy experiences from 1961 to 1963, however, the White House added political advance men to get out a crowd, deal with local political problems, handle decorations, and assist in other details. Some experienced advance men from the Kennedy and Johnson teams of 1960 were used and some new men recruited.

Humphrey advance men, without the advantage of Secret Service support, depended upon a corps of special political recruits, paralleling 1960 practice. Coordination with the President's schedule avoided conflicts and made sure all key events were covered by one of them.

Reflecting the logistical problems of moving a President, with the necessary communications support and a large entourage of newsmen, typical Johnson schedules were tight but sensible. Three speeches a day with perhaps an additional side trip were the normal limit, although the President frequently stopped motorcades to say a few impromptu words and shake hands with crowds which lined his route. A typical schedule, for Thursday, October 8, 1964, shown below, illustrates the detail of movements and the precision of timing necessary to advance a presidential campaign.

The President's campaign style was pure Johnson— southwestern, folksy, filled with traditional political clichés. He made no effort to try the polished phrases of Adlai Stevenson or even the more informal yet eloquent Kennedy style. Neither fit him. As columnists Evans and Novak reported on Election Day:

Never has so much snake oil been applied so generously to such enthusiastic audiences by a man in the White House. Mr. Johnson doesn't make political speeches. He chins with the voters as if he were giving them the Johnson treatment in his parlor down at the old LBJ

THE WHITE HOUSE

SCHEDULE OF THE TRIP OF PRESIDENT JOHN-
SON TO IOWA, ILLINOIS, INDIANA, OHIO, KEN-
TUCKY, TENNESSEE, AND LOUISIANA, OCTO-
BER 7-9, 1964

THURSDAY, OCTOBER 8, 1964

7:30 AM	Press charter departs O'Hare Airport for Gary, Indiana
8:00	PRESIDENT JOHNSON DEPARTS O'HARE AIRPORT FOR GARY, INDIANA (Flying time: 30 minutes) (Press Pool: AP, UPI, ABC, Ed Martin)
8:00	Press charter arrives Gary Airport
8:30	PRESIDENT JOHNSON ARRIVES GARY AIRPORT
8:35	PRESIDENT JOHNSON DEPARTS AIRPORT FOR WASHINGTON HIGH SCHOOL BY MOTORCADE
8:55	PRESIDENT JOHNSON ARRIVES WASHINGTON HIGH SCHOOL
9:45	PRESIDENT JOHNSON DEPARTS WASHINGTON HIGH SCHOOL (Press Pool: AP, UPI, CBS, de Rossett Morrissey)
10:05	PRESIDENT JOHNSON DEPARTS GARY FOR INDIANAPOLIS (Flying time: 1 hour)
10:05	Press charter departs Gary for Indianapolis
11:00	Press charter arrives Indianapolis Airport
11:05	PRESIDENT JOHNSON ARRIVES INDIANAPOLIS AIRPORT
11:40	PRESIDENT JOHNSON ARRIVES DOWNTOWN SQUARE BY MOTORCADE PRESIDENT JOHNSON SPEAKS
12:10 PM	PRESIDENT JOHNSON FINISHES SPEAKING

244

12:20   PRESIDENT JOHNSON ARRIVES ATHLETIC CLUB FOR LUNCH BY MOTORCADE

1:50   PRESIDENT JOHNSON DEPARTS ATHLETIC CLUB FOR AIRPORT

2:10   PRESIDENT JOHNSON DEPARTS INDIANAPOLIS FOR CLEVELAND LAKE FRONT AIRPORT, LOCATED APPROXIMATELY 1 MILE FROM DOWNTOWN CLEVELAND
(Flying time: 1 hour 20 minutes)
Minus 1 hour
(Press Pool: AP, UPI, NBC, Richard Rovere)

2:10   Press charter departs Indianapolis for Cleveland Lake Front Airport

4:00 PM EDT   Press charter arrives Cleveland Lake Front Airport

4:40   PRESIDENT JOHNSON ARRIVES CLEVELAND LAKE FRONT AIRPORT

4:55   PRESIDENT JOHNSON DEPARTS CLEVELAND LAKE FRONT AIRPORT BY MOTORCADE

5:15   PRESIDENT JOHNSON ARRIVES SHERATON-CLEVELAND HOTEL

8:45   PRESIDENT JOHNSON DEPARTS SHERATON-CLEVELAND HOTEL FOR THE CONVENTION CENTER, CLEVELAND PUBLIC AUDITORIUM

9:05   PRESIDENT JOHNSON SPEAKS

9:45   PRESIDENT JOHNSON DEPARTS CONVENTION CENTER FOR DRIVE TO LAKE FRONT AIRPORT

10:10   PRESIDENT JOHNSON DEPARTS AIRPORT FOR LOUISVILLE
(Press Pool: AP, UPI, NBC, Hugh Sidey)

10:40 PM EST   PRESIDENT JOHNSON ARRIVES LOUISVILLE AIRPORT
(Flying time: 1 hour 30 minutes)
Plus 1 hour

11:15   PRESIDENT JOHNSON ARRIVES SHERATON HOTEL BY MOTORCADE

ranch. . . . It is original Johnson—a mixture of Texas frontier and cracker-barrel corn.[5]

The President went out to "press the flesh"—to shake hands, to meet the people in his own way. In Milwaukee he stepped into a neighborhood grocery store to buy "a little hunk of baloney" and to talk to the grocer. In Brooklyn he stopped to greet a large crowd at Nostrand and Flatbush avenues. The *New York Times* caught the flavor:

"I've gone from California to Maine, but I've never seen so many happy faces," he drawled. . . . "This isn't Goldwater country, is it?"

"No!" roared the crowd.

"Well, then, go to the polls Nov. 3 and elect Congressman Murphy," said the President, holding up the hand of Representative John M. Murphy of the 16th District.

"And Bob Kennedy," exhorted the President, thrusting up Mr. Kennedy's arm.

"And don't forget about Hubert Humphrey and Lyndon Johnson, either," cried the President, and the motorcade started off again.[6]

In mid-campaign, Lyndon Johnson unveiled his secret weapon—a weapon only Franklin Roosevelt also had possessed in modern times. His wife proved to be an excellent campaigner who enjoyed politics.

Lady Bird Johnson first demonstrated her national-campaign skills in an officially nonpartisan conservation swing through the West in mid-August of 1964. A visit to the Crow Indian reservation with the Mansfields of Montana, a float trip down the Snake River in Grand Teton National Park with the McGees of Wyoming and Interior Secretary Udall, and the dedication of a National Recreation Area in Utah and Wyoming with the Mosses of Utah were interspersed with effective addresses before capacity crowds at cities along the way. Two Senators who had won in 1958 by the barest of margins regained their seats with ease that November.

As her special contribution to the 1964 campaign, Lady Bird took her own campaign train, the "Lady Bird Special" on a four-day swing through the hostile South, where traditional south-

---

[5] *Ibid.*, November 3, 1964, p. A13.
[6] *New York Times*, October 16, 1964, p. 22.

ern courtesy demanded that she be given the sort of hearing her husband might well have been denied. Traveling 1,682 miles and visiting 80 communities, Mrs. Johnson greeted an estimated 1 million people in Virginia, North Carolina, South Carolina, Georgia, Florida, Alabama, Mississippi, and Louisiana. Her approach was friendly interest, feminine charm, and a straightforward appeal. Typical of her remarks was her statement in Selma, North Carolina:

Ten months ago on a most awful day, my husband became your President. Behind him lay the experience of 12 years in the House of Representatives, 12 years in the Senate, and three years in the Vice Presidency. Into these last ten months, he has poured all the energy, intellect and heart he has to try to keep our country prosperous, preserve peace and plan for a greater America. You can tell what sort of President he will make because you have lived through these ten months along with us. I am proud of his record and I hope you will want to continue it.[7]

The campaign trail had its lighter moments, too. On September 28, Dick Tuck, long-time Democratic funster, planted a pretty brunette "spy," Moira O'Conner, aboard the Goldwater campaign train by passing her off as the representative of a fictitious news service. That night and again the next morning, a newsletter, "Whistlestop," mysteriously appeared under newsmen's compartment doors. Impishly it reported difficulties in getting local Republican leaders to share the Goldwater platform and identified local Republican newspapers which had endorsed Johnson. Unsmiling Goldwater staffers identified Miss O'Conner by midmorning and deposited her on the platform in Parkersburg, West Virginia.[8]

The "spy" incident, in a special way, typifies the difference between Democratic and Republican campaign styles. Democrats get a special delight out of political warfare. Their campaigns are joyful excursions, and their candidates are enthusiastic champions of the cause. In 1928, Al Smith was "The Happy Warrior." Roosevelt's theme song through the 1930's and 1940's was "Happy Days Are Here Again." The crowds in 1948 yelled "Give 'em Hell,

[7] *The Democrat,* October 12, 1964, p. 1.
[8] *The (Washington) Evening Star,* September 29, 1964, p. 1.

Harry," and the President responded, "That's what I'm doin'!" Adlai Stevenson, in more polished style, made famous his wit in 1952 and 1956. In 1960, the Kennedys entered the fray with the special verve of youth and of the Irish.

With typical Democratic exuberance, both the President and Senator Humphrey stumped the nation in 1964. Humor, self-confidence, and the light touch of gaiety gave the Democratic campaign a special quality and appeal. Even the most serious speech had its lighter moments and the candidates proved able to laugh at themselves as well as at their opponents. Thus did Lyndon Johnson make his case to the American people and, by being himself, earn his right to the highest office in the land.

BARNSTORMING WITH NIXON AND LODGE IN 1960

The strategy for the 1960 Nixon-Lodge barnstorming tours was devised by the Vice President and his immediate staff. The convention promise to visit each of the 50 states reflected Nixon's compulsion to expose himself, in person, to as many people as possible. The wisdom of such an exhausting campaign has been reviewed with serious doubt. The Republican presidential nominee's major efforts to transform his image from the "old" Nixon to the "new" may have suffered because of this too-demanding schedule.

It has been argued, in fact, that overscheduling and at times overexposure were two of the Vice President's worst mistakes in the 1960 campaign. When the campaign pace set for a candidate leaves him wan and weak on the night of a national television debate, for example, the crucial importance of the scheduling function is clearly illustrated.

After Nixon had determined his barnstorming strategy and announced it in Chicago in July, tactical decisions were made. In some states, such as Ohio, the state organization would select the places which would be visited and decide the mode of transportation to be used. In other states, such as California, the Nixon staff itself would set the itinerary. After the staff had established the over-all field strategy and made at least tentative plans for the visits to each state, preparations for "advancing" began—plan making for work in advance of the candidate's appearances.

"Advancing" the Republican national candidates has traditionally been handled by the Republican National Committee. In 1960, however, it was decided that this function, like many others, would be assumed by the Nixon-Lodge headquarters. The Vice President's campaign manager, Bob Finch, was well acquainted with the problems in this field since he had been an advance man for the Vice President in the 1956 campaign. Jack Drown, Finch's law partner from Los Angeles, was recruited to help direct the advancing activities.

Shortly after the convention had adjourned, a selected group of people from all over the country was brought to Washington for brief schooling in political advancing. Some were young lawyers, others had been loaned by industry, still others appeared to be just out of college. Sponsored by the Nixon-Lodge headquarters, this school was conducted by men well acquainted with both the technical problems involved in advancing and the political problems of liaison with state and local regular party organizations. These men attempted to impress upon their young students the crucial importance of establishing and retaining good relations with the regular state and local party leaders. As the campaign progressed, more and more people were brought into this activity. These later advance men spent a short period as apprentices in the field and then, armed with a manual, were given an assignment to some city where a Nixon visit was impending.

The advance men's problems with the candidate's movements may be reviewed under the headings of the kinds of transportation: motorcade, train, and air.

THE MOTORCADE

The instructions to the advance men for all categories of trips stressed detail. For example, the Nixon-Lodge representatives were instructed to be very particular about motorcade cars and drivers. The manual read:

Brand new cars should be avoided because of the danger of overheating and the possibility of other mechanical failures. Convertible tops must be checked thoroughly and the cars must be completely decorated before they rendezvous for the motorcade.

Drivers for all except the national candidates' cars were to be young and "fully familiar with the local area and entirely capable of handling their automobile in traffic and in motorcade formation." The driver for the Vice President's car was automatically a Secret Service man, and the driver of Ambassador Lodge's car was always to be supplied by the party headquarters of the host state.

A mid-September telegram to all advance men from H. R. Haldeman (assistant to Jack Drown) instructed the advance man to place his car (in previous practice stationed far ahead of the motorcade) in the motorcade itself. This car was always to contain Haldeman, a police driver, the advance man for that particular visit, and a Secret Service agent, if necessary. In the same telegram the advance men were instructed to make the Nixon car a convertible until further notice. "Schedule top down whenever street crowds are expected, and top up for long highway runs."

Exact provisions for the motorcade lineups were stressed not only in the advance men's manual, but in telegrams sent from Washington, D.C., or from a Nixon staff member traveling with the Vice President's plane.

The plans called for the advance man's car; then a photographer's car (later a flatbed truck or panel truck was specified); Nixon's car; the security car; a car for the wire services; the press buses and several cars for local office holders and dignitaries; staff cars; and a rear-point security car.

By absolute order, the Vice President's car would always contain a Secret Service driver and a Nixon military aide. Only the Vice President and Mrs. Nixon would occupy the second seat. No exceptions were allowed.

Although original orders called for no exceptions to the rule that the press buses must immediately follow the wire-services car, this rule was broken on occasion. Thus, a Haldeman mid-September telegram to all advance men informed them that whenever a candidate for Senator or Governor was riding in the motorcade, his car should precede the press car and follow immediately behind the wire-services car.

Staff men traveling with Nixon rigorously defended this rule on the placement of local and state candidates. They contended that placement of the press bus more than two cars from the Vice President markedly diminished the impact of the crowd's enthusiasm, size, and general reaction—the very things the press should absorb.

As the advance man's manual put it:

If the press cannot see what is going on they cannot write about it. If the candidate stops, the press must be able to get out to be close to him.

To allow local officials to ride in advance of the press bus may serve their personal interest, admittedly sometimes critically important, but it erodes the Vice President's own critically important interest.

Even the speed of the motorcade was predetermined: never below 15 miles per hour even for large crowds, 15 to 18 miles per hour for scattered crowds and up to, but never beyond, the speed limit for open-country driving.

Press relations were often delicate matters for the advance men to handle. The basic instructions were that regardless of the topic involved—a schedule change, a detail of the local program, crowd estimates, or even a possible news item—only one source should pass the word to the news corps. That source was the Vice President's press secretary. Even the local press chairman was requested not to make news announcements after the campaign party's arrival.

Special events called for special patterns of response. When Mrs. Nixon was available for press coverage, the advance men were advised to secure coverage by women reporters, if possible, in preference to men. A customary format for these meetings was developed which included a sitdown for coffee or tea, emphasis on informality, discouragement of photographs after the first few minutes, and an avoidance of the term "press conference" for such affairs. Rather, according to the manual, the language should be "Mrs. Nixon meets the ladies of the press."

Although Nixon advance men were instructed always to check their movements and clear their plans with state and local party leadership, these instructions were somewhat uncertain in the light of other instructions regarding liaison with the regular party headquarters. For example, they were told that the local police should thoroughly understand that orders for motorcade position must come only from the Nixon advance man, his designated agent, or the Vice President's press secretary. A memo stated:

A frequent trick is for the local official to countermand your order, pull his weight on an officer, and remake the motorcade without your knowing it. It has happened too often.

The general procedures used for Nixon advancing obtained for Lodge's campaign tours. The differences consisted mainly in small items, such as the omission of a security car in the motorcade and the reliance upon local police rather than the Secret Service for the personal security of the Ambassador.

The scores of details listed on the Nixon-Lodge checkoff sheets further illustrate the complexity of a presidential campaign tour. Included were such items as: Has the Vice President's room been supplied with copies of all relevant, recent local newspapers? Do the press buses for the motorcade have enough power to keep up with other motorcade cars in hilly and highway driving? Have special phone lines been put in to connect the Vice President's room with his campaign manager and his secretary?

As if these standard checkoff items were not enough to plague the advance men and local chairmen, special-order telegrams were often sent immediately preceding the candidate's arrival. The following, for example, was received by one advance man on September 26:

There should be at least six horns of twenty-five to thirty-watt capacity each for all outside speaker requirements during an engagement. There should also be three sixty-watt amplifiers. There should be two microphones on the speakers' platform for the public-address system. These microphones should be of the directional type. Remember we need a platform twenty-five to thirty feet in front of Nixon that will hold a minimum of four newsreel cameramen. Height is such that cameras are at the Vice President's eye level.

THE TRAIN TOUR

A train tour for a presidential candidate is costly and involved, but most effective when it is necessary to make a strong appeal in a large number of small to medium-sized communities. In 1960, Vice President Nixon boarded a fifteen-car train in Washington, D.C., at 10:00 p.m. on Sunday evening, October 23. York, Pennsylvania, was to be the first of 43 public appearances in five states in a period of six days. Included in these 43 public appearances were 15 major addresses and a statewide television appearance. To illustrate the nature of a train tour, the itinerary for the departure and first day is reproduced on the following pages.

AIR TRAVEL

One of the major problems in advancing a plane tour of various-sized communities is to learn which airport facilities can handle which planes. In addition, information must be obtained on flying times of various types of aircraft under differing conditions. And the question of using military versus civilian airports must also be resolved.

Perhaps the most difficult of the air-tour problems, however, like the one for motorcades and train tours, is who shall be privileged to accompany the tour. Only a few VIP's can be accommodated on the candidate's plane, and as many newsmen as possible must be carried along.

While serving as a state chairman, Ray Bliss solved such problems when any kind of tour came through his state by using what he called tour categories.

First there was the *statewide category,* or what was sometimes termed the *permanent party*—people who ordinarily stayed with the tour during its entire tour through a state. This category included Senators, the governor or candidates for these offices, candidates for or holders of the state constitutional offices, candidates for the state supreme court, the state party chairman, the national committeeman and committeewoman, the chairman of the finance committee in the state, the chairman of the volunteers or citizens group in the state, and the state chairmen of the auxiliary groups (farmers, veterans, minority, women's groups, Young Republicans, and the like).

The second, or *district category,* covered candidates for Congress, state committeewomen and committeemen, chairmen of the district volunteers or citizens group and sometimes cochairmen of

ITINERARY AND SCHEDULE

TRIP OF THE VICE PRESIDENT AND MRS. NIXON

October 23 through October 29, 1960

A. GENERAL INFORMATION

Train will consist of:

1 Pennsylvania Railroad 60′ Baggage Car—RCA to equip for power
1 Pennsylvania Railroad Dormitory Car—Crews
3 Twelve duplex, five bedroom sleepers (N-12, N-11, N-10)
2 Twelve duplex, four bedroom sleepers (N-9, N-8)
2 Three bedroom, one drawing room, 20 lounge seats (Press) (N-7, N-6)
1 Pennsylvania Railroad Diner cleared for Press Room (N-5)
1 Pennsylvania Railroad 48-seat Diner
1 Pennsylvania Railroad midtrain lounge (Reception Car) (N-4)
1 Twelve duplex, five bedroom sleeper (N-3)
1 Twelve duplex, four bedroom sleeper (N-2)
1 Pennsylvania Railroad business car 7504 (N-1)

Total 15 Cars—Capacity 124 in sleepers, based on one person to room.

B. LENGTH OF TRAIN

Each train company has been notified as to the length of the train and will add the length of their engine equipment to that total in order to place a stake for the engineer to line up with.

Pennsylvania Railroad   NOTES

Sunday, October 23

10:00 PM EDT   Depart *Union Station*, Washington, D.C. for York,
               Pennsylvania

Monday, October 24

8:00 AM EDT   Arrive York, Pennsylvania   York pop.: 60,000

               U.S. Senator is Hugh Scott; Candidate for Congress is
               George A. Goodling (19th District)

               Remarks by the Vice President from the rear platform

8:30 AM EDT   Depart York for Harrisburg, Pennsylvania 50 min.—27 mi.

9:20 AM EDT   Arrive Harrisburg, Pennsylvania   Harrisburg pop.: 85,000

               Congressman is Walter M. Mumma (16th District)

               Rally off train at Market Square

9:40 AM   Address by the Vice President

10:10 AM   Depart Market Square for railroad station

10:15 AM   Arrive railroad station

10:20 AM EDT   Depart Harrisburg for Lewistown, Pennsylvania   1¼ hr.—61 mi.

11:40 AM EDT   Arrive Lewistown, Pennsylvania   Lewistown pop.: 15,000

               Brief remarks by the Vice President from the rear plat-
               form

11:55 AM EDT	Depart Lewistown for Huntingdon, Pennsylvania	¾ hr.—37 mi.
11:35 AM EST	Arrive Huntingdon, Pennsylvania	Huntingdon pop.: 8,000
	Candidate for Congress is Irving Whalley (18th District)	
	Brief remarks by the Vice President from the rear platform	
11:50 AM EST	Depart Huntingdon for Altoona, Pennsylvania	50 min.—34 mi.
1:40 PM EDT	Arrive Altoona, Pennsylvania	Altoona pop.: 70,000
	Congressman is James E. Van Zandt (20th District)	
	Remarks by the Vice President from the rear platform	
2:10 PM EDT	Depart Altoona for Johnstown, Pennsylvania	1 hr.—35 mi.
3:10 PM EDT	Arrive Johnstown, Pennsylvania	Johnstown pop.: 58,000
	Candidate for Congress is John P. Saylor (22nd District)	
	Remarks by the Vice President from the rear platform	
3:40 PM EDT	Depart Johnstown for Greensburg, Pennsylvania	55 min.—48 mi.
4:35 PM EDT	Arrive Greensburg, Pennsylvania	Greensburg pop.: 17,000
	Candidate for Congress is William L. Batten (21st District)	
	Remarks by the Vice President from the rear platform	
5:05 PM EDT	Depart Greensburg for Pittsburgh, Pennsylvania	50 min.—31 mi.

5:55 PM EDT   Arrive Pittsburgh (Pennsylvania Station)   Pittsburgh pop.: 650,000

Congressmen are James G. Fulton (27th District) and
Robert J. Corbett (29th District); candidates for Congress
are Arthur O. Sharron (28th District) and Jerome M.
Meyers (30th District)

6:10 PM   Depart station by motorcade for hotel

6:25 PM   Arrive Penn-Sheraton Hotel   **PRESS ROOM:**
                                                            located off lobby

8:00 PM   Depart hotel for Syria Mosque

8:25 PM   Arrive Syria Mosque

8:30 PM   Address by the Vice President

9:30 PM   Depart Syria Mosque for railroad station

9:45 PM   Arrive Baltimore & Ohio Railroad Station

10:00 PM   Board train

these groups, chairmen of district Young Republicans, and chairmen of the district volunteers' youth committee. The *regional category* covered only the regional finance chairman while the fourth, or *county category,* included chairmen of the county central committees, of the county executive committees, of the county finance committees, county chairwomen, county volunteers chairmen and cochairmen, county farm representatives, county Young Republican presidents, and so on.

Insofar as possible, the person in each category accompanied the permanent party only within the category jurisdiction, thus allowing for a maximum effective exposure of the presidential candidate with local and state party leaders and office holders.

BARNSTORMING WITH GOLDWATER AND MILLER IN 1964

SCHEDULING

At the outset of the Republican presidential campaign of 1964, the Campaign Strategy Committee determined a general allocation of time by days that each candidate would spend within a state. The northeastern states were assigned 2.5 days; the Atlantic states and Pennsylvania, 5.5 days; the South and Texas, 10.0 days; the Great Lakes states, 10.0 days; the Plains states, 4.0 days; the western states, 4.5 days; and California, 5.0 days—for a total of 41.5 campaign days. Based on this allocation, a highly tentative schedule was prepared for each of the candidates for stops in each of the states, as well as a particular week of the campaign that such stops would be made. This tentative schedule was placed on plastic maps week by week so that each week could be superimposed on the previous week and the entire picture of the campaign thus developed. One set of maps covered Senator Goldwater's campaign tours, and the other represented Miller's campaign. These maps were projected on a screen at an early meeting of the strategy committee and were fully discussed and approved.

After the general allocation of time and places for each week was approved, a more detailed schedule was developed by the Tour Committee. While these schedules were being developed, the regional directors were in contact with state chairmen or campaign coordinators in the various states to be visited. The first two days of each week were used in developing a schedule for the week which was two weeks ahead. After agreement had been reached on the advance schedule, each senatorial and congressional candidate in the state to be visited was notified by telephone and wire that Goldwater (or Miller) would be in their state two weeks hence.

After the congressional candidates had been notified, a press release was prepared by a member of the press staff of the Republican National Committee who was assigned to cover the Tour Committee, and approved by Chairman Burch, Wayne Hood, Lou Guylay, and Douglas Whitlock, before release. An advance man was then assigned to each stop and ordered to proceed to the place as rapidly as possible. The tour staff of the Goldwater and Miller desks, working with the advance man, then developed the details at each stop on the schedule.

The responsibility for management of tours and advancing in 1964 was placed in the hands of a thoroughly experienced and time-tested "professional," Doug Whitlock. A Washington attorney, Whitlock had organized the nation's first Young Republicans Club in 1928 and had played an important campaign role in 1932, 1940, 1944, 1948, and in 1960. Arranging and directing candidates' schedules, transportation, and advancing for the visits of the party's standard-bearers posed no difficulty for him.

The division itself divided its work into six specific segments: candidate transportation, scheduling, advancing, Goldwater tours, Miller tours, and Ike-Nixon campaign activities.

At the outset of the campaign, a proposed budget of $477,000 was prepared to cover office rent, furniture, communications facilities, office supplies, travel expenses at $150 per day for Eisenhower, Nixon, and Scranton, expenses for advance men at $60 a day ($30 for hotel and meals, $20 for car rentals, and $10 for incidentals), air-rail travel for advance men, salaries for the Tour Committee Washington staff, and the chartered airplanes for Eisenhower, Nixon, Scranton, and other VIP's.

The actual expenditures for the Tour Committee ran closer to $350,000. This budget, incidentally, did not include the leasing of planes or trains for the candidates. It did, however, as noted, provide for chartering airplanes for General Eisenhower, Mr.

Nixon, Governor Scranton, and members of the Goldwater and Miller families.

At the beginning of the campaign it was necessary to recruit men for advancing. Suggestions were received from previous advance men, officials of the Republican National Committee or state committees, personnel in offices of United States Senators or Representatives, recommendations from Goldwater and Miller supporters and volunteers.

A preliminary conference was arranged with each interested person who had been recommended, during which the work of an advance man was briefly outlined. The availability of the prospective advance man for full-time employment away from home, his financial requirements, and his interest in the campaign were discussed. At the same time, the prospect was considered as to personality, ability to make contacts, orderliness of approach, and general adaptability to advance work.

If the prospect appeared to be a person who should be considered, it was suggested he attend the next training session for advance men and learn more about the details of the job before a final decision was reached by either the individual or the Tour Committee. Following this training session, a second conference was held and consideration was given to whether or not the prospect wanted to accept advance work, and a reevaluation of his capabilities for such work was made.

Two training sessions for advance men were held at the beginning of the campaign. The first session was held on August 29-30, 1964. After a general description of the responsibilities of advance men, an informal, "shirt-sleeves" session focused on the advance man's manual. Each section of the manual was read and discussed fully. Then the advance men were addressed by Chairman Burch, Executive Director Grenier, Campaign Director Hood, George Carver of the finance division, and other men who had previous experience as advance men in a presidential campaign.

The manual, or handbook, given to each advance man, was some 150 pages in length and contained all the pertinent data on types of meetings and arrangements the advance men would be called upon to handle. From time to time, additions were made as the requirements of the candidates changed and as experience in the field indicated the need for further directives.

Each advance man was also provided with a briefcase containing such items as car stickers for motorcades, guest passes, a clipboard for notes, biographies and pictures of candidates, expense-report forms, a checklist form, and a thank-you form.

The assistant to the tour director for advance men assigned each scheduled stop to one or more advance men. Because of the great speed of the Boeing *727* jet plane assigned to Senator Goldwater and the *Electra* of Representative Miller, 38 full-time advance men were required to cover the entire campaign of both candidates. Twelve additional advance men were assigned for Mr. Nixon, and 2 for Governor Scranton. Each member of the Goldwater family (Mrs. Goldwater, Barry Goldwater, Jr., and Mike Goldwater) was assigned one advance man to handle details and to prevent local committees from deviating from schedules.

As the campaign developed, it was found expedient to leave certain advance men within a limited number of states. Notably true in Ohio, Texas, and the Midwest, this was due to the frequent stops being made by one or the other of the candidates in these particular areas. The advance man assigned to these areas became acquainted with the local officials and conditions, thus making efficient operation possible. In all cases effort was made to prevent long crisscrossing advance-men assignments in order to minimize expense. Even though there was a seemingly large number of advance men, there was virtually no time when any of the 38 advance men was without an assignment. In fact, several times during the campaign, the Tour Committee was hard-pressed to furnish an advance man to the local committee by the time they desired his services.

TRANSPORTATION PROVISIONS

Senator Goldwater's plane was a Boeing *727* jet leased from American Airlines and fully equipped for communications with TWX and telephone, as well as typewriters and mimeograph machines for staff use. Senator Goldwater's private section was reserved for his immediate party and invited guests, a group usually totaling 16 persons. The remaining seats were allocated to the traveling press. The priority list for political passengers on Senator Goldwater's plane was as follows: First, state chairman and citizens-committee chairman in the state being visited; second, the Governor and/or Senators in the state; third, the congressman in whose district the meeting was being held; fourth, members of the Republican National Committee; fifth, candidates for major office in the state; sixth, the finance chairman in the state; and seventh, the vice chairman in the state. On occasion, a financial contributor or a financial chairman was of such importance that it was felt that his priority should be advanced to fourth or fifth place. This was not the general rule, however.

A Lockheed *Electra* was leased from Eastern Airlines for Representative Miller and was equipped with communications and staff facilities similar to those of Senator Goldwater's plane.

Shortly after the campaign got under way, it became evident that there were not sufficient press seats on Senator Goldwater's plane and a second Boeing 727 was leased from United Airlines for the press. Each member of the press traveling with either candidate was required to pay for his transportation and hotel expenses. The press arrangements were handled by the press section of the Republican National Committee. A $3,600 deposit was required from each news agency against which was charged the cost of transportation for its representative on either of the planes. Mr. Nixon's leased plane, which he used from October 1 to October 31, was equipped with office facilities similar to those of Senator Goldwater. Governor Scranton used his own plane for air travel, and General Eisenhower used chartered planes during his speaking schedule. When not traveling with the Senator, the Goldwater family used a variety of air transportation. Mrs. Goldwater generally traveled by chartered plane; Barry, Jr., by a twin-engine *Aero Commander* made available to him for the campaign; and Mike Goldwater traveled mostly by commercial transportation.

GENERAL PROCEDURE FOR THE CONSTRUCTION OF SCHEDULES

Executive Director Whitlock operated under general policy provisions of the Strategy and Advisory Committee (the group of top campaign advisors who met each Sunday to develop general campaign strategy). The rules for scheduling handed down to Whitlock were as follows:

1. The policy has been established by the Strategy and Advisory Committee that the schedules of both candidates shall be limited to three appearances per day, it being realized that the term "appearance" is intended to describe a period of time for a particular stop rather than a particular type of address.

2. The policy has been established by the Strategy Committee with respect to Senator Goldwater that the schedule may include one appearance by the Senator before a private finance meeting to follow a major speech in a city where the Senator is to remain overnight. However, appearances by the Senator will be limited to finance meetings personally approved by Misters Cordiner or Milbank in accordance with criteria set forth by the Senator.

3. Policy has been established that communications with Governors, Senators, Congressmen and National Committee members will be advisory only, and direct negotiations for scheduling will be conducted with the State Chairman.

4. Responsibilities for the construction of schedules and the decision making process:

    A. The Policy Committee meets at 2 p.m. each Sunday to determine the states to be visited and the specific weeks for appearance in groups of states for two weeks ahead.

    B. A tentative schedule is constructed by the Tour Committee on Sunday based on the decision of the Strategy Committee.

        (1) The tentative schedule is forwarded to the Regional Directors who call the State Chairmen on Monday and Tuesday to determine the cities to be visited in the states on the schedule.

        (2) The Tour Committee on Monday and Tuesday determines from the Transportation Division the "wheels up and wheels down" time for each day of the week under consideration.

    C. The Tour Committee composes the first definitive schedule on Wednesday for general distribution and publication after coordinating the decisions of the Regional Directors and the National Finance Chairman as to specific states and the allocation of time to each appearance after consultation with the Transportation Division.

    D. The Special Assistant to the Chairman for Congressional

Liaison contacts Governors, Senators, and Congressmen on Wednesday to permit announcements of the scheduled appearance.

E. The Tour Committee on Thursday and Friday contacts State Chairmen to determine the nature of the visit of the scheduled appearances and the first tentative allocation of time to specific events. All negotiations with State Chairmen on details and changes to the schedule will be conducted by the Tour Committee.

Decisions should be reached as follows, with respect to these general categories regarding moving the candidates:

1. State and week—Strategy Committee;
2. Town or city within the state—Regional Directors;
3. Allocation of time and nature of visit—Tour Committee;
4. Finance—National Finance Chairman.

The manual for advance men included specific instructions on the development of local schedules. Several such instructions stand out as variants from usual scheduling procedures. For example, no press conferences were to be scheduled except those under the direction of the Washington staff. No stops at small meetings or functions other than the main event were to be scheduled. In drawing up the over-all schedule, the advance men were to keep in mind the probability of impromptu handshaking in the streets or at the rally, but no schedule for any formal reception or handshaking session was to be made.

The candidate was not to be scheduled to eat any meals at a public event. If the candidate was to appear at a breakfast, luncheon, or dinner meeting, he was to be scheduled to arrive after the meal, in time for his speech. No private homes were to be used for overnight or daytime stops, nor were any small, private, off-the-record meetings for finance to be scheduled. (This injunction did create some problems for local party fund raisers.) No fund-raising dinners or other fund-raising events were to be scheduled without explicit instructions from the Washington tour desk.

The over-all day's schedule was to be prepared so that the candidate was in his room at the hotel by 11 o'clock every night. This point was stressed over and over again, probably on the advice of those who had seen what had happened to Nixon during the 1960 campaign when he went for days with virtually no sleep.

No commitments were to be made in advance for factory "drop-bys." If done at all, this had to be done on a last-minute basis. Although the candidates planned to attend church every Sunday during the campaign, no announcements were to be made in advance of church attendance and no invitations accepted for church services.

Private dinners, cocktail parties, or after-meeting social events were not to be accepted, and the local committees were to be aware of this injunction so that they would not schedule anything without the knowledge of the Tour Committee. The advance men were to keep in mind the possibility of a separate schedule for Mrs. Goldwater and Mrs. Miller. Thus, no commitments were to be made in regard to their schedule without prior clearance from the Washington tour office. Separate schedules could be arranged only where appropriate and where they would not appear forced. Those possibilities which were suggested would be interviews with newswomen and visits to hospitals, churches, schools, and orphanages.

GOLDWATER AND MILLER MEET THE PEOPLE

Senator Goldwater and Representative Miller started their campaign on September 3 in Prescott, Arizona—Senator Goldwater's hometown and the spot from which he had initiated his campaigns for the United States Senate. From there, on September 5, the team toured to Lockport, New York—Representative Miller's hometown.

On September 8 and 9, Senator Goldwater spent a short time in San Diego, journeyed to Sacramento and on to Klamath Falls and Eugene, Oregon, and then to Seattle, Washington, for a finance meeting. On Thursday, September 10, he was in Boise, Idaho; Great Falls, Montana; and Minneapolis, Minnesota, for a second finance meeting, and on September 11 he was in Chicago and Rockford, Illinois.

After taking two days' rest on September 12 and 13, Senator Goldwater spent Tuesday, September 15, in Winston-Salem, North Carolina; Atlanta, Georgia; and Orlando, Tampa, and St. Petersburg, Florida. On September 16, the Senator was in Knoxville and Memphis, Tennessee; Macon, Georgia; and Montgomery and Raleigh, North Carolina. On September 17, he was in Greenville,

North Carolina; Shreveport and New Orleans, Louisiana. On Friday he was in Longview, Texas; Springville, Illinois; Evansville, Indiana; and Charleston, West Virginia, and then on to Washington. And so the campaign went: 191 appearances in 45 states supported by his vice-presidential candidate, other Republican leaders, and his family.

Most of Goldwater's campaign was conducted by air travel. But because of the success of the 1960 whistlestop train tour operated throughout Ohio and Illinois, it was decided that there would be several of these in the 1964 campaign. Three were for the presidential canidate, and one for the vice-presidential candidate.

Train #1, Senator Goldwater's first whistlestop train, left Washington the night of September 28. September 29 and 30 were spent in Ohio; October 1 in Indiana, and October 2 and 3 in Illinois, with the train terminating in Joliette. From Joliette, the party moved by motorcade to Wheaton, Illinois, for a rally; thence to O'Hare Airport in Chicago for a return to Washington by air.

Train #2 for Senator Goldwater was operated from Los Angeles to San Diego on Friday, October 23. The trip was scheduled for just over five hours with five intermediate stops.

Train #3 was a one-day trip for Congressman Miller. The train originated in Buffalo, New York, the morning of Saturday, October 24. There were eight speaking stops. The train terminated in Harmon, New York, followed by a motorcade to Westchester County Airport with a "drop-in" stop at the Briarhill Country Club en route. The return to Washington was by air.

Train #4 was a one-day trip for Senator Goldwater across Pennsylvania from Harrisburg to Pittsburgh, on Thursday, October 29, with five intermediate stops.

These trains were highly successful in getting the candidates closer to the people. Goldwater, who had not been enthusiastic about a whistlestop tour, had apparently changed his attitude when he addressed a crowd at Peoria, Illinois, on the morning of Friday, October 2.

This has been a very delightful three days, and we wind up tomorrow on the fourth day in northern Illinois, in Chicago, the first whistlestop tour I ever made as a candidate on a train, and I am happy to admit—having been piloting for 35 years, that I am getting to like this train riding. It is very comfortable. We got to see a lot of wonderful people, and it was so encouraging coming up through Illinois today for in every little town there were people out in their beautifully kept yards, people waving and encouraging us.

The report on the train tours indicated that the press, having been limited by the capacity of the airplane for most of the tour, showed up in exceptionally large numbers for the rail trips. They did have the usual complaints of not being accommodated in cars closer to the candidate—a problem which was not as evident on the one-day trips as it was on the five-day trips, which involved sleeping cars for their use. The policy of collecting in advance from the press was followed for train tours, as it was for plane tours.

Over-all, the scheduling and advancing aspects of the 1964 Republican presidential campaign were handled efficiently and with a minimum of intraparty conflict. The professional and tireless leadership by Douglas Whitlock contributed in large measure to the success of these efforts.

Bibliography

Shadegg, Stephen. *What Happened to Goldwater?* New York: Holt, 1965.

White, F. Clifton. *Suite 3505*. New Rochelle, N.Y.: Arlington House, 1967.

White, Theodore H. *The Making of the President, 1960*. New York: Atheneum, 1961.

White, Theodore H. *The Making of the President, 1964*. New York: Atheneum, 1965.

Chapter X

Financing the Campaign

 It costs at least $10 million to run for President. In 1964, Goldwater forces admitted to spending at least $16 million; Johnson forces, nearly $9 million. In 1960, the Kennedy and Nixon camps reported spending $10 million each. Most observers believe a presidential campaign costs much more.

THE COST OF A PRESIDENTIAL CAMPAIGN

No one really knows how much it costs to run for President. No one has ever kept track of all the costs, and no law requires anyone to do so. The most diligent research by political scientists has turned up only approximations.

In 1964, 107 national-level political committees spent $34.8 million. Of this sum, 18 Republican committees supporting Senator Goldwater disbursed $17,187,000, part as transfers to other candidates and committees. Thirty-two Democratic committees similarly spent $11,973,000, while 31 labor committees added some $3,665,000, largely to aid Democratic causes.[1]

In 1960, 70 national-level political committees spent $25,014,000. Republican committees supporting Vice President Nixon's candidacy reported $11,300,000; Democratic committees

[1] Herbert E. Alexander, *Financing the 1964 Election* (Princeton, N.J.: Citizens' Research Foundation, 1966), pp. 7-8.

backing Kennedy, $10,587,000.[2] In 1956, President Eisenhower's reelection cost his Republican committees a reported $8,900,000, while Stevenson supporters spent an estimated $5,500,000.[3] In 1952, Republicans spent $6,600,000 to elect General Eisenhower, while Governor Stevenson's backers spent $4,500,000.[4]

These figures represent the reported disbursements plus the known debts only of committees operating in two or more states. Much of the expense of presidential campaigning is borne by state and local party organizations which are not obliged to report their expenditures.

Certain other special committees disbursed large sums that should be added to the total available to the candidates. Most notable among them are the labor committees. In 1964, they reported spending $725,000 directly, but had gross receipts of $3,665,000.[5] In 1960, the comparable figures were $843,581 and nearly $2 million. Much of these funds went for registration and get-out-the vote drives, and some funds aided the Republican presidential candidate. The bulk of the money, however, must be counted for Johnson and Kennedy respectively.[6] In 1956, labor groups disbursed $540,735; and in 1952, $797,544—also largely to the benefit of the Democrats.[7]

Winning a presidential nomination costs additional large sums. In 1964, Goldwater forces admitted spending $5,500,000 to capture the Republican nomination. Rockefeller spent $3,000,000. Even Scranton, who entered the lists at the last moment, rolled up an $827,000 bill, while noncandidates like Lodge, Nixon, and Stassen spent between $100,000 and $70,000. The known Republican preconvention bills for these six candidates totaled $9,568,000.

Presidential preference primaries contribute mightily to the cost

---

[2] Herbert E. Alexander, *Financing the 1960 Election* (Princeton, N.J.: Citizens' Research Foundation, 1962), pp. 9-11.

[3] U.S. Congress, Senate, *1956 General Election Campaigns* (Washington: Government Printing Office, 1957), p. 42.

[4] Alexander Heard, *The Costs of Democracy* (Chapel Hill: University of North Carolina Press, 1960), p. 20.

[5] Alexander, *Financing the 1964 Election*, p. 8.

[6] Alexander, *Financing the 1960 Election*, p. 42.

[7] Heard, *The Costs of Democracy*, p. 20.

of winning a nomination. In 1964, the contested California primary alone cost Goldwater and Rockefeller a combined $4,000,000. Even in Oregon, which Goldwater did not contest seriously, the bill for Rockefeller was $490,000; for Goldwater, $109,000.[8]

In 1960, Kennedy forces reported spending $912,500 to win the Democratic nomination. In addition, a family-owned corporation purchased and leased to him a $385,000 airplane.[9] Many costs were picked up by local Kennedy for President preconvention committees. Richard Nixon reported spending $500,000 to win the 1960 Republican nomination, even though he had virtually no serious opposition.[10]

Alexander Heard reports that the 1956 Democratic nomination cost the supporters of Adlai E. Stevenson "at least $1,500,000."[11] Eisenhower preconvention expenditures in 1956 were, of course, unrepresentative inasmuch as there was no contest for the nomination. In 1952, however, Citizens for Eisenhower reported expending $1,200,000 to win the nomination. Heard estimates that the Eisenhower nomination effort cost at least $2,500,000 and that "time, goods, and services contributed without reimbursement . . . had a dollar value running into additional millions."[12] The Stevenson draft in 1952 was not expensive, however, only $20,000 being reported. Stevenson himself spent $1,350, most of it during the Democratic convention. Kefauver, however, who campaigned actively in both 1952 and 1956, spent at least $356,387 in 1952 and nearly $400,000 in 1956.[13]

Why should it take a sizable fortune to win the presidency? The costs of publicity, travel, and staff support are very high.

The single largest bill in a presidential campaign is for television and radio time. In 1964, network and station charges for presidential and vice-presidential candidates alone ran $12,800,000. Goldwater and Miller spent $7,500,000; Johnson and Humphrey, $5,100,000. Of these sums, $1,500,000 went for nomination contests, all but $300,000 of it for Republicans.[14]

[8] Alexander, *Financing the 1964 Election*, pp. 17-35.
[9] Alexander, *Financing the 1960 Election*, p. 16.   [10] *Ibid.*, pp. 21-22.
[11] Heard, *The Costs of Democracy*, p. 341.
[12] *Ibid.*, p. 335.   [13] *Ibid.*, pp. 335-336.
[14] Alexander, *Financing the 1964 Election*, pp. 52-53.

Earlier presidential contests had been much less costly. In 1960, the radio-television bill ran $3,006,102, divided $1,900,000 for the Republican candidate and $1,100,000 for the Democratic.[15] In 1956, the Gore committee reported, the Democrats spent $1,950,000 promoting Stevenson's campaign by television and radio; the Republicans, $2,739,000 for Eisenhower.[16] At least 75 per cent of the money was for television in all three elections. For these sums, the parties received 16 hours and 12 minutes of air time on the three television networks in 1964. In 1960, the candidates purchased 9 hours and 55 minutes over 429 television stations.

Why were radio and television so much more costly in 1964 than in previous years? Basically, less free time was made available to the candidates, and both appealed to wider audiences over more stations. In 1960, the debates between Kennedy and Nixon were made possible by a contribution of 4 hours of prime viewing time by each of the major television networks. In 1964, Congress declined to suspend the equal-time provisions of section 315 of the Federal Communications Act, so no such time offer could be made. In 1964, however, television provided the candidates only 1 hour and 18 minutes of free time. In 1960, in addition to the debates, the networks and individual stations furnished 2 hours and 30 minutes of free time.[17] In 1960, also, both major-party candidates had kept television costs down by favoring regional telecasts which were paid for by state party organizations. In 1956, as in 1964, both had used more costly national telecasts. In 1956, especially, both had chosen to use several 30-minute nationwide telecasts of major addresses.

In 1960, the two national committees saved a fortune on the four debates alone. The networks valued the time at $1,327,520. American Broadcasting Company, which estimated the lowest direct cost for its contribution, a total of $250,000, reported that if the revenue sacrifice by affiliated stations and the administrative and advertising costs had been included, the loss would have been an additional $500,000. If such a ratio is generally justified, the

---

[15] Alexander, *Financing the 1960 Election,* p. 31.
[16] U.S. Congress, Senate, *1956 General Election Campaigns,* p. 9.
[17] Alexander, *Financing the 1964 Election,* pp. 50-60.

debates may have been worth about $4 million! National Broadcasting Company, however, reported its direct cost at $111,130 for each telecast, a total of $444,520. Columbia Broadcasting System reported time and production costs of $633,000 for the four programs.[18]

Other publicity is a heavy consumer of funds. Each party spends about $2 million for pamphlets, buttons, bumper stickers, tabloid newspapers, films, and the like. Campaign literature cost the Democrats an estimated $2 million in 1964,[19] and a reported $1,900,076 in 1956. The Republican bill in 1964 was a reported $1,690,000, and in 1956 $2,187,199. These figures, however, include some costs for senatorial and congressional candidates. In 1960, the Materials Distribution Center of the Democratic National Committee spent $805,303.67 for buttons, tabs, bumper stickers, and a wide variety of literature which represented a major portion of the total Democratic effort for Kennedy. Preparation of such publicity adds to the expense. In 1964, Democrats paid Campaign Aids $435,000[20] and in 1960 paid Jack Denove Productions, Inc., $337,000 for films and tapes.[21]

Travel and transportation create large costs. In 1964, Republicans reported $1,917,629 for travel and air and rail charter expenses. In 1960, the Kennedy campaign cost Democrats an estimated $2,500 a day. Among the costs were three chartered airplanes for the candidate, his staff, and the press. Keeping advance men in the field also cost at least $40 a day per man, and each party had from 20 to 40 men out continuously both in 1960 and 1964.

Staff salaries were up in 1964, the Republican cost being $1,586,672. The number of staff members at Republican headquarters soared to 600. Peak payroll reached $37,500 a week.[22] The Democratic payroll, aided by volunteers from congressional staffs and enjoying automatic Secret Service support for tours by the President and Vice President, ran $23,500 a week. In 1960,

---

[18] Alexander, *Financing the 1960 Election,* pp. 34-35.
[19] Alexander, *Financing the 1964 Election,* p. 50.   [20] *Ibid.,* p. 46.
[21] Alexander, *Financing the 1960 Election,* p. 31.
[22] Alexander, *Financing the 1964 Election,* pp. 45, 48.

the Democratic payroll had reached $50,000 a week during the height of the campaign. Republican figures were reportedly comparable.

In recent years, public-opinion polling has added a new cost to campaigns. In 1964, the Republican National Committee spent $165,400 on polls and surveys. No comparable figures are available for Democrats, but Harris conducted extensive polling efforts for Kennedy in 1960.

THE REGULATION OF PRESIDENTIAL CAMPAIGN FINANCE

Congress long has regulated presidential campaign finance in five important ways.

REPORTS OF EXPENDITURES AND RECEIPTS

Committees operating in two or more states on behalf of candidates for President and Vice President are obliged to report their campaign expenditures quarterly. The Federal Corrupt Practices Act prescribes that the treasurer of each such interstate committee shall file reports with the Clerk of the House of Representatives between the first and tenth days of March, June, and September and before the first day of January each year. In presidential election years, additional reports must be filed between the tenth and fifteenth days before the election and on the fifth day before the election.

The reports must contain the name and address of each person who has made a contribution of $100 or more, in total, during the calendar year; the name and address of each person to whom $10 or more has been paid, together with a statement of the sum, date, and purpose of the expenditure; the total sum of all contributions received; and the total sum of all expenditures made. Reports are cumulative from period to period during the year. Thus the final report on December 31 must cover the entire calendar year.[23]

Such reporting does not tell the whole story and really has more nuisance value than utility. Committees operating within a single

[23] 2 U.S.C. secs. 241-248.

state are exempted. Thus state and county party central committees and independent state and local citizen committees for presidential candidates can handle very large sums without reporting at
all.

The Clerk of the House of Representatives merely keeps such
reports on file for two years. He neither publishes nor analyzes
them. The welter of detail thus collected has been used by a few
scholars who have an interest in political finance, but even they
have found the data largely unenlightening. The public has virtually no knowledge of the procedure or the information thus collected.

LIMITATIONS ON SOURCES OF CONTRIBUTIONS

The Corrupt Practices Act reads:

It is unlawful for any corporation whatever, or any labor organization
to make a contribution or expenditure in connection with any election
at which Presidential and Vice Presidential electors . . . are to be
voted for, or in connection with any primary election or political
convention or caucus held to select candidates for any of the foregoing
offices.

The same section also forbids "any candidate, political committee,
or other person to accept or receive any contribution prohibited by
this section."[24]

Public Law 772 of the Eightieth Congress extended the prohibitions to any person or firm which has entered into a contract to sell
any sort of goods or services to the United States during the life of
the agreement.[25]

Such provisions have invited evasion. The Subcommittee on
Privileges and Elections of the United States Senate in 1957 reported that the United States Chamber of Commerce had circulated widely a publication expressing the legal opinion that the
following political activities could be undertaken by corporations:

(1) Pay salaries and wages of officers and regular employees while
engaged in political activities;

(2) Publish opinions and arguments of a political nature, expressed

[24] 18 U.S.C. sec. 610.
[25] 18 U.S.C. sec. 611.

as the views of the corporation, in any house organ or other printed document circulated at the expense of the corporation;

(3) Purchase radio and television time or newspaper space for the presentation of the corporation's political views;

(4) Use any other means of expressing the political views of the corporate management, publicly or privately;

(5) Encourage people to register and vote, and disseminate information and opinions concerning public issues without regard to parties and candidates.

The committee reported that testimony had been developed which showed that corporations also:

(1) Make use of the advertising or entertainment funds of trade associations for political contributions;

(2) Place advertisements in political publications through public relations firms or advertising agencies;

(3) Make contributions in kind to political candidates (make available to them without pay the use of offices, airplanes, etc.);

(4) Permit the padding of expense accounts with the understanding that political contributions should be made out of the padded amounts; and

(5) Pay or prepay bonuses with the explicit or tacit understanding that part of such remuneration shall be spent in campaign contributions.[26]

Labor unions have taken the same attitude about use of funds from union treasuries. However, the endorsement of Democratic candidates in labor newspapers has led Republican union members to object to such use of their funds. In 1961, the Supreme Court ruled that railway workers, who are compelled by the Railway Labor Act to belong to a railway union, may prevent the union from using their dues for political expressions of which they disapprove.[27]

To avoid these restrictions and yet to mobilize the resources of a large organization, the labor unions have developed independent "committees on political education" which technically are not labor unions, although they usually are headed by labor-union

[26] U.S. Congress, Senate, *1956 General Election Campaigns*, p. 24.
[27] *International Association of Machinists* vs. *Street*, 367 U.S. 740 (1961).

leaders. These committees raise funds from their members for avowedly political purposes, make contributions to candidates, solicit votes, and engage in other direct political action.

Federal employees are free to give to political causes, but they may not solicit funds and they may not be asked to contribute on public property. Presidential appointees and employees of the immediate office of the President are exempted from these restrictions. Similar prohibitions do apply to state employees who are paid in part by federal funds.[28]

The purchase or sale of goods, commodities, or advertising which are designed to raise money for a presidential campaign also is prohibited.[29] Political committees therefore simply offer special buttons, hats, ribbons, banners, pictures, and the like as "gifts" in return for "contributions" of a suggested amount. Tickets to fund-raising dinners and entertainment programs also are cautiously offered "free" in recognition of generous contributions—usually of $100 or more.

The gift subterfuge has had one benefit for the political parties: excise taxes are not charged on the amounts of the gifts. The political committees thereby enjoy the entire benefits of the proceeds.

LIMITATIONS ON AMOUNTS OF CONTRIBUTIONS

Individuals are limited by the Hatch Act of 1940 to a contribution of $5,000 during any calendar year to each presidential candidate and presidential campaign committee.[30] Intended to reduce the influence of wealthy individuals, the provision has only made bookkeeping more complicated for the political parties. An individual who wishes to give more than $5,000 simply divides his money by having his wife and other members of his family give $5,000 each or by distributing such sums among different political committees backing his candidate. Indeed, inasmuch as there is no limit on gifts to state and local committees, or on their transfer of funds to the national committees, the simplest way to make a very large gift is to turn it over to a state central committee for handling.

---

[28] 5 U.S.C. sec. 118 i and k.
[29] 18 U.S.C. sec. 608.   [30] *Ibid.*

LIMITATIONS ON AMOUNTS OF EXPENDITURES

National committees also are limited by the Hatch Act to annual expenditures of $3 million.[31] In ordinary years, when committee operating budgets run from $750,000 to $1 million, the restriction is academic. In campaign years, the restriction is a major handicap to fiscal control.

With presidential campaign costs running more than $10 million, the candidate for President is obliged to establish several other national committees, each of which can spend $3 million. Such an arrangement requires the keeping of several sets of books, the shifting of funds and bills back and forth among committees to keep each one from spending more than the legal limit, and sometimes even the transfer of personnel from one payroll to another. With several treasurers in the act, central fiscal control becomes unnecessarily complex and unwieldy.

Only a partial solution can be found in using the credit of the regular national committee. As a continuing body which must meet outstanding debts, the national committee can postpone paying some bills—for example, printing, telephone, and leased transportation—for 60 days after the election. Being then in a new calendar year, it is free to spend an additional $2 million or so to pay campaign bills.

Because the limitations on amounts of contributions and on amounts of expenditures are not only ineffective but are actually an impediment to responsible fiscal control of presidential campaigns, the President's Commission on Campaign Costs recommended, in April 1962, that both provisions be repealed.[32] In his State of the Union Address in 1966, President Johnson recommended remedial action.

LIMITATIONS ON THE PURPOSE OF EXPENDITURES

Prohibition of the bribery of voters is the only federal limitation on purpose of presidential campaign expenditures. Many states,

---

[31] 18 U.S.C. sec. 609.
[32] President's Commission on Campaign Costs, *Financing Presidential Campaigns* (Washington: Government Printing Office, 1962), p. 17.

however, restrict other actions which affect presidential elections. Thirty-two prohibit the furnishing of intoxicating liquor on Election Day, and fifteen prohibit expenditures to transport voters to the polls, although nine of these exempt the sick and the infirm.

Thirty-one states enumerate permissible expenditures. Some state laws are limited to candidates only, others apply only to political committees. The lists of acceptable purposes run the gamut of ordinary campaign activities and include such items as printing, traveling expenses, rent, salaries, and employing counsel.[33] Such state restrictions, if construed to affect presidential candidates, seem not to have imposed handicaps or to have significantly altered campaigning.

FREEDOM FROM LIMITATIONS ON PERSONAL ACTIONS

Candidates for President and Vice President enjoy a unique personal freedom from regulation. Technically, they are not candidates for office. The candidates being chosen by the people are running for the office of presidential elector. Thus, unlike candidates for Congress, presidential candidates need not report contributions they receive or expenditures they make in their own campaigns. They also face no dollar limitations on the amounts they personally can spend. They are, however, prohibited from receiving contributions from corporations and labor organizations and cannot solicit campaign funds if they are receiving compensation for services from the federal government.

WHO PAYS THE BILLS?

Both major political parties raise their funds for presidential campaigns from the people who have the money: the well-to-do. Small gifts from many people, championed by idealistic political scientists who would like to see the parties freed from dependence upon personal and corporate wealth, are hard to organize and unproductive for the national party organizations.

Two types of small-giver drives have been tried by both parties: mail solicitation of a list of party faithful by the national commit-

---

[33] See U.S. Congress, Senate, *Final Report of the Special Committee to Investigate Political Activities, Lobbying, and Campaign Contributions* (Washington: Government Printing Office, 1957), pp. 327-337.

tee, and direct door-to-door solicitation by local party committees which are expected to hand a share of the proceeds to the national committee. By far the most successful such effort was mounted by Goldwater supporters in the 1964 campaign. By mailing 15,-277,342 requests for small donations and by directing appeals over television, the Republicans obtained 651,000 replies which yielded $5,800,000.[34] Earlier Republican efforts were similarly successful, but less spectacular. In 1963, 100,000 contributors sent in $1,100,000.

Between 1956 and 1960, the Democratic National Committee inaugurated both mail solicitation of "sustaining memberships" of $5-$10 a year and door-to-door "Dollars for Democrats" drives. Both peaked in 1960, the mail solicitation producing a modest $240,000 and Dollars for Democrats a disappointing $120,000. Although reports to the committee indicated that some large sums have been raised door-to-door, most of the money understandably "sticks" in the treasuries of local and state committees on its way up to the national-committee treasury. After 1961, the Democratic National Committee permitted both efforts to languish but did not formally abolish them. In 1966, the sustaining-membership program was revived, more to reinforce voter identification with the party than to provide a major source of funds.

Except for the extraordinary Republican efforts in 1963 and 1964, small gifts have never been sufficient even to keep a national committee operating in ordinary times. In a presidential campaign, even the Goldwater effort of 1964 was short of expenditures by more than $10 million. So both national committees turn to more easily tapped and more lucrative sources—their own state central committees and those who are able to make large personal donations.

THE GIVING CIRCLE

Those who give big money can raise big money. Few people give big money without being asked. These basic rules underlie use of the "giving circle."

Every large community has a group of leading citizens who are quite well-to-do. Well acquainted with one another, operating in

[34] Alexander, *Financing the 1964 Election,* pp. 70-71.

the same social circle, doing business with one another, their families probably intermarried to some extent, these people are the pillars of the local churches, the chairmen of service-organization boards such as the Red Cross and the Camp Fire Girls, the fund raisers for community projects, and the financial angels for their colleges. Their gifts to their several "activities" are tax-deductible and, for those families with very substantial incomes, may even be programed systematically in order to strengthen their influence and to maximize tax savings.

Every few weeks, someone in the giving circle calls on most of the others on behalf of the charity or service in which he is taking a leading part. For the Community Chest, all will be visited. For each church, only identified members will get a call. A regular season for giving for each charity is long since well established: the Community Chest in October, the Tuberculosis Association in December, the Polio Fund in January, and so on. In the course of a year, many members of the giving circle have called on the others on behalf of a project which they have agreed to support.

In September of presidential election years, another round is made, this time by the members of the giving circle who have offered or been invited to be the fund raisers for the presidential candidates of their political parties. Each knows whose pocket-books will be open, for his have been open to them, and each knows who will probably be giving to the other candidate and who may even give to both. Thus the Republican fund chairman does not bother his known Democratic colleagues, and vice versa, unless he suspects that defection is in the wind. One does not use up "credit" with a member of the giving circle needlessly, for the next visit may involve renewal of an insurance policy or a loan for a new building.[35]

Giving circles do not operate just in the $1,000 to $5,000 gift class. Those who give in the $100 to $500 class also operate giving circles, and still more modest levels also flourish. At all levels, however, the principle is the same. He who would raise funds must be one of the circle of givers whom he will solicit.

Big giving starts, then, with the person who has money and who

[35] Heard, *The Costs of Democracy,* pp. 78-84, catches the spirit of this point.

feels a personal responsibility for the success of the campaign. Such a person may be related to the candidate, be a close personal friend, have a great deal to gain or lose by his success or failure, or feel very deeply about the policies he espouses. Motivation is highly complex.

Giving in a presidential campaign is a personal matter, however. Few big givers do so as a matter of habit. Mr. Kennedy could loosen the purse strings of men who never gave to Mr. Stevenson, while Stevenson opened doors which were closed to Mr. Truman before him. So the members of the giving circle in each city act accordingly, expanding the circle or varying their visits as political intelligence dictates.

The essential first move of a candidate who would raise big money is to secure on his team a member of the giving circle in as many major cities as he can. In 1960, John F. Kennedy had a head start over all his competitors. He had brothers-in-law in Chicago and Los Angeles, and close business associates of his father in New York and Philadelphia. The top giving circles of the major cities of the nation were immediately open to him.

THE ASSESSMENT OF STATE COMMITTEES

The other major source of funds for a national campaign is assessment of the state central committees. Each will be asked to raise what the national committee regards as a fair share of the campaign cost.

"Fair shares" may be determined in many ways. Sometimes a scientific formula will be used based on population, numbers of party supporters, and per-capita income. More often the quota is set by the amount raised in a previous campaign—for proved ability to get money is more important than theoretical capacity.

Both sources of funds—the giving circle and the state committees—will be helped in their efforts by formal affairs in their chief cities aimed at the well-to-do. The most common device is the $100-a-plate dinner at which the presidential candidate is the speaker. In recent years, variations on this theme have raised the ante to $250, $500, and even $1,000 a plate where there were enough rich people to hold such exclusive parties. In Washington, D.C., both political parties repeatedly have packed the District of

Columbia Armory with 5,000 guests for $100-a-plate affairs. In 1961, the Democrats added a new wrinkle, the exclusive "President's Club" for those who give $1,000. Originally organized as the "750 Club" to wipe out the party's debt from the 1956 election, the club built up to 4,000 members in 1964. Members enjoyed personal contact with the President, special privileges at the national convention, invitations to White House affairs, and occasional special briefings or seminars on public issues. Republicans also charged from time to time that members received other benefits in the form of government contracts and relief from enforcement of the laws, which Democrats vehemently denied. A similar Republican $1,000 "Associates Program" had 1,500 contributors in 1964. Former President Eisenhower assisted similar efforts in 1965 with a picnic for $1,000 contributors at his Gettysburg farm.[36]

WHO THE BIG GIVERS ARE

The big givers are the leading industrial families of the United States, the officials of their industries, professional men who serve them, the men who lead their employees, and the leaders in law, medicine, entertainment, and advertising. Few farmers are big givers and virtually no career public servants are in that class.

In 1964, twelve leading families, including such famous names as Du Pont, Field, Ford, Mellon, Rockefeller, and Vanderbilt, gave $602,926. In 1960, these same families gave $646,521, and in 1956 $1,153,735. Most was given to Republican causes in all three elections, but in 1964 all but four gave some funds to the Democrats, bringing their gifts to the Johnson camp to $133,500. In 1960, Democrats received only $78,850, and in 1956 only $107,109 from the big twelve.

Individuals who contributed a total of more than $10,000 each also increased in 1964: 130 persons gave a total of $2,161,905, 52 exclusively to Republicans, 65 exclusively to Democrats, and 13 to both parties. In 1960, there were 95 such givers who contributed $1,552,009. In 1956, 111 gave $2,300,000; and in 1952, 110 gave $1,936,870. Except in 1964, most of the money went to Republi-

---

[36] Alexander, *Financing the 1964 Election,* pp. 77-84.

can causes.[37] Thus, in most recent presidential campaigns, a handful of wealthy persons was able to give more than the combined efforts of thousands of small contributors. The much smaller cost and effort required to reach the few big givers point to the basic reasons for continued political-party dependence upon them.

Do the same people give year after year? Generally they do not. Of the 130 big givers in 1964, only 17 were in the $10,000 gift class in 1952, 1956, and 1960. Twelve of the regulars were Republican, four Democratic. One switched to Johnson in 1964.[38]

Executives of the nation's leading corporations and their trade associations have been another major source of presidential campaign funds. In 1956 the Gore committee revealed that 199 officers of the nation's leading corporations gave $1,936,847.[39] Giving by business leaders may have declined and shifted, however, in both 1960 and 1964. A comparison of officers of 13 major trade associations for all three elections reveals that from a high of $751,914 in 1956, their giving dropped in 1960 to $493,465 and in 1964 to $468,218. At the same time, the proportion going to Democrats rose dramatically. From a mere $8,000 in 1956 and $62,255 in 1960, it jumped to almost half—$225,790—in 1964.[40]

Although some labor leaders give in sums of $500 or more, principally to Democratic causes, labor generally prefers to raise political funds as it collects dues and to spend its money through its own Committee on Political Education. Relations between COPE and the Democratic National Committee ordinarily are close and cordial, however.

THE REPUBLICAN FINANCIAL ORGANIZATION

Since 1937 the Republican National Finance Committee has served as the central financial organ for the party. It was obvious after the debacle of 1936 that a major rebuilding job was necessary if the Republicans were to come back. Rebuilding a national institution is a costly process. Thus it was that the Republican

---

[37] *Ibid.,* pp. 84-90. See also Alexander, *Financing the 1960 Election,* pp. 59-61, and U.S. Congress, Senate, *1956 General Election Campaigns,* p. 12.

[38] Alexander, *Financing the 1964 Election,* pp. 84-90.

[39] U.S. Congress, Senate, *1956 General Election Campaigns,* pp. 12-15.

[40] Alexander, *Financing the 1964 Election,* p. 92.

National Finance Committee was created to coordinate financial planning for the national committee, the Senatorial Campaign Committee, and the Congressional Campaign Committee.

Selected for the job of restructuring the financial apparatus of the Republican Party was Carlton G. Ketchum of Pittsburgh. His role in the rebuilding process emphasized the early recognition of the need for professional staff men in the financial phase of party political work. Ketchum, though a dedicated Republican, was not a politican per se. He was, rather, an eminently successful fund raiser.

THE REPUBLICAN SYSTEM

Under Ketchum's direction the Republican National Finance Committee assigned to individual state finance committees annual quotas which they were expected to raise and send to the national finance committee. The actual quota assigned to a given state was based on the electoral vote of the state, the population, the Republican vote in the last election, the personal income tax paid by the state's residents, the number of occupied dwellings, and the purchasing power of the state's population.

Having learned how much it owed the national party organization, the state party leadership was to determine its own needs for the next year and add this amount to the national figure. Each county finance committee was then assigned by the state finance committee an equitable share of this combined state-national figure. To this figure it would in turn add the costs of its own local operation in order to compute the total amount it must raise to meet its obligations.

Ideally, all Republican fund raising in a county was to be undertaken by that county's finance committee. The fund-raising program became, under Ketchum's plan, similar to the annual United Fund drives for support of various social agencies in most large cities.

The unified nature of the campaign theoretically eliminated the possibility of a given party member being asked to donate more than once to the Republican Party during any given year. The state finance committee was to function as the centralized control center not only to set county quotas and work out agreements with county finance committees, but also to provide assistance in the form of professional fund raisers working out of the state finance committee.

A third cardinal feature of the Republican program was the separation of the fund-raising function from the "political" activities of the party. There were good reasons for this separation. Experience over the years had clearly indicated that good political leaders are often not good money raisers; conversely, good money raisers may not be the best public spokesmen for a party. Thus the political leaders of the operating units of the party were instructed to submit an estimate of their needs for a given year and, subject to negotiation with the finance committees (county, state, and national), a final budget was to be arrived at which the finance committees then undertook to provide.

These innovations wrought by Ketchum set the pattern for Republican fund raising from 1937 on. They introduced professionalization in the political fund-raising area and provided for continuous, year-round programing of the party's finance efforts.

Failures were bound to occur in such a neat system. The extent to which Republican fund raising approached the Ketchum ideal has varied from state to state and in some states from year to year. In few states do all of the counties agree to accept the "united-giving" program. Some state finance committees cannot raise the necessary funds to pay their quota to the national finance committee or to meet their commitment to their own state party executive committees.

Another problem encountered in the administration of the unified fund drive is the independent fund drive for a particular candidate. Such drives sabotage, in effect, the party's attempt at a united effort, but the party can do little about them. During a presidential year, volunteer or citizen committees are especially likely to be in the field raising money in competition with the regular finance committees, although they are formed primarily to attract funds and votes from citizens not likely to respond to a purely partisan approach.

FINANCING, 1960-1963

Despite these unavoidable variations, the Republican fund-raising plan has worked well and the Republican national committees entered the presidential campaign of 1960 in a fairly strong financial position. Their treasury had a small surplus left over from their 1959 budget, and they benefited handsomely early in the year from a series of highly successful fund-raising dinners honoring President Eisenhower. When all the bills were in, however, and all the figures tallied, the Republicans discovered at the end of the campaign that they had amassed a net debt of slightly over $700,000. Excluding state and local committee expenditures, costs for the national Republican presidential campaign amounted to $11,300,000 in 1960. Where did the money come from to pay this large bill?

Unlike so many of the 1960 Republican presidential campaign operations, Republican fund raising was centered at the Republican National Committee headquarters, more precisely in the Republican National Finance Committee. Setting an original campaign goal of $7,800,000, the finance committee actually raised over $8,000,000. Added to this was $500,000 raised by national Nixon-Lodge Clubs, $2,300,000 raised by the Volunteers for Nixon-Lodge, and almost $375,000 raised by miscellaneous Republican committees. The grand total was $11,180,000.

Two sources supplied most of this $11,180,000. *Large individual gifts* to the Republican National Committee, the Congressional Campaign Committee, the Senatorial Campaign Committee, and the Independent Television Committee totaled $6,213,766. *Fund-raising dinners* supplied most of the rest. Eighty-three "Dinners with Ike" netted the national party $1,800,000; thirty-six "campaign dinners" yielded $1,200,000 for the presidential campaign; and twenty-three additional fund-raising affairs turned in an estimated $1,250,000.

Despite their $700,000 campaign deficit, the Republicans started 1961 with cash balances amounting to roughly $500,000 distributed among the three national committees. Their plans called for a 1961 fund-raising goal of $2,500,000 which would retire their debt and allow them ample funds for the upcoming 1962 congressional campaign.

To raise this money the Republicans concentrated on a program which gave associate membership in the national party to every $1,000 contributor. A congressional dinner, again featuring Eisenhower, was also used in June of 1961. It netted roughly $450,000 for the 1962 congressional election campaign.

But the heavy reliance on these emergency devices, such as the Ike dinners, had provoked the long-time advisor to the Republican National Finance Committee, Carlton Ketchum, to insist that extra effort be placed on improving the unified fund drives at the state and county levels. He argued against what he thought was an overemphasis on direct national solicitation. But many states were not meeting their national quotas. Where could the national Republican Party turn?

One direction pointed clearly toward broadening the financial base of the party. Both major parties had spent considerable time with such programs as Dollars for Democrats and Neighbor to Neighbor during the 1950's; and there had been some local successes (Hennepin County, Minnesota, for example, had set a Neighbor to Neighbor goal of $60,000 in 1960 and raised $94,000). But since a relatively small percentage of these funds reached Washington, this program did not seem to offer promise of substantial funds. Some national party leaders began to look toward the use of a direct-mail solicitation from the national party headquarters.

Such a plan had been used by the Democratic National Committee since 1957 and by some state Republican committees as well. It was not entirely new to the Republican National Finance Committee either, for late in 1959, Spencer T. Olin, then chairman of the Republican National Finance Committee, experimented with the idea of a direct-mail solicitation campaign from the national party headquarters. The experiment was a request for a small contribution from those who could not participate in a Dinner for Ike. Though the effort had only a limited financial success, Olin was helping to set the stage for a national party sustaining-membership program. In an extremely interesting and informative interoffice memorandum, Olin outlined the problems and prospects for such an effort. He reported encouraging returns from a test mailing but commented on two problems. First, many people got two or more appeals. Such duplication is inevitable, since many people are on more than one mailing list, especially commercial mailing lists. It would be costly to try and almost impossible to eliminate these duplications. Second, all but a few mailing lists are mixed— Democrats, Republicans, and whatnot—and cannot be sifted. So prominent Democrats inevitably get Republican fund appeals;

and quite often they use them in public ridicule of the Republicans. Olin was not disturbed by either problem.

A program of solicitation by direct mail for sustaining memberships ultimately was established in 1962, with the joint support of the Republican National Committee, the Republican Senatorial Campaign Committee, the Republican Congressional Campaign Committee, and the Republican National Finance Committee. A contribution of $10 entitled the donor to a year's subscription to *Battle Line,* the national committee's regular publication, and a sustaining-membership card issued from the Republican Party national headquarters.

The success of the Republican sustaining-membership program was much greater than expected. In the first year of its operation, more than $900,000 was raised in this way. In 1963, it brought to the national headquarters slightly more than $1 million. And in 1964, receipts from this source reached $1,029,075 by the time of the national convention in early July.

But these funds were used mainly for current expenses by the national committee. A series of major fund-raising dinners in January 1964 was necessary to retire the last $225,000 of indebtedness remaining from the 1960 campaign. By the time the national convention was called to order in July, however, the heavy expenses of preparing for the convention and gearing up for the campaign itself had placed the national committee in debt again to the extent of $217,000.

FINANCING, 1964

When the national nominating convention adjourned, it appeared that Republican fund raising would be a formidable task in 1964. The primary campaigns had been extremely costly, and general public opinion after the two nominating conventions held Johnson a sure winner. Some of the traditional Republican "big money" from the East had already begun to find its way to the Johnson campaign by early September.

Perhaps it was this concatenation of factors that led both Republican Finance Chairman Ralph Cordiner and candidate Goldwater to insist on a presidential campaign run in the black. Cordiner, a retired Chairman of the Board of General Electric, had accepted the finance-committee chairmanship on that basis, and although such an approach was very much in the tradition of solid conservative business practice, it hardly fit the fluctuating fiscal demands of a presidential campaign.

To mount an effective television-radio-press offensive requires committing choice time and space months ahead of the time when the money is actually in hand. Thus when Cordiner was handed a campaign budget for $7,000,000 in September, he promptly moved to cut back a number of costly television spot announcements because he could not see where the money would come from to pay for them. But the money did come. As John Bailey, chairman of the Democratic National Committee, said of the Republicans, "They wound up with a vote deficit and a financial surplus."[41]

In total, the Republicans raised over $18.5 million which was an increase of $7 million over their 1960 contributions. Of this $18.5 million, 46 per cent came from 650,000 contributors who gave contributions ranging from a few cents to $100. Only 28 per cent of the total dollar value of Republican contributions came in sums of $500 and more.[42]

The Republicans at the national level were able to maintain financial support from many of their usual sources as well, but the dramatic response to their massive direct-mail drive and effective television appeal for funds constituted a major breakthrough in presidential campaign funding.

The major sources of Republican funds in 1964 were as follows: direct mail, $5.8 million; state payments, $2.7 million; dinners, $2.5 million; associates, $2.2 million, Dean Burch television appeal, $1.3 million; Los Angeles television, $1.2 million; miscellaneous, $800,000; raised direct by Congressional Campaign Committee, $450,000.[43]

When the 1964 contributions base and voter support is compared with that of 1952, it is interesting to note that although the Eisenhower candidacy drew electoral support of almost landslide proportions, the Republican National Committee received contri-

---

[41] Joseph A. Loftus, "Democrats Form Negro Vote Unit," *New York Times*, January 20, 1965.
[42] Alexander, *Financing the 1964 Election*, p. 11.
[43] *Ibid.*, p. 71.

butions from only 17,500 contributors and the national Citizens for Eisenhower-Nixon garnered support from only 20,000 contributors.[44]

One of the more interesting aspects of the financial side of the 1964 election is that 72 per cent of the Republican total contributions was received in sums of less than $500, compared with 30 per cent for the Democrats.[45]

In light of the widely forecast defeat for Senator Goldwater, it was remarkable that so much money was raised from so many individuals for his campaign.

As Herbert Alexander has suggested:

To some extent a large number of contributors to national level Republican committees must have reflected the political polarization within the Republican Party in 1964. Goldwater supporters tended to give directly to Washington to avoid normal Republican state finance channels whereby funds would be shared with moderate candidates for other offices. Nor were moderate Republicans anxious to have portions of their funds shared with the national campaign, so individual moderate candidates and not state party committees benefitted from their contributions.[46]

Aside from the campaign itself, the cost of the primary campaigns was an interesting and important financial aspect of the 1964 presidential campaign. Efforts to nominate Senator Goldwater cost at least $5.5 million.

In the time from January to July, 1964, the Goldwater national campaign raised more money ($4.75 million) than did the national Republican Party Committees ($3 million) which were suffering from uncertainty as to whom the Presidential nominee would be. Funds for the Goldwater candidacy for nomination came from more than an estimated 300,000 contributors.[47]

Unlike many other presidential prenomination campaigns, those seeking the Republican nomination for Goldwater did not spend large sums of money for contests in states holding a presidential

---

[44] Heard, *The Costs of Democracy*, p. 45.
[45] Alexander, *Financing the 1964 Election*, p. 11.
[46] *Ibid.*, p. 12.   [47] *Ibid.*, p. 18.

preference primary. Instead, major expenditures were for publicity and organizational expenses in states which selected their national delegates at state conventions.

About $200,000, or 7 per cent of funds spent by the Goldwater for President Committee from January to July, 1964, went to primary contests, whereas about $470,000 or 52 per cent of total funds were transferred by·the Kennedy national command to state primary campaigns in 1960.[48]

Substantial sums were spent on behalf of the other potential Republican presidential nominees in 1964. Supporters of Rockefeller spent some $2,927,135; Scranton supporters expended $827,035; efforts to nominate Lodge cost over $100,000; Nixon, $71,800; Stassen, $70,000; and the Margaret Chase Smith candidacy cost $1,171.[49] Senator Smith's announcement indeed suggested that her candidacy would be a "test whether one has to have a million dollars to go into a primary [and] whether you can go in without an organization."[50]

Although both Goldwater and Miller insisted that their campaign be run organizationally out of the national committee and that it be financed from the same office, the limitation of $3 million on expenditures made it necessary to establish a number of special finance organizations through which contributions in excess of this amount could be spent. These organizations included the Republican National Committee, the National Finance Operations, the National Congressional Committee, the Congressional Booster Club, the Senatorial Campaign Committee, the Republican Television Committee, the National TV Committee, plus five miscellaneous campaign committees most of which raised money to support moderate and liberal Republican candidates for state and national offices.

All of the Goldwater finance operations were controlled from the national committee with the exception of the national Television for Goldwater-Miller Committee which was located in Los Angeles.

The major expenditures by the various Republican committees

[48] *Ibid.,* p. 19.   [49] *Ibid.,* 23ff.
[50] Quoted in *ibid.,* p. 29.

for publicizing its standard-bearers included $5.6 million for television and radio time and production; printing and reproduction, $555,000; printed advertising, $530,000; promotion and campaign supplies, $380,000; motion pictures, $128,000; and outdoor productions, $100,000.[51] Of the television time, 60 per cent went for spot announcements and 40 per cent for programs of longer duration.[52] One publicity item, an innovation for presidential campaigns, was a $300,000, eight-page advertisement in the October issue of *Reader's Digest.*

An increased expenditure for public-opinion polls and surveys was shown in the 1964 Republican campaign with some $165,400 being spent for this purpose. Of this amount, $136,000 was spent at one opinion-poll organization alone.[53] Surveys for the Republican national campaign included

a panel study, with four waves of interviewing among a national cross-section of voters, some trial-heat surveys in selected states, a measurement of the Goldwater campaign trip through Southern cities, a study of the Goldwater whistlestop campaign in the Midwest, a measurement of the TV campaign commercials of both the Democrats and Republicans and a number of special analyses.[54]

The costs for the highly successful direct-mail appeals and television appeals were substantial. Although direct-mail appeals brought in some $5.8 million for the campaign, the investment in postage and printing and in purchasing the use of mailing lists and services was more than $1 million. Even though there was an unexpectedly high response from the direct-mail campaign, the percentage response in 1964 was not as high as it had been for the Republican sustaining-membership fund in 1962 or 1963.[55]

Alexander has pointed out that in terms of meeting the state quotas there were some actual increases in 1964 from state party sources and some decreases. For example, eight southern states increased their percentage, but Florida, North Carolina, and

---

[51] Alexander, *Financing the 1964 Election,* p. 49.

[52] *Ibid.,* p. 54.   [53] *Ibid.,* p. 73f.

[54] Thomas W. Benham, "Polling for a Presidential Candidate: Some Observations on the Campaign," *Public Opinion Quarterly,* XXIV (1965), p. 185.

[55] Alexander, *Financing the 1964 Election,* p. 71.

Tennessee decreased theirs; California increased quota performance from 78 per cent in 1960 to 118 per cent in 1964, but New
York decreased from 132 per cent to 62 per cent; some large
states—Illinois, Ohio, Pennsylvania, Michigan, and Minnesota—
decreased, while Indiana, Oklahoma, and Wisconsin increased.
However, of ten New England and Middle Atlantic states, seven
decreased, with only Maine, Vermont, and New Jersey showing
increases; of eleven Pacific and Mountain states every one increased its percentage though Oregon and Washington were up
only slightly while increases in Arizona, Idaho, Montana, and
New Mexico were substantial; Nevada rose from meeting 42 per
cent of its 1960 quota to 262 per cent of the 1964 quota. For all
states and the District of Columbia, Puerto Rico, and the Virgin
Islands, the Republican quota performance record in 1964 was
105 per cent, compared with 113 per cent in 1960. As compared
with the 1960 presidential campaign, Goldwater ran ahead of
Nixon in six of the seven geographic regions of the country and
in 35 of the 50 states.[56]

The Republicans and the Democrats raised almost identical
amounts from fund-raising dinners and special events during the
1964 campaign. The amount was $13.3 million each. This figure
covers dinners and events for county, state, and national candidates and thus concerns fund-raising efforts far beyond the presidential campaign.[57]

Of the more than 6,700 individuals who contributed $500 and
over in 1964, 3,400 were contributors to the Democratic campaign. This group gave some $7.2 million. Approximately 3,000
$500-and-over gifts were from Republican contributors, for a total
of $3.7 million.[58]

In conjunction with the direct-mail campaign, efforts to broaden
the base continued at the local level through the Republican Neighbor to Neighbor drive. This program was in operation, however, in
only some areas of the country in 1964. The Minnesota Republican Party received some $360,000 from this source in 1964 in
comparison to $340,000 raised in 1962 and $216,000 raised in
1960 from the same source. In Ohio, more than $200,000 was
raised from this program in 1964.[59]

[56] *Ibid.,* p. 73.   [57] *Ibid.,* p. 81.   [58] *Ibid.,* p. 84.   [59] *Ibid.,* p. 91.

FINANCING SINCE 1964

The aftermath of the 1964 campaign was unusual in that there was a cash surplus both at the Republican National Committee and in the national Television for Goldwater-Miller Committee. Although many Republicans requested that the national Television for Goldwater-Miller funds be turned over to the National Republican Committee, such requests fell on deaf ears and the funds were ultimately used to support conservative candidates in organizational contests and in primary elections in 1965 and 1966.

One of the adverse effects of the 1964 presidential campaign was the breakdown of the unified fund-raising structure developed at such pains since 1937. Fortunately for the Republican Party, this rupture did not appear to be a continuing one, since state and national efforts to return to the unified fund-raising methods in 1965 proved to be largely successful.

At the same time, some splinter groups were raising funds of their own which did hamper the development of the unified fund-raising program supported by the national committees. On the liberal-moderate side, nine organizations joined together in the Council of Republican Organizations. At least three of these groups solicited funds from known moderate and liberal Republicans. On the conservative side, the establishment in 1965 of the Free Society Association, supported by Barry Goldwater, also detracted from the success of Republican fund-raising drives.

For years the Republican National Committee and the Congressional and Senatorial Campaign Committees have been in a somewhat competitive position for financial support. In 1965, however, Ray Bliss brought these groups together through a series of meetings with the leaders and staffs of the three national party committees. For the first time the total national Republican fund-raising program began to take on the semblance of unity with direction.

Vigorous national-committee efforts coupled with those of the Congressional and Senatorial Campaign Committees allowed the national party organizations to move into the 1966 campaigns with substantial surpluses—a major factor in the significant victory of the Republican Party in the 1966 midterm elections.

DEMOCRATIC FISCAL IMPROVISATION

The Democratic Party has never developed a separate, systematic fund-raising system comparable to the Republican. In part, the failure has been deliberate. Observing the power which the fund chairmen wielded within the Grand Old Party, Democratic leaders avowed preference for a system which kept authority in the hands of the duly elected county and state chairmen. In part, the failure was due to the Democrats' special problems in raising funds. In the South, the party could seek money from the general business community which the Republican finance system taps in the North. Elsewhere, it depended upon lone Democrats among the businessmen, on labor, on special industries such as entertainment and beverages, and on public employees. Systematization of such sources did not promise to be greatly more productive than the old order.

FUND RAISING, 1964

The Democratic National Committee seems always to be in debt. So perennial is this condition that its having money in the bank is headline news. On August 22, 1964, Columnist Drew Pearson cheerfully reported:

> For the first time since the days of Andrew Jackson, the Democratic Party is beginning a national convention with money in the bank.
> It has $5 million now on deposit and $10 million in sight before election day.[60]

By Election Day, the national committee again had a deficit of $1 million.[61] But that was a major improvement over 1960. The Kennedy campaign ran $3,800,000 in the red—the all-time record. Stevenson's 1956 campaign debt was $750,000 and was still unpaid in 1960. Between 1952 and 1956, to wipe out the 1952 debt, Governor Stevenson made numerous appearances before fund-raising dinners. Even in 1948, President Harry Truman closed his

---

[60] *Washington Post,* August 22, 1964, p. E23. The Democratic National Committee, however, never admitted to more than being in the black.

[61] Alexander, *Financing the 1964 Election,* p. 46.

successful campaign in the red, but a flood of postelection checks, many with preelection dates, closed the gap.

In 1964, the Democrats found campaign financing the easiest in history. The circumstances of the campaign, however, not hard work or good organization, wrought the change. The Republican choice of Goldwater as their presidential nominee drove many regular Republican contributors into the Johnson camp. For the first time, the Democratic candidate basked in the warmth of many generous gifts from wealthy contributors.

So substantial was Republican fiscal defection to the Johnson camp that specialists in campaign finance have called it "the switch in campaign giving."[62] For the first time, the Democratic Party reported more individual contributions of $500 or over than the Republican—3,400 to 3,000.[63] Individual contributors with long records of Republican giving turned up in Democratic lists. For example, of the 183-man Business Council, composed of the key leaders of the nation's business world, 63 gave $500 or more in 1960 or 1964. Of this number, only 5 gave to Democratic causes in 1960, and their combined contributions totaled only $20,000, while 44 members gave $165,110 to Republican committees that year. In 1964, by contrast, 32 council members gave a total of $135,450 to Democratic causes, while 36 remained steadfastly Republican but gave only $87,100. Many of the latter targeted their giving to non-Goldwater candidates and committees.[64]

Democratic fiscal fortunes also were aided substantially by the tactical situation itself. Mass Republican defections from Goldwater soon made abundantly clear that Johnson would win handily. The Democratic National Committee therefore deliberately kept down presidential campaign expenses and passed funds to candidates for Congress to win the President a commanding legislative majority as well.

Key to Democratic fund raising in 1964 was the President's Club, composed of those who contributed $1,000 or more. Led by Arthur B. Krim of New York, who had rendered the same service

[62] Herbert E. Alexander and Harold B. Meyers, "The Switch in Campaign Giving," *Fortune*, November 1965.

[63] Alexander, *Financing the 1964 Election,* p. 84.

[64] Alexander and Meyers, "The Switch in Campaign Giving."

to Mr. Kennedy, the President's Club swelled to an all-time record of 4,000 members.

State quotas, long a mainstay of Democratic finance, were abandoned and replaced by direct negotiations with state central committees. The states responded with $2,300,000[65]—a figure double the quotas of the late 1950's.

Drives to attract small givers centered on a version of the sustaining-membership program. One million mail solicitations, some enclosing a blank check made out to the Johnson-Humphrey Committee, produced 50,000 contributors—a figure comparable to the 1960 effort.

Supporting these efforts was a well-established system of $100-a-plate dinners and galas across the land. Spurred by the big Kennedy debt, the national committee had started immediately on inaugural eve in 1961 with a $100-a-seat gala which featured Frank Sinatra, Peter Lawford, then the President's brother-in-law, and many other stars of stage and screen. One-quarter of the debt was erased that single night. There followed a series of $100-a-plate dinners across the land in celebration of Jefferson's birthday. The following January, a whole series of $100-a-plate victory dinners marked the anniversary of the Inauguration. Another $100-a-seat gala in 1963 on the second anniversary of the Inauguration virtually erased the debt, but the 1964 gala was postponed until late spring by the President's assassination.

The Democratic National Committee also apparently made money on its 1964 convention—a most unusual occurrence. Normally, the host city puts up money to pay convention expenses and earns revenue by publishing the convention program, which produces both advertising and sales income. This time, however, Atlantic City put up $625,000 in cash—normally enough to pay for a convention—and the Democratic National Committee published the program. Democratic spokesmen reportedly claimed that the convention cost an unprecedented $2 million and that the bulk of the proceeds went for its expenses. However, at least $50,000 of convention profits went to the Public Affairs Institute for Negro-registration drives.[66]

---

[65] Alexander, *Financing the 1964 Election*, p. 76.   [66] *Ibid.*, pp. 40-41.

Democratic fund-raising efforts in 1964 were atypical, however, and many details have never been made public. The experiences of the two previous campaigns may therefore be more instructive.

FUND RAISING, 1956-1960

Fund-raising efforts between 1956 and the nomination of John F. Kennedy in 1960 reflected the "party-responsibility" concepts of National Chairman Paul Butler. Butler wanted the Democratic Party to become an effective vehicle for the promotion of liberal causes. To accomplish that end, he concluded that the national committee needed as much financial independence as it could muster.

Butler therefore appointed a full-time finance director to work with the treasurer, systematized assessment of state central committees, and introduced two promising small-givers drives. He also introduced a system of regional representatives of the national committee who were to work with the state committees in organization, finance, and other party purposes.

Assessment of state central committees, which had been customary but apparently rather irregular, was set at $1,187,500 per year, a sum calculated to pay committee operating expenses and retire the 1956 campaign debt by 1960. Based more on past performance than on any equitable formula, the quota system soon encountered pressure for reform and rationalization. Early in 1960, after much negotiation, a new quota formula was announced which was based on the number of Democratic voters in each state, the number of Democratic incumbents, and other acceptable criteria.

Collecting the money from the state committees proved to be a more formidable task. As Butler's leadership became more and more unpopular, fewer and fewer states bothered to meet their quotas. By June 30, 1960, when Butler published his last report on quota standings, covering the entire period from 1957 to mid-1960, only eight states and territories had paid in full: Maryland, the Virgin Islands, South Dakota, Wyoming, the District of Columbia, Delaware, New Jersey, and Florida. Maryland's 164 per cent of its share had been paid almost wholly by Montgomery County, adjoining the District of Columbia, with the proceeds from its extraordinarily successful Dollars for Democrats drives. However, on the basis of quarterly installments, half of the states were virtually up to date. Seventeen states had paid less than half.

Butler rewarded the faithful states by assigning them front seats at the convention and by giving them the best Los Angeles hotels. The Illinois delegation, by contrast, found itself in the back of the Sports Arena and consigned to a hostelry without air conditioning "just off skid row."

In a last desperate effort to bail the national committee out of debt by convention time, Butler announced a special "750 Club" which was to enjoy special facilities and special privileges at Los Angeles. Membership in the club was obtained by a $1,000 donation to the national committee. Hard work on the 750 Club program and last-minute quota payments, encouraged by the assignment of housing and seats at the convention, reduced the debt somewhat by the opening of the campaign.

The small-givers drives likewise met with but limited success. Door-to-door solicitation by county central committees was labeled the Dollars for Democrats drive. Operated yearly beginning in 1957, it asked individual Democrats to give $1, $5, or $10 to local precinct workers during the early fall each year. Participating counties were to keep one-third of their proceeds and pass two-thirds on to the state central committees. The states similarly were expected to keep one-third and pass on the rest to national headquarters.

Despite clever promotion and hard work, the national committee never won cooperation from all of the states. Even the most successful states—like California, Arkansas, and Washington—never had full participation from all counties. County central committees which conscientiously tried the drive, however, raised substantial sums. Montgomery County, Maryland, annually led the nation with from $30,000 to $40,000 in proceeds. But even small counties, among them Whitman County, Washington, raised 25 cents per Democratic voter and were able to pay all party assessments from the one annual drive.

From 1957 through 1959, the drive brought the national committee from $45,000 to $106,000 a year. It peaked in 1960, yielding $121,059.92, although additional funds probably reached the committee without proper identification and were credited to other sources. To derive such a return, the national committee distributed 400,000 certificate books to 48 state and territorial drives and to county drives in two nonparticipating states. Circumstantial evidence strongly suggests that the Dollars for Democrats program was much more successful than the national committee ever knew. A sampling of returned books suggested strongly that several times the sum the committee received may have been raised in 1960. If so, most of the money probably stayed where it was collected to meet local party expenses.

Mail solicitation was labeled the "sustaining-membership" program. Democrats were asked to contribute $10 a year to finance the national committee. Peak success again came in 1960, when 600,000 mailed requests yielded $240,000.

FUND RAISING AND FISCAL MANAGEMENT, 1960

Fund raising for the Kennedy campaign used three basic sources: the giving circle was tapped in as many cities as possible, state central committees were assessed quotas double their 1956 contributions, and the regular small-giver efforts were carried through.

Before the convention, Paul Butler had established a National Finance Committee which was to raise funds for the campaign. Chairing it were Roger Stevens of New York and Sydney Solomon of St. Louis. Each state chairman had been asked to appoint one or two persons to represent his state on the finance committee, and most had done so. On the Saturday following the nominations, the finance committee met for the first and only time in the Biltmore Hotel in Los Angeles. Thirty-seven persons showed up and agreed to bend every effort to raise funds. Illinois enthusiastically proposed a very large fund-raising dinner in the near future. Beyond the individual efforts of the committee members, however, the finance committee itself did not function further in the campaign.

Retained as national-committee treasurer, Matthew H. McCloskey promptly undertook to assess the states. He and Finance Director Dennis Jensen arranged eight regional meetings, to each of which were invited the members of the National Finance Committee, national-committee members, state chairmen, and Dollars for Democrats chairmen of several states. Representatives from all but eight or nine states attended one of the meetings. Quotas were agreed upon. The new formula was set aside and McCloskey instead asked each state to raise twice the sum it had contributed to the Stevenson campaign in 1956. Under this plan, little would be expected of states which had done little for Stevenson. McCloskey therefore judiciously raised the sights for those states which had obviously not done what they could.

To follow up the regional fund-raising conferences, a meeting was held at the Mayflower Hotel in Washington, D.C., which Senators Kennedy, Johnson, and Jackson, Adlai Stevenson, and former President Truman attended. Agreement was reached to promote a series of $100-a-plate dinners in key centers across the country as a major fund-raising device.

From the beginning, both Matthew McCloskey, treasurer of the national committee, and Stephen Smith, the effective treasurer of Citizens for Kennedy-Johnson, knew they would have to divide the costs between them and that both would probably spend to their legal limits. McCloskey started with the added handicap of having used nearly a third of his limit to pay the debts and run the preconvention affairs of the national committee. Thus at least one other major committee would have to handle part of the expenses.

The basic steps in preventing a campaign deficit are to impose budget and accounting controls centrally and to enforce rigid economy. In an effort to simplify procedure and to maintain some vestiges of central control, the comptroller's office of the national committee installed a form of automatic data processing which was made available to Citizens for Kennedy-Johnson. Early receipts and expenditures were run through the national committee's books. In mid-October, as the national committee approached its spending limit, everyone on its staff was fired and immediately retained by the Citizens for Kennedy-Johnson. All incoming contributions of any size were signed over to the citizens group by Treasurer McCloskey. Bills similarly were redirected. The citizens' accounting team was moved from the Esso Building to the fifth floor at 1737 L Street and processed its receipts and expenditures through the national committee's machines.

To control budgets, Ralph Dungan and Richard Donohue tried to set spending limits for each unit of the committee. Successful to a degree with the new auxiliary units, they faced the problem of having several units with separate treasuries and several old units of the committee which expected to clear expenditures through the chairman's office.

On September 21, Chairman Jackson also sought to impose central budgetary controls by assigning William H. Perkins the task, but recognized the organizational dilemma he faced by confining Perkins' function to "the orderly and economic use of the Committee's funds."

Both national-committee treasurer McCloskey and citizens-committee treasurer Smith appear to have exercised independent judgment about clearing expenditures. McCloskey seems to have taken the position that he should pass on expenditures inasmuch as the national committee ultimately would have to meet all unpaid bills. Smith also appears to have believed that he should pass judgment as long as Citizens for Kennedy-Johnson was paying the bills. As a result, some projects were approved by one man only to be disapproved by the other.

The national committee itself compounded the financial problems. Many persons were able to spend money without having to worry about where it came from. For example, because there was no central personnel system, department heads were permitted to set salaries independently. Stipends for clerical help were kept within reason, but professional salaries in several instances reached the absurd—with a few persons even being granted $500 a week until review by the finance department ended the practice. Also, although cash advances were used for men sent out of Washington on committee business, credit cards for airlines, telephones, and food also were issued. Abuse followed. The committee received food bills charged to a restaurant across the street from headquarters and discovered that a few of its irresponsible representatives had occupied extremely expensive hotel rooms to which they had ordered generous quantities of food and drink. One man even sent the committee a doctor bill!

At the height of campaign pressure early in November, the national committee discovered that it had been getting money from an unexpected source: a forger in Spokane, Washington. With a fine impartiality, he had sent generous checks to both the Democratic and the Republican National Committees and had signed the names of prominent local party leaders whom he apparently thought were not being generous enough. On one $700 check, simulating the victim's handwriting, he even added, "Pour it on!"

Miscalculations and needless expenses probably account for a very minor portion of the debt. The debt came because campaign costs were up. It came because the Kennedys were determined to conduct a thorough campaign, better advertised than in 1956, better advanced, better staffed, and better supported with auxiliary efforts.

A $3,820,000 debt gets on the books because some companies extend credit. Television and radio stations give no credit. Cash must be paid to the station 48 hours before air time or the show doesn't go on. Credit in 1960 came especially from printing concerns which enjoyed generous contracts, from airlines which rented airplanes and crews to the committee, and from the telephone company which tolerated an intolerable bill.

Bibliography

Alexander, Herbert E. *Financing the 1960 Election*. Princeton, N.J.: Citizens' Research Foundation, 1961.

Alexander, Herbert E. *Financing the 1964 Election*. Princeton, N.J.: Citizens' Research Foundation, 1966.

Alexander, Herbert E. *Regulation of Political Finance*. Berkeley, Calif.: Institute of Governmental Studies and Citizens' Research Foundation, 1966.

Alexander, Herbert E. *Responsibility in Party Finance*. Princeton, N.J.: Citizens' Research Foundation, 1963.

Alexander, Herbert E., and Harold B. Meyers. "The Switch in Campaign Giving," *Fortune,* November 1965.

Heard, Alexander. *The Costs of Democracy*. Chapel Hill: University of North Carolina Press, 1960.

Hennessy, Bernard. *Dollars for Democrats, 1959*. New York: McGraw-Hill, 1960.

Johnston, Felton M., and Richard D. Hupman. *Factual Campaign Information*. Washington: Government Printing Office, 1964.

U.S. Congress, Senate. *Election Law Guidebook 1964*. Washington: Government Printing Office, 1964.

U.S. Congress, Senate. *Final Report of the Special Committee to Investigate Political Activities, Lobbying, and Campaign Contributions.* Washington: Government Printing Office, 1957.

U.S. Congress, Senate. *1956 General Election Campaigns.* Washington: Government Printing Office, 1957.

U.S. President's Commission on Campaign Costs. *Financing Presidential Campaigns.* Washington: Government Printing Office, 1962.

Chapter XI

The Meaning of a
Presidential Election

Presidential elections in the United States have many meanings. They determine, of course, who will fill the office of President. They also reveal the current status of the balance of political power between the two major parties, indicate the general policy thrust which the electorate accepts, and determine which groups will have access to the seats of power. They also may disclose shifts in group alignment, and reveal the distribution of liberal and conservative sentiment in the nation.

For professional politicians, presidential elections also are tests of organizational efforts and campaign techniques. They test the power of organizations to deliver the vote, prove the worth of fund-raising tactics, demonstrate the utility of special-group appeals, and offer opportunities to try out new techniques to win votes and new gadgets to improve communications or travel.

The American arena-of-compromise political system, however, precludes many interpretations of presidential elections which some theoreticians would like to make. Presidential elections neither approve nor disapprove the philosophy of a political party. They render no mandate to enact or to reject a party platform. Rarely, too, do they determine a specific issue unless it has been clearly a central focus of debate between the major-party candidates.

The meaning of any presidential election, therefore, must be interpreted both in terms of the underlying balance of political power in which the election took place and in terms of the issues and personalities that shaped the contest. Even so, each American presidential election is unique and may answer some questions which will never be confronted again.

The basic American political framework has been exceedingly stable. The rules for success which Thomas Jefferson first perceived and applied are still valid. Only one party can win the presidency, and thus only two can seriously contend for power. Given the widely varied social and economic conditions in the United States, ideological parties or sectional parties have no chance to capture the presidency. Success, then, can come only to a broadly based arena-of-compromise party which can muster a majority of the votes in enough states to gain a majority in the electoral college. The candidate for President of a party which has such a majority, and can deliver the votes at the polls, can be elected President. Nothing his opponent can say or do will change the outcome.

The basic political balance of power between the two major parties also has been remarkably stable. Changes have come only at great intervals in the Republic's life and, since the party system really has been established, only upon very great and deeply stirring issues: the Civil War and the Great Depression. Barring another similarly catastrophic change of human circumstances, the existing balance of party power is likely to continue indefinitely; for in arena-of-compromise parties, dissident members of the majority have more to gain from sharing power than from contending for it.

Thus the essential politics of future presidential elections are quite predictable, even if the candidates and the issues are not. The real contests will be between the candidates of the two major parties, and for the foreseeable future they are likely to continue to be the Democratic Party and the Republican Party. The Democratic candidate normally will enter each presidential contest with the advantage of the majority behind him. Because that majority is widely distributed and well placed in the pivotal states, his basic effort must be directed to uniting his party behind him and getting all Democratic voters to the polls on Election Day. If he can win independents and even moderate Republicans, so much the better. The most tangible consequence of such broad support will be the election of a greater majority of his fellow partisans to the Congress.

The Republican candidate normally will face an uphill battle. Not only must he unite all Republicans, but he must attract independent voters and make some inroads among nominal Democrats. Without such a broad, basically nonparty appeal, no Republican candidate can win the presidency no matter how well he is financed or how well he organizes his campaign.

Most elections, then, are likely to be reaffirmations of power for the majority. A few, however, will be deviating elections in which the minority breaks, temporarily, the majority party's control of the federal government.

When the Democratic candidate is the incumbent President, he is very likely to win the election. Only a series of blunders which drive important segments of his own party to the Republican candidate or induce them to field a third-party candidate can bring about his defeat.

Republican opportunities to elect a President therefore ordinarily come at the end of a Democratic President's second term of office when a nonincumbent successor must be chosen. If, at such a time, the minority party can select a figure with broad appeal and a well-established national reputation which generally is above partisan political consideration, it can make a serious bid for power.

Unfortunately, within both parties, ideologues work feverishly to "sharpen the intellectual differences" between the parties. Within the Democratic camp the liberals would have every candidate in their image, and thus needlessly risk defection by conservative and even moderate Democrats. Paul Butler's chairmanship of the Democratic National Committee from 1954 to 1960 is a classic recent illustration of the consequences of such ideological leadership within the Democratic Party.

Republicans, on the other hand, bear a conservative cross. The ideological right can see no cause but its own and apparently still believes—despite the devastating demonstration of 1964—that the country has a great conservative majority which stays at home on

Election Day rather than choose between a progressive Democrat and a "me-too" Republican. Devoted and dogmatic, they believe so firmly that they must rescue their nation from Communism that they are willing to give endless hours and large sums of money to control the regular organization of the Republican Party. Against such efforts, only the hardiest pragmatists can prevail.

Republican moderates, therefore, can hope to nominate a candidate only by the greatest exertion within their own ranks during election year. Early union behind an outstanding candidate with broad appeal at an election when success seems possible is the first prerequisite. The second is systematic and determined organization to carry precinct caucuses, county conventions, and state conventions to control delegate votes, paralleled by thorough organization to carry presidential preference primaries. Without such efforts to control the Republican nominating procedure, Republican national conventions will be controlled by the conservative regular organizations and will nominate Alf Landons and Barry Goldwaters. Such candidates await but one fate: defeat of landslide proportions as the Democratic candidate easily unites all his own followers, captures the independents, and even attracts liberal Republicans.

Thus the strongest candidates for both parties are the moderates. They are strongest precisely because they are best able to unite their own party and to appeal to independent voters and to moderates of the other party.

When the Democratic candidate is a moderate, he poses the gravest possible threat to Republican hopes. He is almost certain to attract part of the independent vote, and although he always risks defection from his own radical left, the Republican candidate has little hope of winning it.

When the Republican candidate is a moderate, he poses the greatest possible challenge to Democratic hopes. He, too, can appeal to the independent vote, and although he likewise faces defection from his radical right, he need not fear its joining the Democrat against his cause.

Only occasional presidential elections, consequently, are potentially deviating elections. Ordinarily, at least four conditions need to be present to give the minority-party candidate a better-than-even chance for victory. First, he must be a moderate with a national reputation. Preferably his reputation should have been gained outside of politics and have a very broad appeal, or if gained in politics, must be "reform" and "nonparty" in character.

Second, he must face a nonincumbent majority-party candidate who is attempting to succeed a majority-party President. Thus the minority candidate can appeal to the accumulated discontents of special groups who have failed to get what they wanted or have been aggrieved during the current administration.

Third, he preferably should face a representative of the extreme ideological wing of the majority party. Thus, when the Democratic Party is the majority, the Republican candidate is best served if the Democrat is an ideological liberal.

Fourth, the incumbent majority-party President needs to have lost favor in the eyes of the American people by committing blunders or by getting involved in difficult international situations from which he cannot extricate the country. If the minority-party candidate can seriously offer the ability to correct the blunders or resolve the problems, he can make a very serious bid for power.

Once the minority-party candidate is in office, he has an excellent chance to win reelection. Thus one deviating election is very likely to be followed by a second.

These basic conditions have applied to all deviating elections in the past century. Thus it is possible to look to the immediate future in presidential elections and to offer some elementary predictions within the basic political framework and the balance of political power between the parties.

The election of 1968 has all the earmarks of a reaffirmation-of-confidence election. The incumbent majority-party President is likely to seek reelection. He is a moderate. Although he has alienated part of his own left wing because of entanglement in the Vietnam war, he is not likely to face a Republican "peace" candidate. Indeed, the two major parties are most likely to offer the electorate little choice on that issue, leaving peace advocates to field a third-party candidate or choose the "lesser of two evils." However, since the peace advocates are in general liberal Democrats who back the President's domestic program, they are likely to provide little assistance to the Republican nominee. With low unemployment and a high standard of living at home, the incumbent majority-party President enjoys an enormous advantage, even over a moderate minority-party candidate. Only a national challenge from a truly distinguished third-party peace candidate could tip the scales sufficiently to bring about the conditions necessary for a deviating election.

The election of 1972, on the other hand, is likely to have several elements characteristic of a deviating election. The two most prominent apparent candidates for the majority party now appear to be Vice President Hubert Humphrey, leader of the liberal wing, and Senator Robert Kennedy, who has been trying to offer a more liberal position than President Johnson, especially on the Vietnam war and race relations. Although both have established national reputations, neither can preempt the middle of the road from a moderate "nonparty" Republican candidate, especially one who can convincingly offer the ability to cope effectively with some continuing thorny national problems, such as urban affairs or race relations. By 1972, twelve years of Democratic rule will have built a substantial number of special-group grievances. Thus, barring death or major events which change the lineup of potential candidates, 1972 appears to offer Republicans the best opportunity since 1956.

The election of 1976, again barring death or major changes of public affairs, is most likely to return to office the victor in the 1972 campaign. Thus, if 1972 reaffirms confidence in the Democrats, so, too, probably, will 1976. If 1972 is a deviating election, the Republican victor is very likely to repeat in 1976. Should the latter be the case, 1980 will replay the pattern of 1960 and offer the Democrats an excellent chance to recover the White House.

Yet candidate selections are not always rational. The majority party can enhance the prospects for a deviating election by nominating a champion of its own extreme wing who would alienate independents and moderates. On the other hand, the minority party can "blow" a promising opportunity by nominating a candidate of its radical wing who would insure the certain election of any candidate of the majority. In 1952, the Republicans nominated Dwight D. Eisenhower only with the greatest internal exertion, although all of the conditions conducive to a deviating election were present. Had Senator Robert Taft, the leader of the conservative wing, been the Republican nominee, the majority-party candidate might well have won.

All this adds up to one basic conclusion: A major political party in the United States must obey the basic rules of the American arena-of-compromise political system if it would succeed, whether it be in the majority or the minority. The candidates themselves, and the issues they espouse, can make a difference, but only if the underlying power system and the political conditions are favorable.

THE DEEPER MEANING OF THE ELECTION

Electing a President in the United States is boisterous, expensive, exhausting, and contentious. Sometimes, in the past, it has been bitter and even crude. Observers from other lands often find it bewildering and dismaying.

Great leaders are bombarded by their opponents with whispered ridicule and extravagant criticism. They are promoted by their followers with lavish phrases and exaggerated claims. The voters are reminded of their own discontents and prejudices as well as of their own ideals and legitimate desires.

The presidential election itself can fall at a time when issues must be invented for debate or in the midst of war when division at home is a luxury the nation can ill afford. On the other hand, the election can precipitate a great decision, as it did in 1860, or enable the nation to chart a new course in grappling with human problems, as it did in 1932.

Despite their noise and evident tumult, American presidential elections have been regular, orderly, and free. Every four years since the adoption of the Constitution in 1789, on the first Tuesday after the first Monday in November of years which are divisible by four, the United States has held a presidential election.

Thirty-five different men have served as President. Twenty-seven were elected to the office directly. Eight were elected Vice President and became President upon the death of their predecessors. Of the latter, four subsequently won election as President in their own right. Eleven Presidents were elected to two terms, the constitutional limit since 1951. Only one, Franklin D. Roosevelt, was elected President four times, in 1932, 1936, 1940, and 1944. Roosevelt died in April 1945, after serving 12 years and one month. The briefest service was by William Henry Harrison, who died April 4, 1841, just one month after taking office.

Some Presidents have changed the course of American history and left a memorable mark in the development of world freedom. Among them were George Washington, Thomas Jefferson, Andrew Jackson, Abraham Lincoln, Theodore Roosevelt, Woodrow Wilson, and Franklin D. Roosevelt. Others have preferred to let history take its course and have gone largely unremembered. Party label has been no guide to greatness. Distinguished Presidents have been Federalists, Democratic Republicans, Republicans, and Democrats.

The election of a President of the United States is the largest free electoral decision taken regularly in the world. In the election of 1964, more than 70 million Americans decided which of two men would hold the office.

Each such decision demonstrates that a free people can entrust the greatest political power and the most overwhelming military might the world has ever known to an elected leader who will wield his authority constitutionally and responsibly and surrender it in course when his term expires. It also confirms the continuing ability of a free people to chart the course of government. Such demonstrations of human capacity to organize and direct a stable society and at the same time to preserve the rights and dignity of individuals have been the hope of the world for nearly two centuries.

When George Washington was chosen first President of the United States, democracy was a daring experiment in a small new republic, a collection of former British colonies that clung along the eastern shores of the vast and largely uninhabited North American continent. Across the Atlantic, the glittering capitals of Europe were controlled by hereditary monarchs who viewed the new nation and its democracy with suspicion, distrust, and open hostility. Among them, the wise and shrewd knew enough of history and of men to suspect that its survival and its success would someday bring an end to absolutism and colonialism.

Yet the little nation, with its brand-new written Constitution, the first in the political history of the world, was also part of all that had gone before. It did not wish to withdraw from the western world in which it had so recently won its freedom or to repudiate the civilization it had acquired. Its representative legislature, its many religious beliefs, its concept of due process of law, its freedom of speech, its beliefs in the rights of man—all the basic ideals of the new democracy—were drawn from the long struggle for freedom which was still being waged in England. The speech, the literature, the art, and the music of the new Americans also tied them with their ancestral Europe.

The firm establishment of an effective national government for the American states and of a workable democratic method for the free and orderly change of political power in a republic marked a turning point in world history. Henceforth, mankind would be "yearning to breathe free," to follow the trail which Washington and Adams and Jefferson would blaze. The demand for independence and freedom would not wait long. The spark would fall later that year in France, and the flame of freedom would spread on and on until, a century and three quarters later, more than one hundred free and independent nations would sit in council at the United Nations in New York.

Successive American presidential elections have reflected the struggles of a growing nation as it developed the natural resources of its continent, battled slavery and secession, built an unparalleled industrial system, wrestled with the social and economic problems of an urban society, and tried to shoulder the frustrations of a world leadership it had not sought. Today the presidency and the system by which it is filled stand as a monumental achievement in the development of human freedom. The nation which created the office of President, assigned to it the great powers it possesses, and supported it with the political, economic, and military might of the greatest of world powers did all these things to preserve its revolutionary ideals of freedom and independence. These ideals have become not only America's ideals, but the ideals of free peoples everywhere.

Consequently, each presidential election can be said to represent for the United States and for mankind more than a mere partisan contest for control of the executive branch of government in one nation. Although the nomination and the campaigning are cast in a partisan and nationalistic mold, and the outcome is interpreted as a victory for one candidate and his policies, each election is, in its deepest meaning, a demonstration of the continuing ability of a free people to allocate great power by orderly, constitutional means. Presidential power, thus determined and thus controlled, is freedom's guardian, for Americans and for free men everywhere.

Appendix I

The Selection of Delegates to the National Conventions

State	Method of Selection
Alabama	Democrats at Presidential Primary; Republicans at State and District Conventions
Alaska	State Convention
Arizona	State Executive Committee
Arkansas	State Committee
California	Presidential Preference Primary
Colorado	State and District Conventions
Connecticut	Democrats at State Convention; Republicans at State and District Conventions
Delaware	State Convention
District of Columbia	Presidential Preference Primary
Florida	Presidential Preference Primary
Georgia	Democrats by State Committee; Republicans at State Convention
Hawaii	State Convention
Idaho	State Convention
Illinois	State Conventions for At Large Delegates; Presidential Preference Primary for District Delegates
Indiana	State and District Conventions
Iowa	Democrats at State Convention; Republicans at State and District Conventions
Kansas	State and District Conventions
Kentucky	Democrats at State Convention; Republicans at State and District Conventions

State	Method of Selection
Louisiana	State Central Committees
Maine	Democrats at State Convention; Republicans at District Conventions
Maryland	State Convention (delegates not chosen at Presidential Preference Primary)
Massachusetts	Presidential Preference Primary
Michigan	State and District Conventions
Minnesota	State and District Conventions
Mississippi	State Convention
Missouri	Democrats at State Convention; Republicans at State and District Conventions
Montana	State Convention
Nebraska	State Convention for Delegates at Large; Presidential Preference Primary for District Delegates
Nevada	State Convention
New Hampshire	Presidential Preference Primary
New Jersey	Presidential Preference Primary
New Mexico	State Convention
New York	State Convention or State Committee for At Large Delegates; Primary Election for District Delegates. No Presidential Preference Voting
North Carolina	Democrats at State Convention; Republicans at State and District Conventions
North Dakota	State Convention
Ohio	Presidential Preference Primary
Oklahoma	State and District Conventions
Oregon	Presidential Preference Primary
Pennsylvania	State Central Committee for At Large Delegates; Presidential Preference Primary for District Delegates
Rhode Island	Primary Election. No Presidential Preference Voting (optional with the political parties)
South Carolina	State Convention
South Dakota	Presidential Preference Primary
Tennessee	State and District Conventions
Texas	State Convention
Utah	State Convention
Vermont	State Convention
Virginia	Democrats at State Convention; Republicans at State and District Conventions
Washington	State Convention
West Virginia	Presidential Preference Primary
Wisconsin	Presidential Preference Primary

State	Method of Selection
Wyoming	State Convention
Canal Zone	Democrats only at Territorial Convention
Puerto Rico	Commonwealth Convention
Virgin Islands	Territorial Convention

SOURCE: Richard D. Hupman and Eiler C. Ravnholt, *Nomination and Election of the President and Vice President of the United States* (Washington: Government Printing Office, 1964).

Appendix II

Electoral Votes:
1956, 1960, 1964

State	1956 Dem.	1956 Rep.	1956 Other	1960 Dem.	1960 Rep.	1960 Other	1964 Dem.	1964 Rep.
Alabama	10		1	5		6		10
Alaska					3		3	
Arizona		4			4			5
Arkansas	8			8			6	
California		32			32		40	
Colorado		6			6		6	
Connecticut		8		8			8	
Delaware		3		3			3	
District of Columbia							3	
Florida		10			10		14	
Georgia	12			12				12
Hawaii				3			4	
Idaho		4			4		4	
Illinois		27		27			26	
Indiana		13			13		13	
Iowa		10			10		9	
Kansas		8			8		7	
Kentucky		10			10		9	
Louisiana	10			10				10
Maine		5			5		4	
Maryland		9		9			10	

State	1956 Dem.	1956 Rep.	1956 Other	1960 Dem.	1960 Rep.	1960 Other	1964 Dem.	1964 Rep.
Massachusetts		16		16			14	
Michigan		20		20			21	
Minnesota		11		11			10	
Mississippi	8					8		7
Missouri	13			13			12	
Montana		4			4		4	
Nebraska		6			6		5	
Nevada		3		3			3	
New Hampshire		4			4		4	
New Jersey		16		16			17	
New Mexico		4		4			4	
New York		45		45			43	
North Carolina	14			14			13	
North Dakota		4			4		4	
Ohio		25			25		26	
Oklahoma		8			7	1	8	
Oregon		6			6		6	
Pennsylvania		32		32			29	
Rhode Island		4		4			4	
South Carolina	8			8				8
South Dakota		4			4		4	
Tennessee		11			11		11	
Texas		24		24			25	
Utah		4			4		4	
Vermont		3			3		3	
Virginia		12			12		12	
Washington		9			9		9	
West Virginia		8		8			7	
Wisconsin		12			12		12	
Wyoming		3			3		3	
Totals	73	457	1	303	219	15	486	52

Popular Votes Cast for President: 1956, 1960, 1964

State	1956 Dem.	1956 Rep.	1960 Dem.	1960 Rep.	1964 Dem.	1964 Rep.
Alabama	280,844	195,694	324,050	237,981	—	479,085
Alaska	—	—	29,809	30,953	44,329	22,930
Arizona	112,880	176,990	176,781	221,241	237,765	242,536
Arkansas	213,277	186,287	215,049	184,508	314,197	243,264
California	2,420,135	3,027,668	3,224,099	3,259,722	4,171,877	2,879,108
Colorado	263,997	394,479	330,629	402,242	476,024	296,725
Connecticut	405,079	711,837	657,055	565,813	826,269	390,996
Delaware	79,421	98,057	99,590	96,373	122,704	78,093
District of Columbia	—	—	—	—	169,796	28,801
Florida	480,371	643,849	748,700	795,476	948,540	905,941
Georgia	441,094	216,662	458,638	274,472	522,557	616,600
Hawaii	—	—	92,410	92,295	163,249	44,022
Idaho	105,868	166,979	138,853	161,597	148,920	143,557
Illinois	1,775,682	2,623,327	2,377,846	2,368,988	2,796,833	1,905,946
Indiana	783,908	1,182,811	952,358	1,175,120	1,170,848	911,118
Iowa	501,858	729,187	550,565	722,381	733,030	449,148
Kansas	269,317	566,878	363,213	561,474	464,028	386,579
Kentucky	476,453	572,192	521,855	602,607	669,659	372,977
Louisiana	243,977	329,047	407,339	230,980	387,068	509,255
Maine	102,468	249,238	181,159	240,608	262,264	118,701
Maryland	372,613	559,738	565,808	489,538	730,912	385,495
Massachusetts	948,190	1,393,197	1,487,174	976,750	1,786,422	549,727
Michigan	1,359,898	1,713,647	1,687,269	1,620,428	2,136,615	1,060,152
Minnesota	617,525	719,302	779,933	757,915	991,117	559,624
Mississippi	144,453	60,685	108,362	73,561*	52,591	356,447
Missouri	918,273	914,299	972,201	962,221	1,164,344	653,535
Montana	116,238	154,993	134,891	141,841	164,246	113,032

* State carried by third-party electors in 1960 with 116,248.

State	1956		1960		1964	
	Dem.	Rep.	Dem.	Rep.	Dem.	Rep.
Nebraska	199,029	378,108	232,542	380,553	307,307	276,847
Nevada	40,640	56,049	54,880	52,387	79,339	56,094
New Hampshire	90,364	176,519	137,772	157,989	182,065	104,029
New Jersey	850,337	1,606,942	1,385,415	1,363,324	1,867,671	963,843
New Mexico	106,098	146,778	156,027	153,733	194,017	131,838
New York	2,750,769	4,340,340	3,830,085	3,446,419	4,913,156	2,243,559
North Carolina	590,530	575,062	713,136	655,420	800,139	624,844
North Dakota	96,742	156,766	123,963	154,310	149,784	108,207
Ohio	1,439,655	2,262,610	1,944,248	2,217,611	2,498,331	1,470,865
Oklahoma	385,581	473,769	370,111	533,039	519,834	412,665
Oregon	329,204	406,393	367,402	408,060	501,017	282,779
Pennsylvania	1,981,769	2,585,252	2,556,282	2,439,956	3,130,228	1,672,892
Rhode Island	161,790	255,819	258,032	147,502	315,463	74,615
South Carolina	136,372	75,700	198,129	188,558	215,700	309,048
South Dakota	122,288	171,569	128,070	178,417	163,010	130,108
Tennessee	456,507	462,288	481,453	556,577	635,047	508,965
Texas	859,958	1,080,619	1,167,932	1,121,699	1,663,185	958,566
Utah	118,364	215,631	169,248	205,361	219,628	180,682
Vermont	42,549	110,390	69,186	98,131	108,127	54,942
Virginia	267,760	386,459	362,327	404,521	558,038	481,334
Washington	523,002	620,430	599,298	629,273	779,699	470,366
West Virginia	381,534	449,297	441,786	395,995	538,087	253,953
Wisconsin	586,768	954,844	830,805	895,175	1,050,424	638,495
Wyoming	49,554	74,573	63,331	76,551	80,718	61,998
Totals	26,027,983	35,609,190	34,227,096	34,107,646	43,126,218	27,174,898

INDEX

Abshire, David, 79
Advance scheduling of campaign tours, 233-236
Advertising in presidential campaigns, 192-194
  See also specific Democratic and Republican campaigns
AFL-CIO Committee on Political Education, 171, 283
Aging, problems of, 83, 183-184, 221
  See also Social security
Agriculture, 90, 166, 171, 182, 184-186, 201, 204, 221
Ahlgren, Henry, 206
Alcorn, Meade, 75, 127, 128
Alexander, Herbert E., 41n, 192, 268n, 269n, 270n, 271n, 272n, 279n, 282n, 283n, 289n, 290n, 291n, 292n, 295n, 296n, 297n
All Americans Council, 163
Allocation of delegates: *See separate listings* Democratic *and* Republican National Convention Delegates
American Association for the United Nations, Inc., 75
American Broadcasting Company, 223, 271
American Council for Judaism, 75
American Enterprise Association, 112
American Farm Bureau Federation, 75

American Friends of the Captive Nations, 75
American Heritage Foundation, 155
American Israel Public Affairs Committee, 75
American-Latvian Association, 75
American Legion, 75
American political parties:
  coalitions, 2, 158, 159, 160, 162
  decentralization of, 3-4
Americans for Democratic Action, 75
AMVETS, 75
Anderson, Robert B., 164
Arena of compromise:
  effect on campaigns, 14-16
  political parties, 3, 4, 7, 16, 306
  in Republican Party, 65, 67, 162
  system, 7, 305, 311
  theory, 5
Arends, Leslie, 80
Arth, Carol, 132
Ashbrook, John, 140, 141
Associates Program, 282
Authoritarianism, 198

Babcock, Richard, 185
Bailey, John, 98, 101, 289
Baker, Bobby, 212, 212n
Balance of power between parties, 306

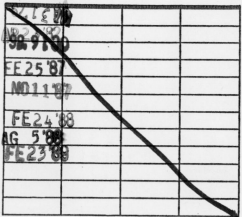